THE LOST JOY OF RAILWAYS

REMEMBERING THE GOLDEN AGE OF TRAINSPOTTING

D&C

David and Charles

THE LOST JOY OF RAILWAYS

REMEMBERING THE GOLDEN AGE OF TRAINSPOTTING

JULIAN HOLLAND

D&C
David and Charles

Ivatt Class 2 2-6-2 tank No. 41206 has just arrived at Lyme Regis with the 4.21pm train from Axminster on 9 August 1963. The previous day Ronnie Biggs and his mates had gone down in history by stealing £2.6m in the Great Train Robbery!

Another great train robbery was when the much-loved S&D north of Templecombe came under Western Region management and through trains from the North to Bournemouth were diverted via other routes. Here, BR Standard Class 4 4-6-0 No. 75007 waits to depart from Bath Green Park with the 4.35pm train to Templecombe on 10 August 1963.

A DAVID & CHARLES BOOK
Copyright © David & Charles Limited 2009

David & Charles is an F+W Media, Inc. company
4700 East Galbraith Road
Cincinnati, OH 45236

First published in the UK in 2009

Text copyright © Julian Holland 2009
Photographs copyright © see page 250

Julian Holland has asserted his right to be identified as author of this work in accordance with the Copyright, Designs and Patents Act, 1988.

The publisher has endeavoured to contact all contributors of text and/or pictures for permission to reproduce. If there are any errors or omissions please notify the publisher in writing.

A catalogue record for this book is available from the British Library.

ISBN-13: 978-0-7153-3199-6
ISBN-10: 0-7153-3199-X

Printed in China by Shenzhen RR Donnelley Printing Co. Ltd
for David & Charles
Brunel House, Newton Abbot, Devon

Director of Editorial and Design: Alison Myer
Commissioning Editor: Neil Baber
Editorial Manager: Emily Pitcher
Editor: Tim Hall
Art Editor: Martin Smith
Proofreader: Ian Mitchell
Production Controller: Ali Smith

Visit our website at www.davidandcharles.co.uk

David & Charles books are available from all good bookshops; alternatively you can contact our Orderline on 0870 9908222 or write to us at FREEPOST EX2 110, D&C Direct, Newton Abbot, TQ12 4ZZ (no stamp required UK only); US customers call 800-289-0963 and Canadian customers call 800-840-5220.

previous page
The shed yard at King's Cross in the days when engine shed security was somewhat more lax than today and spotters could get closer to the engines they so admired. The object of the boy photographer's attention on 27 July 1960 appears to be the appearance of Edinburgh Haymarket Class 'A3' No. 60037 'Hyperion', a rare sight at Kings Cross if ever there was one. Also in attendance is 'A3' No. 60059 'Tracery', 'A4' No. 60025 'Falcon' bearing 'The Elizabethan' headboard and 'A4' No. 60014 'Silver Link'. What a line up!

CONTENTS

Seen on the way back home after a day's trainspotting at Basingstoke, 'Castle' Class 4-6-0 No. 5076 'Gladiator' heads a Cheltenham to Paddington train at Reading on 31 August 1963. With the diesel hydraulic invasion well under way this sighting was a pleasant surprise indeed!

The handwritten notebook list (left margin):

7086 shed.	7318 goods	31796 sidings	×	×	×
1444 e.c.s. for Swanseas	3693 "spa" to Glos.	31617 "	×	P	×
61153 Local to Birm.	5054 Worcester-Gloster Local	30825 "	P	×	×
4564 shed.	D1726 goods	CHURCHDOWN 27/6/64			
911 wow.	D134 Bristol-Newcastle	45221 Glos.-Worcester Local	P	×	×
1721 shed.	44965 Birm.-Pengam	4958 Local for Chelt.	×	×	
ER 26/6/64	7024 wow-Penzance				
45 goods	GLOSTER 27/6/64	9471 "Spa" to Chelt.	—	×	
93 "	73028 shed.	75024 Local for Worcester	—	×	
125 Local	73091 "	7024 Penzance-wow.	×	P	
24 shed.	5939 "	48026 goods	√	√	
9 goods in siding	1444 to Swansea	6859	×	√	
24 on way to S.Wales	9620 shed.	48424 "	×	√	
7	3737 goods	92112 "	×	√	
9	92003 "		√	√	
2 "	3775 Chalford	GLOSTER 28/6/64	√	√	
	D7050 shed.	D7595 excursion	√	√	
		GLOSTER 30/6/64	√	√	
"	8471 Chelt-Padd.	D7578 Light	√	√	
	9471 shed.	4929 goods	√	×	
27/6/64	D7061 Padd.	3745 Chelt-Padd.	×	×	
goods	31810 sidings	GLOSTER 19/6/64	—	×	
		4438 goods	×	√	

INTRODUCTION

As a young lad I was surrounded by railways. Across the road from where we lived in Gloucester was the ex-Midland Railway line to Bristol and Birmingham; behind us was the branch line down to Gloucester Docks and the Gloucester Railway Carriage & Wagon Company's Works; in the attic was an 'O' gauge clockwork railway built by my father. Boys' books and magazines were awash with railway subjects and the weekly *Eagle* comic with its centrefold cutaway, often a railway subject, was always eagerly awaited. Unlike today, railways then were still an important part of everyday life and the long and complicated journey to our holiday destination each year was pure joy.

I distinctly remember the first time I went trainspotting. Having just passed my 11-plus exam I went on to attend secondary school where many of my classmates, aided by a plethora of Ian Allan books and magazines, had already been bitten by the craze. I was determined that the next Saturday I would catch the bus down to Gloucester Central and Eastgate stations to investigate this phenomenon. I have still got my Sterling No. 3 notebook and a pencil from that portentous day in 1957 when I hung around the stations, taking in the smell of smoke, steam and oil – I was hooked! Penzance, Paddington, Newcastle, Wolverhampton Low Level, Birmingham Snow Hill, Manchester and Sheffield were among the distant and seemingly romantic destinations of the trains that I saw on that day. There was no stopping me after that, and over the next ten years I travelled far and wide, usually in the company of like-minded friends, to nearly every far-flung corner of British Railways in search of that elusive locomotive number or to travel on a soon-to-be-closed line. Even the introduction of those dastardly diesels failed to dampen my enthusiasm!

This has all been swept away by a combination of political machinations, the powerful road transport lobby, profit-seeking, and bland modernity. Yes, we still have our railways but the pure joy and camaraderie that they once engendered in my generation has long gone. Surprisingly there are still many trainspotters out there but their innocent hobby is being increasingly threatened by 'Big Brother' health and safety legislation and the perceived spectre of terrorism.

The Lost Joy of Railways is unashamedly nostalgic. It is a time machine that will carry the reader back to those innocent, glorious years when railways were still an integral part of our everyday lives. The book is divided into the six regions of British Railways and within each of these chapters are the stars of the show – the locomotives themselves, and favourite top spots and engine sheds that were a magnet to every trainspotter – many now a distant memory but which are brought back to life with photographs, ephemera and authentic personal notebooks stuffed with lists of loco numbers. Records of trainspotting trips and the final days of steam are also included along with feature pages on railway works, scrapyards, dastardly diesels and, last but not least, the locomotives that escaped the cutter's torch.

(below) In 1963 a large area of former WR territory in the Midlands and West Wales came under LMR management. Here, 'Hall' Class 4-6-0 No. 6907 'Davenham Hall' sports the new 6D shedplate while on station pilot duties at Shrewsbury on 18 April 1964.

(left) Soon to become a bit of a celebrity Peppercorn 'A2' Pacific No. 60532 'Blue Peter' gets ready for its next turn of duty at Dundee Tay Bridge shed (62B) on 30 July 1964.

The early 5200 numbered 'Black Fives' were mainly Central Division ones and so proved very difficult for spotters in the Midlands, being allocated to such far away depots as Newton Heath, Liverpool Bank Hall, Accrington, Low Moor Bradford and Huddersfield. Here the local spotters pay attention to the activities on the footplate of No.45212 which was a Fleetwood-allocated engine in 1952 but when this picture was taken was allocated to Bolton Plodders Lane - a depot not noted for its Black Fives.

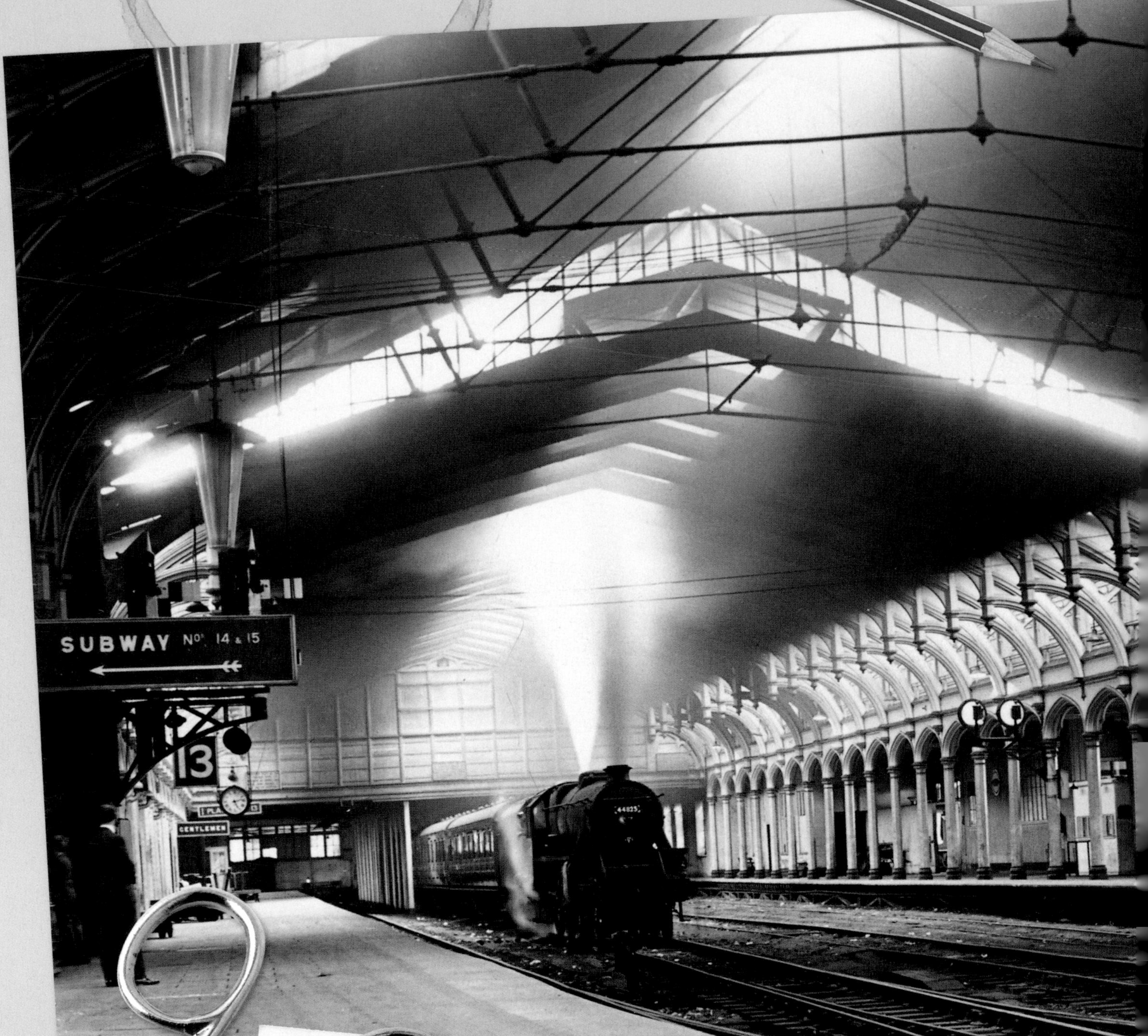
SUBWAY No. 14 & 15
13
GENTLEMEN

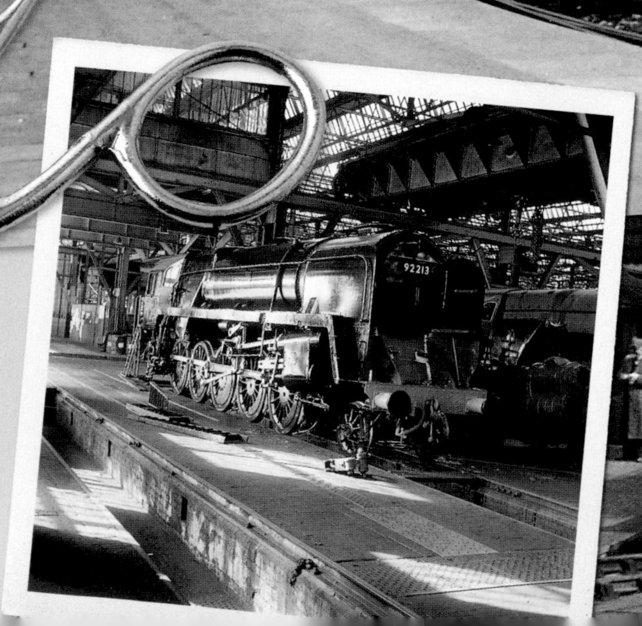

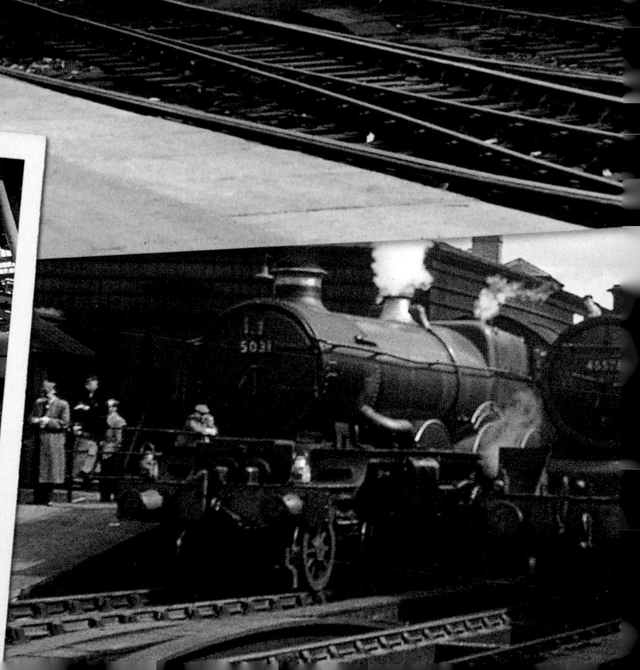

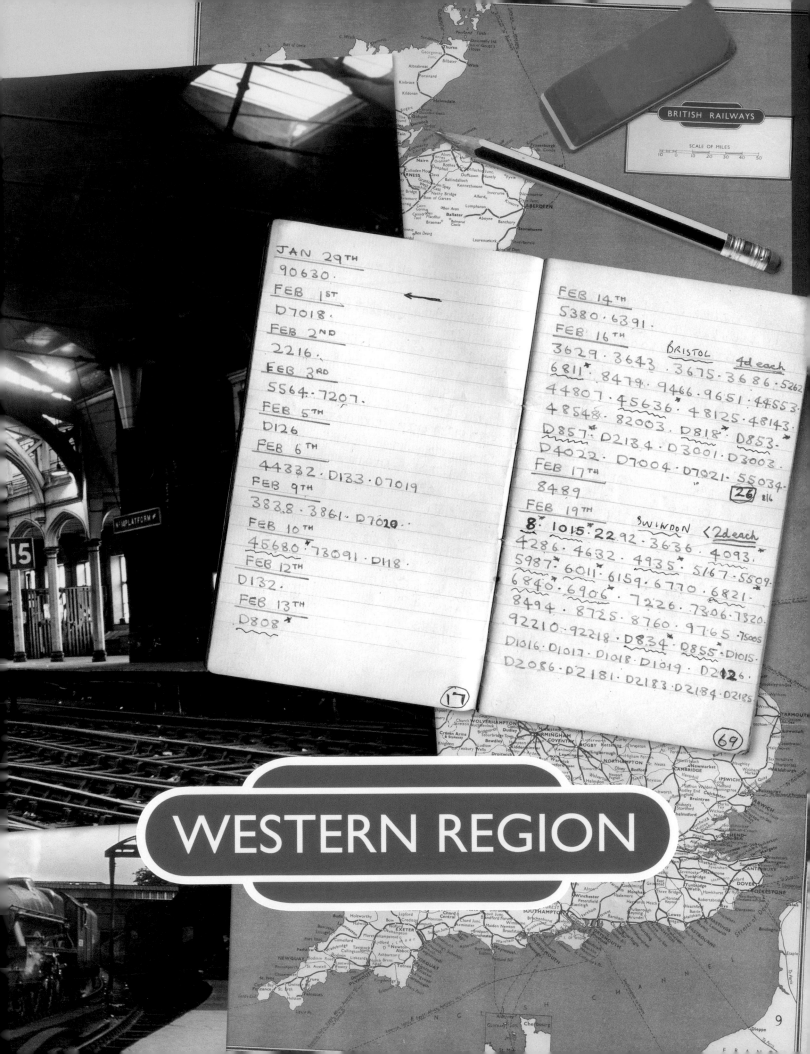

WESTERN REGION

One of the first batch of BR Standard 7P6F 'Britannia' Pacifics built at Crewe in 1951, No. 70020 'Mercury' is seen at Paddington having arrived from the west in the late 1950s. 'Mercury' went on to Carlisle Kingmoor and Willesden sheds before ending its days in 1967 at the Shettleston scrapyard.

London Paddington

THE GATEWAY TO THE WEST, PADDINGTON STATION BECAME THE LONDON TERMINUS OF THE GWR IN 1838. THE PRESENT STRUCTURE WITH ITS 14 PLATFORMS AND GRACEFUL GLAZED ROOF AND WROUGHT IRON PILLARS WAS DESIGNED BY ISAMBARD KINGDOM BRUNEL AND COMPLETED IN 1854.

This busy station not only served the towns of the Thames Valley and Chilterns but was also the starting point for many of the famous named trains to the West. By the late 1950s the list of these steam-hauled trains was impressive and included the world-famous 'Cornish Riviera Express' to Penzance, 'The Mayflower' to Plymouth, 'The Merchant Venturer' to Weston-super-Mare, 'The Bristolian' non-stop to Bristol, 'The Capitals United Express' non-stop to Cardiff, 'The South Wales Pullman' to Cardiff, 'The Torbay Express' to Kingswear, 'The Pembroke Coast Express' to Pembroke Dock, 'The Inter-City' to Wolverhampton, 'The Red Dragon' to Carmarthen, 'The Cheltenham Spa Express' to Cheltenham Spa, 'The Royal Duchy' to Penzance, 'The Cambrian Coast Express' to Pwllheli and Aberystwyth and 'The Cathedrals Express' to Hereford.

At the same time Paddington was a Mecca for trainspotters with Old Oak Common shed providing

The date is March 24, 1951 and 'Castle' Class No. 4096 'Highclere Castle' stands at Platform 9 with the empty coaching stock of a train for Bristol Temple Meads. To the right, 'King' Class No. 6005 'King George II' is just arriving at Platform 10 with an express from Birmingham Snow Hill.

The diesel-electric powered Blue Pullmans provided a 1st Class service between Paddington and Bristol, and Paddington and Wolverhampton Low Level. An additional service to Cardiff and Swansea was introduced in 1961. Following the transfer of Blue Pullmans from the LMR in 1967 additional services were introduced from Paddington to Bristol and Oxford. The service to Wolverhampton LL was withdrawn in 1967 and to Bristol and Swansea in May, 1973.

Complete with train reporting number Z48 and Hawksworth tender, 'Castle' Class 4-6-0 No. 5054 'Earl of Ducie' at the head of an Oxford University Railway Society special at Paddington in May 1964. Less than 12 months later steam had disappeared from Paddington. No. 5054 was allocated to Worcester shed (85A) but was transferred to Gloucester in September 1964 and withdrawn.

top link 'Castles' and 'Kings' for the main line expresses and the more humble 6100 Class 2-6-2 tanks for suburban duties along with the unique Hawksworth-designed 1500 Class 0-6-0 tanks for empty coaching stock movements.

This period also saw for the first time the introduction of diesel-hydraulic locomotives on the main line expresses. Beginning with the five original North British A1A-A1A 'Warship' Class in 1958 diesel numbers started as a trickle but had ended as a flood by the early 1960s when the D800 B-B 'Warship' Class and the later D1000 C-C 'Western' Class took over many of the main line duties. By March 1965 the changeover was complete and Old Oak Common shed was closed to steam. Now, even those diesel loco-hauled trains are a distant memory with only the ageing HSTs providing a link back to those fascinating times.

By 1974 even the 'Western' (Class 52) diesel-hydraulics were looking rather shabby. Here, at Paddington on March 30, No. 1040 'Western Queen' stands at Platform 1 with the 10.25 from Birmingham New Street while No. 1070 'Western Gauntlet' has just arrived at Platform 2 with the 08.35 from Penzance. No. 1040 was built at Crewe in 1962 and scrapped in 1976 while No. 1070, also built at Crewe but in 1963, was scrapped in 1979.

ON SHED

LOCO SHED BOOK
abc
SPRING 1964
2'6

BRITISH RAILWAYS
Locoshed Book
IAN ALLAN
shed allocations for all
British Railways locomotives
3/-

Old Oak Common

A classic scene inside Old Oak Common shed in September 1955. Ex-GWR 'Star' Class 4-6-0 No. 4061 'Glastonbury Abbey', along with others of its class, was soon to be withdrawn. Only one, No. 4003 'Lode Star', has been preserved and can be seen in the National Railway Museum in York.

The principal steam shed for the Western Region in London, Old Oak Common was opened by the GWR in 1906 on a site adjoining the Grand Union Canal just west of Paddington station. The nearest station was Willesden Junction (LMR and LTE) which was about ten minutes' walk away.

The largest engine shed on the GWR, it contained a total of four turntables, all of them under the cover of a pitched and glazed roof. Since closure to steam on March 22, 1965, part of it was retained as a stabling point for diesel locomotives and multiple unit trains.

A difficult shed to visit without a permit, Old Oak Common's October 1961 allocation of steam locomotives included 13 'King' Class 4-6-0s and 35 'Castle' Class 4-6-0s all kept in tip-top condition for hauling the principal expresses, such as the 'Cornish Riviera', 'Bristolian' and 'Red Dragon', and 11 'Halls', 14 'Modified Halls', 3 '4700' Class, 8 large 'Prairies' and a varied assortment of 49 0-6-0 tanks.

Photographed inside Old Oak Common roundhouse on January 26, 1964, '4700' Class 2-8-0s Nos 4704 and 4701, both 81A locos, wait for their imminent demise in a few months' time. Introduced between 1919 and 1923 this class of nine locos was the most powerful heavy freight engines built by the GWR but were often used to haul heavy expresses to the West of England on summer Saturdays. None of this class was preserved.

Ex-GWR 0-6-0 tanks wait for their next turn of duty inside Old Oak Common shed on May 11, 1963. On the left is '9400' Class No. 9495 which was built at Swindon after Nationalisation in 1949. In the centre is '9700' Class No. 9706 one of seven locos in this class which were introduced in 1933 and fitted with condensing apparatus for working through the tunnels of London Transport's Metropolitan Line.

(left) Two Old Oak Common locos wait for their next turn of duty inside the shed, c.1959. In the foreground is 'Modified Hall' 4-6-0 No. 7903 'Foremarke Hall' which was built at Swindon by BR in 1949 and withdrawn from Cardiff East Dock shed (88L) in June 1964. Fortunately the loco was saved from Woodham's scrapyard at Barry in 1981 and has since been preserved. Behind it is 'King' Class 4-6-0 No. 6029 'King Edward VIII' (when built in 1930 it was named 'King Stephen') which wasn't so lucky and was scrapped in 1962.

While Old Oak Common closed to steam in 1965 it continued life as a diesel stabling point. Seen here on 3 November 1973 are 'Western' Class diesel hydraulics (Class 52) Nos 1054 'Western Governor' and 1057 'Western Chieftain' and, nearest the camera, 'Hymek' (Class 35) diesel hydraulic No. 7022. Now that steam had disappeared the prefix 'D' had been painted out on two of the locos' numberplates.

Oxford

THE CITY ONCE POSSESSED TWO STATIONS: THE GWR'S GENERAL STATION, OPENED IN 1852, AND THE LNWR'S REWLEY ROAD STATION, OPENED IN 1851 AND CLOSED IN 1951.

Having just replaced a Southern Region loco, ex-LMS 'Jubilee' 4-6-0 No. 45581 'Bihar and Orissa' heads north out of Oxford station with a train from the south coast on 20 July 1963. Built by the North British Locomotive Company in 1934 and allocated to Farnley (55C) for many years, No. 45581 was withdrawn and scrapped in 1966. By contrast a fairly new diesel multiple unit can be seen approaching the station from the Banbury direction.

Oxford was unique on the Western Region as a focal point for trains from more than two regions (as witnessed at places such as Shrewsbury, Gloucester, Salisbury and Exeter). These inter-regional trains brought 'foreign' locomotives from the Southern Region via Basingstoke and Reading, the Eastern and Midland Regions via the former L&NWR route from Cambridge via Bletchley and the Eastern (subsequently Midland) Region from the former Great Central main line via Woodford Halse and Banbury. Consequently it was not uncommon to see the native former GWR locos rubbing shoulders with SR 'Battle of Britain' or 'West Country' Pacifics, ER Class B1s or even ex-LNWR 0-8-0 goods locos.

In addition to the regular appearance of these 'foreigners', the WR was well represented by 'Castles' on the 'Cathedrals Express' and other Paddington to Worcester and Hereford turns, 'Halls' and 'Granges' on mixed-traffic duties to Worcester, Banbury, Birmingham, Reading and Basingstoke, and the plain-Janes of heavy freight such as the 2800 Class 2-8-0s. Quite a heady mix which also included branch line trains from Fairford and Princes Risborough and has now disappeared forever.

During the last month of steam on the Western Region, decrepit 'Modified Hall' 4-6-0 No. 6993 'Arthog Hall' (minus nameplates) passes through Oxford with an up coal train on 12 December 1965. No 6993 was built at Swindon in 1948 and finally ended up allocated to Oxford shed (81F) before being withdrawn less than three weeks after this photo was taken. The loco was scrapped at Cashmore's, Newport in 1966.

Built at Swindon in 1950, 'Manor' Class 4-6-0 No. 7824 'Iford Manor' has just taken on water at Oxford before resuming its journey southwards with the 10.30 Birmingham Snow Hill to Hastings train on 20 July 1963. This summer-Saturdays train followed an interesting route southwards via Reading General, Guildford, Redhill, Brighton, Eastbourne, Bexhill Central and St Leonards (Warrior Square). No. 7824 was built at Swindon in 1950 and withdrawn in 1964.

Ex-GWR 'Hall' Class 4-6-0 No. 6923 'Croxteth Hall' brings a down fitted freight into Oxford by Hinksey gasworks. No. 6923 was built at Swindon in 1941 and spent its last years allocated to Oxford shed (81F) before being withdrawn at the end of 1965. It was scrapped at Cashmore's, Newport, in May 1966.

WESTERN REGION

Oxford

The ex-GWR shed at Oxford was located on the west side of the line north of the station and was about five minutes' walk via a footbridge over the Oxford Canal.

Originally opened in 1854 by the Oxford, Worcester & Wolverhampton Railway (later absorbed by the West Midland Railway and then the GWR in 1863), the shed was not only home to a varied selection of ex-GWR locos in the '50s and early '60s but was also regularly visited by 'foreigners' from other regions while hauling trains from and to the Southern, Midland and Eastern Regions.

With just under four months to go before withdrawal, decrepit 'Grange' Class 4-6-0 No. 6848 'Toddington Grange' (minus name and numberplates) is coaled up at Oxford shed on September 9, 1965. Built at Swindon in October 1937 No. 6848 was cut-up at Cashmore's scrapyard, Newport, in 1966.

Oxford shed was often visited by 'foreign' locos from the Southern, Eastern and London Midland Regions. Here, in August 1954, ex-LNER Class 'D16/3' 4-4-0 No. 62585 has arrived on shed after working a passenger train over the cross-country route from Cambridge. Known as 'Claud Hamiltons' after the first loco of this type (D14 introduced by the Great Eastern in 1900), the last D16/3 in service, No. 62613, was withdrawn from March shed in 1960. Note the crew having their tea break and the ex-GWR AEC railcar, or 'Flying Banana, on the right of the picture.

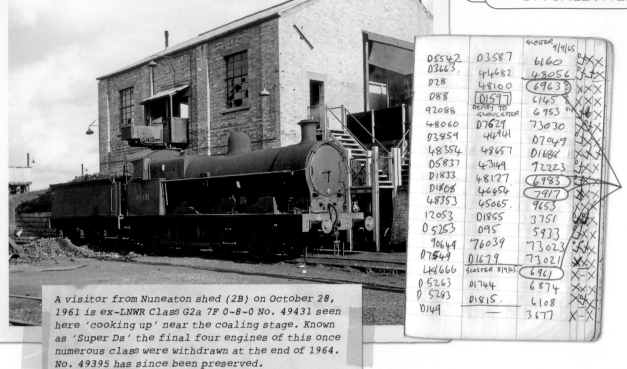

A visitor from Nuneaton shed (2B) on October 28, 1961 is ex-LNWR Class G2a 7F 0-8-0 No. 49431 seen here 'cooking up' near the coaling stage. Known as 'Super Ds' the final four engines of this once numerous class were withdrawn at the end of 1964. No. 49395 has since been preserved.

Apart from a 'Hymek' and a Brush Type 4 all of the locos spotted on a visit to Oxford shed on 9 September 1965 were steam. With just under four months to go before the 'end' a total of 30 locos were noted including six 'Modified Halls' Nos. 6961, 6963, 6983, 6998 (since preserved), 7912 and 7917.

In the 1950s and early '60s it would have been common to see SR Bulleid Light Pacifics, ex-L&NWR 7F 0-8-0s or ER 'B1' 4-6-0s rubbing shoulders with WR 'Halls' or 'Granges'. Oxford's allocation in October 1961 consisted of 9 'Halls', 5 'Modified Halls', 6 BR Standard Class 4 4-6-0s, 3 '1400' 0-4-2 push-pull tanks, 13 large 'Prairies', 2 '5101' Class 'Prairies' and 10 0-6-0 pannier tanks.

In January 1966 the shed became the last ex-GWR to close to steam. The shed was Oxford's only sub-shed Fairford and was usually home to a Class 7400 or 5700 0-6-0 tank. For such a small shed it is unusual that it had a 55ft. turntable which was used to turn the tank locomotives so they did not run bunker first. The shed closed in June 1962 at the same time as the 25-mile branch line that it served.

Ex-GWR '2800' Class 2-8-0 No. 3855 looks rather the worse for wear at Oxford shed in March 1965. By this date, with only nine months to go before the end of steam on the Western Region, most locos were kept in a very sorry state with their brass name and number plates already removed away from temptation and the wandering hands and spanners of spotters!

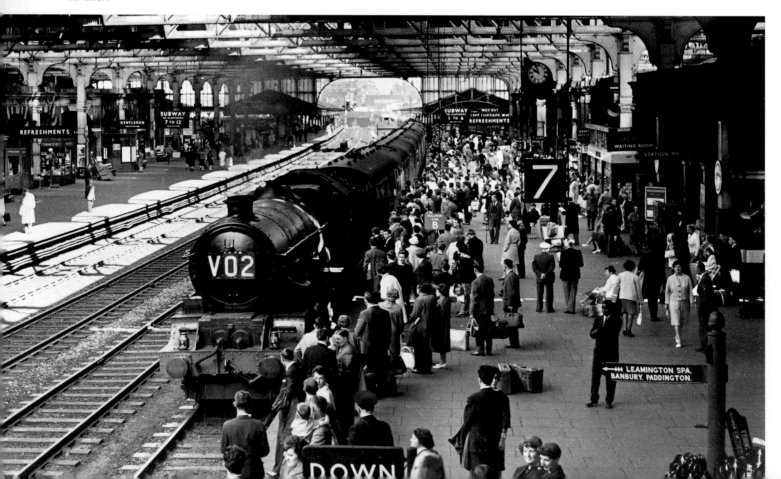

Birmingham Snow Hill

OPENED BY THE GWR IN 1852, BIRMINGHAM SNOW HILL WAS ONE OF TWO PRINCIPAL STATIONS IN THE CITY (THE OTHER BEING NEW STREET) AND SERVED THAT COMPANY'S MAIN LINE TRAINS TO LONDON PADDINGTON, SHREWSBURY, CHESTER AND WEST WALES.

A busy scene on Platform 7 of Snow Hill station on August 18, 1962 as ex-GWR 'King' Class 4-6-0 No. 6002 'King William IV' arrives with the 6.30am train from Birkenhead to Paddington. Judging by the clock the train is only about a minute late and will, no doubt, leave punctually at 10am. Allocated to Wolverhampton Stafford Road (84A) No. 6002 was built at Swindon in 1927 and was withdrawn from service only a month after this photo was taken.

It was rebuilt and enlarged twice, firstly in 1871 with an overall glazed roof and, secondly, in 1912 with improved facilities. Sadly, with the diversion of all main line trains to New Street in 1967, Snow Hill's days were numbered and this grand building and adjoining Great Western Hotel were demolished in the 1970s. Since then a much smaller and modern station has been reopened on the site to serve cross-city trains and, more recently, through trains to London Marylebone.

Snow Hill was a great place for the trainspotter in the late 1950s and early 1960s. Highlights of each day included 'The Inter-City' express from and to Paddington (normally hauled by a 'King' Class 4-6-0), the dual-portion 'Cambrian Coast Express', normally 'King' or 'Castle'-hauled between Paddington and Shrewsbury, to and from Paddington and West Wales and 'The Cornishman', also 'Castle'-hauled between Wolverhampton Low Level and Bristol Temple Meads, to and from Wolverhampton LL and Penzance. In addition to other passenger services to Shrewsbury, Wrexham, Chester, Worcester via Stourbridge Junction and

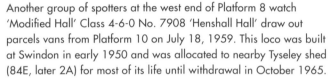

Another group of spotters at the west end of Platform 8 watch 'Modified Hall' Class 4-6-0 No. 7908 'Henshall Hall' draw out parcels vans from Platform 10 on July 18, 1959. This loco was built at Swindon in early 1950 and was allocated to nearby Tyseley shed (84E, later 2A) for most of its life until withdrawal in October 1965.

In ex-works condition local engine 'Grange' Class 4-6-0 No. 6861 'Crynant Grange' heads through Snow Hill with an up freight on May 11, 1961. This loco was built at Swindon in early 1939 and was withdrawn from Tyseley shed in October 1965.

South Wales via Stratford-upon-Avon (often operated by twin AEC railcars Nos 33 and 38 plus corridor second complete with buffet facilities and then Swindon-built 'Cross-Country' diesel multiple units), Snow Hill also witnessed a succession of freight trains through its centre roads. The short-lived 'Blue Pullman' diesel multiple unit service to and from Paddington was also introduced in September 1960. It was very rare to see locos from other regions at Snow Hill apart from the odd football special which could bring 'foreigners' from both the Southern and Midland Regions.

Watched by two trainspotters, 'Castle' Class 4-6-0 No. 5082 'Swordfish' heads the 'Cambrian Coast Express' at Snow Hill in 1959. Built at Swindon in 1939 this loco was originally named 'Powis Castle' but was renamed early in 1941 along with 10 other members of its class to commemorate World War II British aircraft. Allocated to Old Oak Common (81A) No 5082 was withdrawn in July 1962.

ON SHED

85 A

Worcester

The ex-GWR shed at Worcester was located just north of Shrub Hill station in the triangle formed by the lines to Hereford and Droitwich. For the enthusiastic trainspotter it was just a 10 minute walk from Shrub Hill or quarter of an hour from Foregate Street station.

The shed, once also home to several of the ex-GWR AEC diesel railcars, consisted of two separate buildings totalling seven roads and in October 1961 had an allocation of 3 '2251' Class, 4 'Prairies', 3 '5600' Class, 6 Moguls, 6 'Halls', 5 'Modified Halls', 5 'Granges', 10 0-6-0 pannier tanks of various types, 2 BR Standard Class 4, 3 BR Standard Class 2 and last, but not least, 9 'Castles'. These were kept in tip-top condition for working 'The Cathedrals Express' and other main line services between Hereford, Worcester and Paddington. Included in this list were No. 7005 'Sir Edward Elgar' – named after the local composer – and No. 7007 'Great Western' – so named as it was the last steam engine built by the GWR before Nationalisation.

Even by 1962 the diesel-hydraulic invasion hadn't reached Worcester to any great extent and the Worcester-line trains remained some of the last to be steam-hauled out of Paddington. The shed was closed to steam at the end of 1965. Sub-sheds of Worcester were Evesham (closed 1961), Honeybourne (closed 1965), Kingham (closed 1962) and Ledbury (closed 1964).

This panoramic view of Worcester shed, circa 1962, clearly shows its triangular layout north of Shrub Hill station. Included in this view are several 'Castles' and 'Granges', a 'Manor', a '2251' Class 0-6-0 and a 'Black Five'. Worcester was the last WR shed to operate 'Castle' Class locos for regular main line express duties to Paddington.

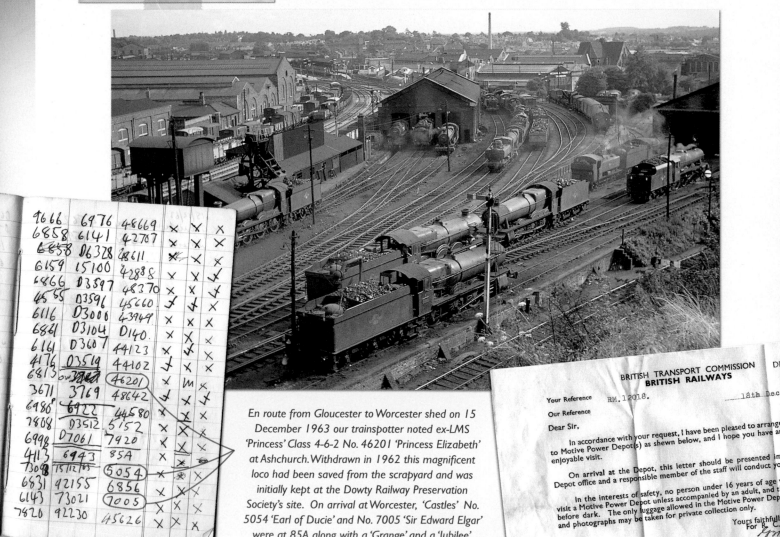

En route from Gloucester to Worcester shed on 15 December 1963 our trainspotter noted ex-LMS 'Princess' Class 4-6-2 No. 46201 'Princess Elizabeth' at Ashchurch. Withdrawn in 1962 this magnificent loco had been saved from the scrapyard and was initially kept at the Dowty Railway Preservation Society's site. On arrival at Worcester, 'Castles' No. 5054 'Earl of Ducie' and No. 7005 'Sir Edward Elgar' were at 85A along with a 'Grange' and a 'Jubilee'.

BRITISH TRANSPORT COMMISSION
BRITISH RAILWAYS

Your Reference   RM.12018.   18th Dec.

Our Reference

Dear Sir,

In accordance with your request, I have been pleased to arrange for
to Motive Power Depot(s) as shewn below, and I hope you have an
enjoyable visit.

On arrival at the Depot, this letter should be presented immedi
Depot office and a responsible member of the staff will conduct you rou

In the interests of safety, no person under 16 years of age will b
visit a Motive Power Depot unless accompanied by an adult, and the vis
before dark. The only luggage allowed in the Motive Power Depot wi
and photographs may be taken for private collection only.

Yours faithfully,
For B. C. HIL

Motive Power Depot to be visited	Date	Time
Worcester	6.1.63	9.30am

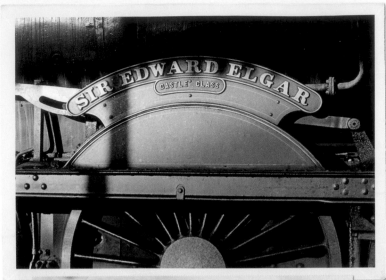

A busy scene at Worcester on February 17, 1962
with '8100' Class 2-6-2 tank No. 8107 and a '9400'
Class 0-6-0 pannier tank being moved around the
yard by a '5700' Class 0-6-0 pannier tank. On
the left another '5700' Class 0-6-0 pannier tank
receives some minor attention from the driver.
With a total of ten locos the '8100' Class were
rebuilds of the '5100' Class and were introduced
in 1938. Two of them were allocated to 85A in 1962
but none of this class was preserved.

Worcester was very proud of its nine 'Castles'
and kept them in immaculate condition up until
1964. Star among them was No. 7005 'Sir Edward
Elgar' which could regularly be seen in action
on the 'Cathedrals Express' to Paddington. Built
at Swindon in 1946 and originally named 'Lamphey
Castle', No. 7005 spent its working life at
Worcester until withdrawal in September 1964.

With still very few diesels in
evidence, our trainspotter noted
a further five 'Castles' on his visit
to 85A on December 15, 1963
– No. 5022 'Wigmore Castle', No.
7000 'Viscount Portal', No. 7023
'Penrice Castle', No. 7025 'Sudeley
Castle' and No. 7031 'Cromwell's
Castle'. Three of these, Nos. 5022,
7000 and 7031 had already been
withdrawn from service.

The ultimate in 'Castle' development – fitted with
a double chimney and four row superheater No. 7004
'Eastnor Castle' was allocated to 85A when seen at
the shed in February 1962. Built in 1946 this loco
was withdrawn in January 1964. In addition to Nos.
7004 and 7005, Worcester was home to seven other
'Castles' – Nos. 7002, 7006, 7007, 7011, 7013,
7023 and 7027 – by the end of 1961.

Swindon Works

WESTERN REGION

LOCATED TO THE WEST OF SWINDON STATION IN THE FORK BETWEEN THE SWINDON TO GLOUCESTER AND SWINDON TO BRISTOL MAIN LINES, SWINDON WORKS WAS THE PRINCIPAL LOCOMOTIVE, CARRIAGE AND WAGON WORKS FOR THE GREAT WESTERN RAILWAY AND, FROM 1948, THE WESTERN REGION OF BRITISH RAILWAYS.

PART OF No. 4 SHOP—CARRIAGE BODY BUILDING

Swindon Works

sh Railways
ERN REGION

Obviously taken on a Sunday when the workforce was at home this grandstand view of the erecting shop at Swindon Works was taken in May 1963. Steam loco production at Swindon ceased in 1960 although repairs continued for a few more years. The building of diesel hydraulics continued until 1965 but the Works finally succumbed to rationalisation and finally closed after 145 years' service in 1986.

The last Great Western express passenger engine built at Swindon was 'Castle' Class 4-6-0 No. 7037 'Swindon' which was built in 1950 and fittingly named to commemorate the works of her birth. Here she stands alongside fellow class member No. 5094 'Tretower Castle' undergoing repair in Swindon's famous 'A' shop in the mid 1950s.

By 1962 Swindon Works was not only repairing main line steam locos but was also building new diesel hydraulics. On a visit to the main erecting shop on 3 November our trainspotter noted 10 new 'Westerns' in various stages of construction along with two (D1037 and D1042) recently delivered from Crewe. Of note on the steam side were four 'Castle' Class 4-6-0s (Nos. 7012 'Barry Castle', 7024 'Powis Castle', 7032 'Denbigh Castle' and 7011 'Banbury Castle') receiving attention.

Opened in 1841, the Works transformed what was then just a rural village to a large railway town. Under the GWR's famous locomotive superintendents - Daniel Gooch, Joseph Armstrong, William Dean, G. J. Churchward, C. B. Collett and F. W. Hawksworth - the Works turned out firstly such broad gauge giants as the single-wheeler 2-2-2 and 4-2-2 express locos followed by the famous standard gauge 'City' and 'County' Class 4-4-0s, 'Star', 'Castle' and 'King' Class 4-6-0s and, at its peak in the 1930s, employed around 14,000 people.

Following nationalisation in 1948 Swindon turned its hand to building many of the BR Standard Class locos including 45 Class 3 2-6-2 tanks (Nos 82000-82044), 80 Class 4 4-6-0s, 20 Class 3 2-6-0 (Nos 77000-77019) and 53 Class 9F 2-10-0 including the last steam loco to be built for BR, No. 92220 'Evening Star'. The ill-thought-out Modernisation Plan of 1955 brought more work for Swindon including the building of 38 of the 'Warship' Class diesel-hydraulics (Class 42 D800-D832 and D866-D870) between 1958 and 1961, 35 'Western' Class diesel-hydraulics (Class 52 D1000-D1034) between 1961 and 1964 and 56 of the short-lived

Swindon Works built the entire class of 80 BR Standard Class 4 4-6-0s in the early 1950s. Here, on 27 September 1951, a near-complete loco is hoisted high in the main erecting shop to be paired up with its front bogies. Fondly remembered for their work on the Cambrian mainline in Wales during the last years of steam six members of this class have since been preserved.

Swindon also built 53 of the BR Standard Class 9F 2-10-0 heavy freight locos. Here, No. 92213 is seen nearing completion in the main erecting shop in 1959. The last steam loco to be built at Swindon, also a 9F, and the last to be built by BR was the now-preserved No. 92220 'Evening Star' which was named in a ceremony at Swindon on March 18, 1960.

Type 1 diesel-hydraulics (Class 14 D9500-D9555) between 1964 and 1965 along with some of the more successful Class 03 0-6-0 diesel shunters and diesel multiple units – including some of the Inter-City, Cross-Country and trans-Pennine units. The last main line diesel locomotive to be broken up at Swindon was BR Sulzer Type 2 No. 25157 in March 1987.

Swindon was always popular with trainspotters in the 1950s and 1960s and armed with a permit it was possible to have a comprehensive guided tour of the Works, scrap line and engine shed on a Sunday. A tour of the Works only was available without a permit on Wednesday afternoons in the school summer holidays. Sadly, while the scrapyard continued cutting up main line diesels for a while longer, the Works closed in 1986 and all that is left to remind us of its illustrious past is the STEAM Museum of the Great Western Railway with its resident exhibits No. 4073 'Caerphilly Castle' and No. 92220 'Evening Star' and the former Engineer's Office which is now the headquarters of English Heritage.

Swindon built 35 of the 'Western' Class 52 diesel-hydraulics between 1961 and 1964. Although magnificent looking machines, the 'Westerns', along with the other types of diesel hydraulics, were plagued with unreliability and consequently had a very short life. Here, on 1 February 1975, the cab of No. 1007 'Western Talisman' and the body shell of No. 1019 'Western Challenger' end their days in the Swindon scrapyard.

Shrewsbury

PARTIALLY BUILT OVER THE RIVER SEVERN, SHREWSBURY'S ORNATE STATION WAS OPENED IN 1848 BY THE SHREWSBURY & CHESTER RAILWAY. WITH THE OPENING OF LINES TO CREWE AND BIRMINGHAM THE STATION SOON CAME UNDER THE JOINT CONTROL OF THE GWR AND THE LNWR.

Still an important junction, Shrewsbury was once a favourite haunt of trainspotters in the 1950s and 1960s. Numerous locomotive types from both the Midland and Western Regions rubbed shoulders here, with 'Royal Scots', 'Jubilees' and even 'Coronation' Pacifics being fairly common sights working through trains to the Midland Region via Crewe. LMR classes including 'Jubilees', 'Black Fives', Stanier 8F 2-8-0s and Fowler 2-6-4 tanks were also seen at work on trains to Swansea (Victoria) via the remote Central Wales Line – including the famous Swansea to York mail train. WR locomotive types ranged from 'Castles', 'Halls', 'Granges'and 'Counties' on trains to Birmingham, Chester and on the North-West route to Bristol

Seen at Shrewsbury on April 18, 1964, ex-LMS 'Jubilee' Class 4-6-0 No. 45577 'Bengal', carrying the shed code 6D, waits to depart with a train for Swansea Victoria via the Central Wales Line. A year earlier Shrewsbury's shed code had changed from 89A to 6D following BR regional boundary changes.

Ex-LMS Fowler 2-6-4T tank No. 42309 arrives at Shrewsbury with a train from Swansea via the Central Wales Line on May 6, 1960. This loco was built at Derby in 1928 and was withdrawn from Carnforth shed in September 1964.

Shrewsbury was a trainspotter's paradise as witnessed here on June 11, 1963 when 'Coronation' Class Pacific No. 46251 'City of Nottingham' visited the station. The loco is seen here having just turned on the triangle around Severn Bridge Junction signal box. Allocated to Crewe North (5A) No. 46251 was repainted in BR red livery in November 1958 and carried this until withdrawal in October 1964.

and Cardiff via Hereford and the beautifully turned-out 'Manors' which hauled the 'Cambrian Coast Express' from Shrewsbury to Aberystwyth and Pwllheli. Despite being diesel-hauled from Paddington (usually by Brush Type 4s - later Class 47) from 1963, the last leg of this named train to West Wales continued to be steam-hauled up to 1967 – in their last season, these trains were hauled by BR Standard Class 4 4-6-0s and 2-6-0s. The continuous stream of north-south freight trains trundling through Shrewsbury station along with branch trains to Bridgnorth via the Severn Valley added to this rich tapestry.

In August 1958, ex-LMS 'Jubilee' Class 4-6-0 No. 45578 'United Provinces' waits to take over a West to North express which has just arrived from Hereford behind ex-GWR 'Castle' Class 4-6-0 No. 5031 'Totnes Castle'. The 'Jubilee' was built by the North British Locomotive Co. in 1934 and withdrawn in 1964. The 'Castle' was built at Swindon in 1934 and withdrawn in 1963.

Cardiff

OPENED BY THE SOUTH WALES RAILWAY IN 1850, CARDIFF GENERAL STATION WAS REBUILT IN ITS PRESENT FORM BY THE GWR IN 1932. IT IS THE LARGEST STATION IN WALES.

'Castle' Class 4-6-0 No. 7027 'Thornbury Castle' enters Cardiff General at the head of the inaugural down 'Pembroke Coast Express' on Monday, June 8, 1953. Having left Paddington at 10.55am this train would reach its destination at Pembroke Dock at 5.26pm. No. 7027 was built at Swindon in 1949 and withdrawn in 1963. Fortunately it was bought by Dai Woodham in 1964 and has subsequently been saved for the preservation movement.

Cardiff has always been an important railway hub with local trains to the Welsh Valleys and long distance services to Fishguard via Swansea and Carmarthen, Bristol, Portsmouth and London Paddington via the Severn Tunnel, the north via Newport, Hereford and Shrewsbury and the Midlands via Gloucester. Although still a very busy station, the scene during the 1950s and 1960s was very different.

Named expresses such as the 'Capitals United Express', 'The South Wales Pullman', 'The Pembroke Coast Express' and 'The Red Dragon' were in the charge of Cardiff Canton's 'Kings' or 'Castles' and for a few years at the end of the '50s also in the capable hands of the 12 'Britannias' that were also allocated to that shed. 'Halls', 'Modified Halls' and 'Granges' completed the line up on many of the other cross-country services and it was a daily occurrence to see SR malachite green livery coaches in Cardiff on the through service to Portsmouth Harbour via Bristol and Salisbury. Between the summer of 1961 and May 1973 the 'South Wales Pullman' to Paddington was operated by a Blue Pullman diesel train. Until the introduction of dmus in the early 60s many of the local Valley services were handled by 5600 Class 0-6-2 tanks. Goods traffic through Cardiff was exceptionally heavy with the long

26

With only six months to go before withdrawal, 'Castle' Class 4-6-0 No. 5043 'Earl of Mount Edgcumbe' passes Pengam Junction, Cardiff with an up express on June 30, 1963. This loco was built at Swindon in 1936 and originally named 'Barbury Castle'. Fitted with a double chimney and four row superheater in 1958 this loco ended its days at Cardiff East Dock shed. Fortunately No 5043 was sold to Dai Woodham in 1964 and subsequently saved for preservation by the Birmingham Railway Museum in 1973.

coal and iron ore trains in the charge of 2800 Class 2-8-0s, 4200 Class 2-8-0 tanks, 7200 Class 2-8-2 tanks, ex-WD Class 2-8-0s and the Standard 9F 2-10-0s.

The year 1962 was a turning point for Cardiff's band of trainspotters when Cardiff Canton steam shed was closed and all of its remaining allocation transferred to Cardiff East Dock shed (88L). A new diesel depot was opened at Canton and soon Cardiff General was humming with the sound of 'Western' and 'Hymek' diesel hydraulics, soon to be followed by Brush Type 4 and English Electric Type 3 diesels. Steam was finally ousted from the Cardiff area by the summer of 1965.

Steam had long disappeared from Cardiff by February 25, 1968 as Brush Type 4 (Class 47) D1597 hauls the empty coaching stock of the recently arrived 11.10am from Manchester. Seen all over the UK, the Class 47 diesels were one of the most successful main line types built for BR with a total of 512 built between 1962 and 1968.

Loading the up mail for Paddington on a cold February morning in 1953 at Cardiff General station. The first special mail train in Britain was operated by the GWR in 1855 but, since January 2004, all mail traffic has gone by road or air.

The Miracle of Barry Scrapyard

THE STORY OF DAI WOODHAM'S SCRAPYARD AT BARRY IN SOUTH WALES IS WELL KNOWN BUT WITHOUT HIM THE MAJORITY OF BRITAIN'S PRESERVED STEAM LOCOS WOULD NOT BE WITH US NOW.

It all started in 1959 when Woodham's took their first delivery of Western Region withdrawn steam locos from Swindon - four 5300 Class Moguls and one 3100 'Prairie' tank. In these early days the scrapyard could keep pace with deliveries but as time went on the numbers steadily increased, not only from the Western Region but also, by 1964, from the Southern and London Midland Regions. In total, between 1959 and 1968, Woodham's bought 297 steam locos but scrapped less than a third.

The answer for this reprieve was simple – Woodham's had also bought vast amounts of redundant goods wagons and brake vans from BR and these were easier to dispose of than steam locos. These could wait until later but by then the growing railway preservation movement had other ideas and soon these rusting hulks were being carted off for their rebirth on preserved lines throughout the UK. Britain's railway enthusiasts have much to thank Dai Woodham for as he inadvertently saved 213 steam locos. Many of them lay rusting at Barry for over 20 years with the longest resident being ex-GWR 2-6-2 tank No. 5552 which arrived in May 1961 and was liberated in June 1986 – more than 25 years on 'death row'.

A sad scene at Woodham's scrapyard in Barry, South Wales following the end of steam on British Railways as an ex-LMS Black Five makes an impassioned plea.

Some of the early arrivals at Dai Woodham's scrapyard at Barry. Here a long line of Western Region 0-6-0 pannier and 2-6-2 Prairie tanks make a sad sight in August 1961. Fortunately, of the 297 withdrawn steam locos bought by Woodham's between 1959 and 1968 only 80 were actually dismantled and scrapped. The rest is history!

Thousands of locomotives passed into private scrapyards during the 1960s and most disappeared within months, but despite Woodham's receiving some 297 engines, few were scrapped and this 'stay of execution' enabled preservationists to build up funds and save types which would otherwise have become extinct. The centrepiece in this view of Woodham's sidings is SR 'U' Class 2-6-0 No. 31625 which arrived in June, 1964. She lay in the scrapyard for 16 years, until purchased for preservation in 1980.

Although Woodham's bought a total of 28 SR Bulleid Pacifics only two, Nos. 34045 and 34094 were actually scrapped. Here, unrebuilt 'West Country' No. 34094 'Mortehoe' is seen being cut up on January 10, 1965.

Western Region locos saved include 11 'Hall', five 'Castle', two 'King', six 'Modified Hall' and eight 'Manor' 4-6-0s. Representatives of the Southern Region, particularly Bulleid Pacifics, fared even better as most of them were withdrawn towards the end of steam on BR and include 10 'West Country', eight 'Battle of Britain' and 10 'Merchant Navy' Pacifics. Even two Somerset & Dorset Joint Railway 7F 2-8-0s and the unique BR 8P Pacific No. 71000 'Duke of Gloucester' were fortunately saved for posterity.

Woodham's bought 35 ex-LMS steam locos between 1964 and 1968. Of these only two, Ivatt 2-6-2 tanks Nos. 41248 and 41303, were cut up. The rest were saved for preservation including 'Jubilee' Class 4-6-0 No. 45690 'Leander' seen here at Barry on April 24, 1965. This now-famous loco, one of only four of its class to be preserved, was withdrawn from Bristol Barrow Road (82E) in March 1964, arrived at Woodham's in July and left for preservation in May 1972.

A visit to Woodham's on April 7, 1963 found 31 condemned steam locos, all WR types. The stars of the show were the 'King' Class 4-6-0 Nos 6023 'King Edward II' and 6024 'King Edward I'. They had arrived at Barry late in 1962. No. 6023 spent 22 years at the yard before being saved for preservation in 1984. No. 6024 was saved in March 1973, after 10 years on 'death row'.

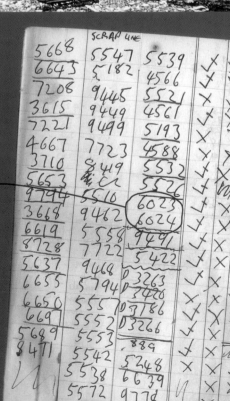

88 A Cardiff Canton

Located just to the west of Cardiff General station and originally opened by the GWR in 1882 and considerably extended by them in 1925 and 1931, Canton shed was the principal main line steam shed in Cardiff and was given the code 86C until 1960. It was about 10 minutes walking time from General station.

Along with the regular 'Kings' and 'Castles' allocated for top link jobs on expresses to Paddington, Canton was also allocated 12 'Britannia' Class 4-6-2s for a short while in the late 50s and early 60s until they were reallocated to Carlisle Kingmoor (12A) and Aston (21D). In October 1961 Canton's impressive allocation included 7 '2800' Class 2-8-0s, 5 '4200' Class 2-8-0 tanks, 3 Moguls, 19 0-6-0 pannier tanks of various types, 2 'Manors', 5 'Granges', 3 'Modified Halls', 21 'Halls', 15 'Castles', 3 'Kings', 7 ex-WD 2-8-0s and 11 BR Standard 9F 2-10-0s including No. 92220 'Evening Star' – the last steam locomotive to be built by BR.

After closure to steam in September 1962 a new diesel depot was opened on the site and all of Canton's remaining steam locomotives were reallocated to Cardiff East Dock (88L). The new diesel depot serviced 'Hymek' and 'Western' diesel-hydraulics and the English Electric Type 3 (later Class 37) and Brush Type 4 (later Class 47) diesels for many years.

Ex-GWR '4575' Class 2-6-2 tanks Nos. 5572 and 4578 at the end of the fire-dropping and coaling queue at Canton shed on September 6, 1953. Fourteen of these locos were saved for preservation, of which 13 were rescued from the nearby Barry scrapyard.

Ex-GWR '2800' Class 2-8-0 No. 2876 pollutes Cardiff's skies at Canton in March 1961. This heavy freight loco was built at Swindon in 1919 and spent the majority of its life allocated to various South Wales sheds before being withdrawn from Newport Ebbw Junction shed in early 1965. Preservation groups have saved 16 of these fine locos, of which 15 were rescued from the famous Barry scrapyard.

Ex-Alexandra (Newport and South Wales) Docks & Railway Company 2-6-2 tank No. 1205 is seen here a year after withdrawal at Canton shed on 18 July 1957. The A. D. & R. Company and its 39 locos, including No. 1205, became part of the GWR in 1922 when the two companies were merged.

88 L Cardiff East Dock

Located in Cardiff's Docklands, Cardiff East Dock shed was a 30 minute walk for the trainspotter from General station past Bute Docks and Roath Basin.

Built by the GWR in 1931, the shed was originally coded 88B until 1958 and provided steam motive power for the extensive rail network around Cardiff's Docks. It later became a diesel depot (code CED) with an allocation in October 1961 of 40 of the standard BR 0-6-0 shunter and the entire class of 1948 Swindon-built 0-6-0 shunters numbered 15101 to 15106. Destined for early closure, Cardiff East Dock's fortunes revived in September 1962 when it received the remaining steam locos displaced by the closure of Canton shed.

Until closure in August 1965 it was common to see a motley collection of decrepit ex-GWR main line steam locos around the shed – for instance on Sunday April 7, 1963 there were 44 steam locos (all ex-GWR except for one Stanier 8F 2-8-0) including 2 'Counties', 2 'Granges', 6 'Halls', 2 'Modified Halls' and 7 'Castles'.

Heavy freight workhorses of BR line up outside Cardiff East Dock on July 6, 1965 – less than a month before closure of the shed. Two Standard Class '9F' 2-10-0s, including 92166, and Stanier '8F' 2-8-0 No. 48636 await their next turn of duty. Then allocated to Birkenhead (6C) the '9F' was finally withdrawn in November 1967.

The three other 'Castles' seen on that trip in 1963. Note also the presence of two 'County' Class 4-6-0s and the trainspotter's comment about Cathays shed (88M)!

The filthy task of cleaning the smokebox of a Stanier '8F' 2-8-0 at Cardiff East Dock shed in March 1963. Despite our nostalgia for steam the cleaners must have jumped for joy when diesels were introduced.

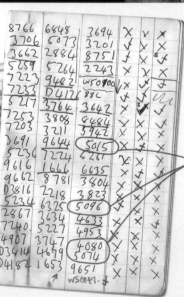

A 'foreign' visitor seen at Cardiff East Dock in July 1964 was SR 'U' Class 2-6-0 No. 31613 which was making its own way to Cohen's breaker's yard at Morriston in Swansea. On the right is 'County' Class 4-6-0 No. 1010 'County of Caernarvon' which was also withdrawn that month after only 18 years' service from Swindon shed (82C).

Four of the seven 'Castles' found at Cardiff East Dock (88L) during a Warwickshire Railway Society 'shed bash' to South Wales on April 7, 1963.

31

ON SHED

87 D

The bleak line-up of stored locos at Swansea East Dock on October 27, 1963 - from left to right former Powlesland & Mason 0-4-0 saddle tank No. 1151, ex-Cardiff Railway 0-4-0 saddle tank No. 1338, 2-8-0 tank No. 4264, 0-6-0 pannier tanks Nos. 3781 and 6724 and 2-8-0 tank No. 5237.

Swansea East Dock

Swansea East Dock was a good 20 minute walk from Swansea High Street station or, alternatively, a ride on a United Welsh bus heading towards Neath.

The shed was opened by the GWR in 1893 and provided locos for the extensive rail network serving Swansea Docks and associated heavy freight trains. The shed's allocation of 48 locos in October 1961 were all tank engines and included 28 0-6-0 pannier tanks of various types, 4 '4200' 2-8-0 tanks, 3 '7200' 2-8-2 tanks, and '5600' 0-6-2 tanks. To traverse the sharp curves around the docks the shed was also home to the two ex-Powlesland & Mason 0-4-0 saddle tanks Nos 1151 (built 1916) and 1152 (built 1912) and ex-Cardiff Railway 0-4-0 saddle tank No. 1338 dating from 1898. No. 1152 was soon withdrawn and the shed was allocated two unusual 'foreigners' in the shape of ex-LMS 0-4-0 saddle tank No. 47003 and ex-Lancashire & Yorkshire Railway 0-4-0 saddle tank No. 51218 of 1901 vintage.

Set in a bleak, windswept landscape Swansea East Dock finally closed in June 1964. Sub-sheds of Swansea East Dock were Gurnos (closed 1962) and Upper Bank (closed 1963).

Far from its home territory in northern England veteran OF 0-4-0 saddle tank No. 51218 stands forlornly out of use at Swansea East Dock in October 1963. Designed by John Aspinall for the Lancashire & Yorkshire Railway and introduced in 1901, this loco's short wheel base enabled it to traverse the sharp curves that abounded around Swansea Dock's rail system. Previously allocated to Bristol Barrow Road (82E) before moving to Swansea, No. 51218 was fortunately preserved and can now be seen on the Keighley & Worth Valley Railway.

Another, more modern, 'foreigner' allocated to Swansea East Dock in October 1963 was ex-LMS 0-4-0 saddle tank No. 47003. Built by Kitson & Co of Leeds for the LMS the first five members of this class were introduced in 1932. A further batch of five locos with extended side tanks and increased coal space were built at Horwich by British Railways in 1953. Formerly allocated to Hasland shed (18C), No. 47003 and the other nine members of this class had all been withdrawn by 1966. Sadly, none was preserved.

Another Kitson-built loco to be seen at Swansea East Dock was 0-4-0 saddle tank No. 1338. Here, seen out of use in October 1963, the loco was built in 1898 for the Cardiff Railway and spent its life on shunting duties around the docks of South Wales. Fortunately, this diminutive loco has since been preserved and can be seen at the Didcot Railway Centre.

With only eight months to go before closure Swansea East Dock shed was a rather sad place to visit in October 1963. Fortunately, the four short-wheel base 0-4-0 saddle tanks were still there, although three of them were stored out of use by then.

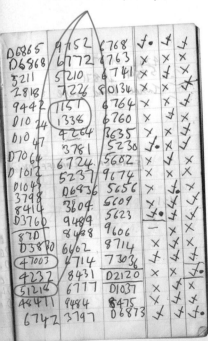

Although of a standard GWR design originally introduced in 1929, 5700 Class 0-6-0 pannier tank No. 6777, seen here at Swansea East Dock shed in October 1963, was one of only 15 members of this class built in 1950 after Nationalisation. The standard GWR shunting loco, a total of 863 were built of which 16 have been preserved.

Day Tripper

Carmarthen 25/02/1963

It was the half-term holiday and I, along with a trainspotting friend, decided to set off from Gloucester for a shed bash in South Wales. The main object of the exercise was to find the last 'Castle' Class loco still needed to underline in my Ian Allan ABC Combined Volume – No. 4081 'Warwick Castle'. By early 1963 steam-hauled passenger trains were on the decline but we were lucky with the first leg of our journey to Cardiff as the train was hauled by 'Hall' Class 4-6-0 No. 4929 'Goytrey Hall', an 85B loco at that time. Other sections of our journey to Carmarthen and back saw diesel haulage in the shape of 'Hymek' and 'Western' diesel hydraulics.

Calling in at Duffryn Yard (87B), Neath (87A) and Llanelly (87F) sheds on the way we finally arrived at Carmarthen where, joy oh joy, we found No. 4081 tucked away out of use at the back of the shed. I sneaked a rusty old split pin from the running plate as a memento and still carry it with me today. One of the first batch of 'Castles' built at Swindon in 1924, No 4081 had already been withdrawn a month earlier.

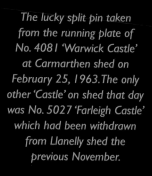

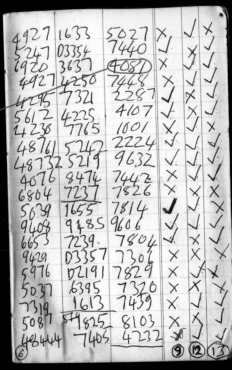

The lucky split pin taken from the running plate of No. 4081 'Warwick Castle' at Carmarthen shed on February 25, 1963. The only other 'Castle' on shed that day was No. 5027 'Farleigh Castle' which had been withdrawn from Llanelly shed the previous November.

With train reporting number 1M34 'Castle' Class 4-6-0 No. 7011 'Banbury Castle' heads northwards through Churchdown on 15 August 1964 with a Saturdays-only train for Wolverhampton Low Level. The 'Castle' was withdrawn from Oxley shed (2B) in February 1965.

Churchdown 15/08/1964

Situated midway between Cheltenham and Gloucester, Churchdown station was a great place for trainspotting on a summer Saturday in 1963 and 1964. A constant procession of Saturdays-only trains from the Midlands and North of England to holiday destinations in Devon and Cornwall brought a wide selection of, by then, fairly run-down motive power, including 'Castle', 'Jubilee', Royal Scot, 'Britannia', 'Black Five' and even the occasional 'B1'.

The summer of 1964 was the last year of steam-haulage on these trains, many of which had travelled down the soon-to-be-closed GWR route from Wolverhampton Low Level via Honeybourne and Cheltenham Malvern Road.

For a few hours of the afternoon of August 15, 1964

'Jubilee' Class 4-6-0 No. 45697 'Achilles' of Leeds Holbeck shed (55A) heads through Churchdown on the same day with a southbound troop train. Built at Crewe in 1936 'Achilles' was withdrawn from Holbeck shed in September 1967.

WESTERN REGION

HOLIDAY RUNABOUT TICKETS

ISSUED ON ANY DAY FROM

28th APRIL to 26th OCTOBER, 1963

Available for ONE WEEK from date of issue

PROVIDE

UNLIMITED TRAVEL IN HOLIDAY AREAS

SECOND CLASS FARES

Area No. 6 .... 20s. 0d. each

a mixture of motive power was spotted at Churchdown ranging from 'Peaks' and 'Black Fives' on the Midland line trains to a couple of 'Jubilees', a 'Castle' and a 'Grange'. The Cheltenham St James to Gloucester trains were still in the hands of ex-GWR pannier and 'Prairie tanks'. On September 5 that year the very last 'Castle'-hauled Penzance to Wolverhampton (LL) train was hauled through Churchdown behind No. 5063 'Earl Baldwin'.

Highlights of the afternoon's session at Churchdown on August 15, 1964 was ex-GWR Class '5101' 2-6-2 tank No. 4100 piloting a failed 'Peak' diesel, D162, towards Gloucester Eastgate on a southbound express! 'Castle' Class No. 7011 'Banbury Castle' was seen on a Wolverhampton (LL) train, 'Jubilee' Class No. 45697 'Achilles' on a southbound troop train and No. 45622 'Nyasaland' on a northbound express.

Sharpness Branch

The 1960s saw the closure of rural stations, branch lines and secondary routes throughout Gloucestershire. 1964 was a particularly black year and the imminent closure of the Sharpness branch led to a last visit on 25 August.

Waiting at Berkeley Road station on that sunny afternoon was ex-GWR '1400' Class 0-4-2 tank No. 1472 of Horton Road shed (85B) and an auto-coach. Departure to Sharpness was delayed until the arrival of the up and down connecting trains on the Midland main line – 'Castle' Class No. 5055 'Earl of Eldon' duly arrived from Bristol while BR Standard Class 5 No. 73037 finally sauntered in with the stopping train from Gloucester. However, there were no joining passengers!

With an intermediate stop at Berkeley, the trip to Sharpness and back was quickly over but there was just time to see Fowler '4F' 0-6-0 no. 44123 on a branch goods. The line closed to passengers just over two months later.

(Left) No. 1472 and auto-coach wait at Berkeley Road as 'Castle' Class No. 5055 'Earl of Eldon' departs with a stopping train to Gloucester. (Top right) The driver of the Sharpness train scratches his head while waiting for the Bristol-bound connecting train to arrive at Berkeley Road. (Bottom right) The missing spans of the Severn Railway Bridge which was put out of action by a collision from a barge in 1960. Until that date trains from Berkeley Road continued across the bridge to Lydney.

Gloucester

ONCE SERVED BY BOTH THE GWR AND MIDLAND RAILWAY, GLOUCESTER FEATURED IN THE FAMOUS 19TH CENTURY BREAK-OF-GAUGE CARTOON WHEN IT WAS AN IMPORTANT TRANSHIPMENT CENTRE BETWEEN BRUNEL'S BROAD GAUGE AND THE STANDARD GAUGE OF THE MIDLAND RAILWAY.

With Gloucester Cathedral in the distance and viewed from the long overbridge linking Eastgate and Central stations ex-LMS 'Jubilee' Class 4-6-0 No. 45668 'Madden' manoeuvres a train out of the carriage sidings at Gloucester, c.1960. Built at Crewe in 1935, 'Madden' ended its days at Burton shed (17B) before being withdrawn at the end of 1963.

For the young trainspotter in the late 1950s and early '60s Gloucester couldn't fail to impress. With two engine sheds and two through stations it was here that a wide range of ex-GWR and ex-LMS locos could be seen at work. On the ex-GWR side was Central station and Horton Road shed. From here the top-link working was the 'Cheltenham Spa Express' and other unnamed trains to Paddington via Swindon always hauled by a gleaming 85B 'Castle'. Trains to Newport and Cardiff were usually in the capable hands of 'Halls' while the single-track route to Hereford saw a varied selection ranging from Class 4300 Moguls to 5101 Class 2-6-2 tanks. Interspersed were the 1400 Class 0-4-2 tanks on the Chalford auto trains and either 9400 Class 0-6-0 or 5101 Class 2-6-2 tanks on the short run to Cheltenham St James and ex-GWR AEC railcars on the Ledbury branch. Heavy freight to and from South Wales and the Midlands was usually in the capable hands of Class 2800 2-8-0s and Class 7200 2-8-2 tanks and the continuous stream of iron-ore trains from Banbury to South Wales were usually headed by BR Standard 9F 2-10-0s or ex-WD 2-8-0s. By 1965 nearly all main line operations were in the hands of the 'Warship', 'Western' and 'Hymek' diesel-hydraulics, Brush Type 4 and English Electric Type 3 diesels.

Gloucester Eastgate station (linked to Central station by a very long footbridge) and Barnwood shed served the distinctly separate

Sheffield Millhouses (41C) engines were a fairly common sight at Gloucester working trains down to Bristol. Here, ex-LMS 'Royal Scot' Class 4-6-0 No. 46164 'The Artists' Rifleman' (in a fairly decrepit condition and minus nameplates) departs from Gloucester Eastgate with a summer-Saturday train for the north in September 1962. This loco was built at Derby in 1930 and was withdrawn soon after this photo was taken.

'Hall' Class 4-6-0 No. 4929 'Goytrey Hall' passes its homes shed at Horton Road as it heads an FA Cup Final special to Wembley in 1961. The loco spent its last six years allocated to 85B until withdrawal in March 1965.

ex-MR route from Birmingham to Bristol. Here 'Black Fives', 'Jubilees', unrebuilt 'Patriots', Standard Class 5s and Class 2P 4-4-0s and 4F 0-6-0 goods engines were the order of the day until overtaken by the 'Peak' diesel invasion of the early 60s. Highlights of each day were named trains such as the 'Pines Express' and 'Devonian' – usually 'Jubilee' or 'Black Five'-hauled – and 'The Cornishman' – always hauled by an immaculate Wolverhampton Stafford Road (84A) 'Castle'. The Docks branch, usually worked by diminutive ex-MR Deeley 0-4-0 tanks, also saw brand new London Underground stock, BR diesel railcars and coaching stock for far-flung parts of the British Empire such as Sierra Leone and Nigeria emerging like new full-size toys from the Gloucester Railway Carriage & Wagon Works.

The twilight of steam in Gloucester during 1963 and 1964 also saw the introduction of filthy and run-down 'Britannias' and 'Royal Scots' on the summer-Saturday trains from the Midlands and the North to the south west via Bristol. All local stopping and branch trains were withdrawn in late 1964 and steam had virtually disappeared by the end of 1965. Gloucester Eastgate clung to life but it was closed at the end of 1975 and then demolished.

A Gloucester Horton Road 'Castle' waits to depart from Central station with an express from Cheltenham (St James) to Paddington, c.1960. The Cheltenham to Paddington workings, including the 'Cheltenham Spa Express', were headed by large 'Prairie' or '9400' Class tank engines as far as Gloucester Central. Here a usually immaculate 85B 'Castle' would back down on to the rear of the train before heading off towards Swindon and Paddington.

ON SHED

Gloucester Horton Road

Built by the GWR in 1854 and subsequently enlarged in 1921 this 6-road shed still possessed 35 steam locomotives as late as 1965. Walking time from Central station was about 10 minutes. Entry to the shed, through a hole in the fence, was not difficult for trainspotters!

In October 1961 Gloucester's allocation included 4 of the '1400' Class 0-4-2 tanks for the Chalford auto trains, 6 '2251' Class, 13 'Prairies' mainly for use on the Cheltenham St James run, 7 Moguls, 2 '5600' Class, 19 0-6-0 pannier tanks of various types, 5 'Halls', 3 'Modified Halls' and 8 'Castle' Class 4-6-0s which were used mainly on the Cheltenham Spa to Paddington expresses including the 'Cheltenham Spa Express', a descendant of the pre-war 'Cheltenham Flyer'.

Possessing one of the largest nameplates of any steam locomotive on BR, a regular on this run was No. 5017 'The Gloucestershire Regiment 28th, 61st' – originally 'St Donats Castle' and renamed in 1954 after that regiment's heroic stand at the Battle of the Imjin River during the Korean War. Horton Road closed to steam on the first day of 1966.

Sub-sheds of Horton Road were Brimscombe (closed 1963), Cheltenham Malvern Road (closed 1963), Lydney (closed 1964) and Ross-on-Wye (closed 1963). Brimscombe shed usually housed a 'Prairie' tank which was kept there for banking heavy freight trains up Sapperton Bank. Lydney and Ross-on-Wye supplied locos for duties on the network of lines in the Forest of Dean.

Happier days at Horton Road. Ex-GWR '1400' Class 0-4-2 tank tops up with water prior to working an auto train to Chalford and back on May 15, 1964. In the background are '4300' Class 2-6-0 No. 6349 and '4500' Class 2-6-2 tank No. 4564. The Chalford auto train, the delightfully rural line to Hereford and all local stopping train services were all withdrawn by the end of that year.

By July 1963 the diesel-hydraulic invasion had reached Horton Road. Here, only four months old, 'Western' Class D1056 'Western Sultan' rubs shoulders with two 85B regulars – 'Modified Hall' 4-6-0 No. 6993, 'Arthog Hall' and 'Hall' Class 4-6-0 No. 5951, 'Clyffe Hall'.

85C Gloucester Barnwood

A typical Midland Railway roundhouse, Barnwood shed was opened in 1890 and closed in May 1964. For the trainspotter walking time from Eastgate station was about 15 minutes and access was fairly easy along a cinder path from Tramway Crossing. Engines awaiting the cutter's torch were usually stored on a long siding to the west of the shed. Barnwood's allocation provided motive power in the form of ex-MR, ex-LMS and BR Standard types for local passenger services to Bristol and Worcester, the Dursley, Nailsworth and Tewkesbury branches and local trip workings

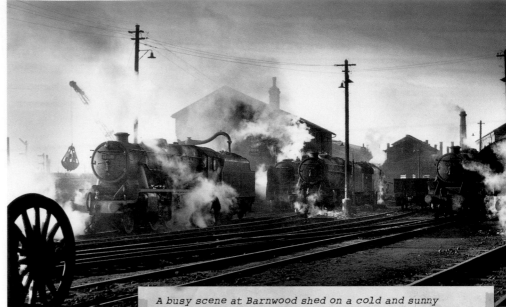

A busy scene at Barnwood shed on a cold and sunny December morning in 1962. Getting up steam from left to right are 8F 2-8-0s Nos. 48420 and 48182 and 'Black Five' 4-6-0 No. 44819.

to Bristol Road gasworks and Gloucester Docks. The shed's allocation in October 1961 included the following 'maids of all work': 2 ex-MR Deeley 0-4-0 dock tanks, 5 ex-MR Johnson 3F 0-6-0s, 7 ex-LMS 4F 0-6-0s, 2 'Jinties' and 3 BR Standard Class 5 4-6-0s.

Sub-sheds of Barnwood were Dursley (closed 1962) and Tewkesbury (closed 1962).

Both allocated to Barnwood shed where they were photographed at rest on November 26, 1961. On the left is ex-MR Johnson 3F 0-6-0 No. 43645 which was a familiar sight pottering up and down the docks branch and on other local freight trains. On the right is ex-LMS Fowler 0-6-0 No. 44209 which travelled further afield and could occasionally be seen working local passenger trains to Bristol.

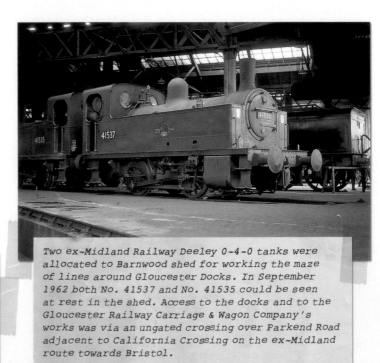

Two ex-Midland Railway Deeley 0-4-0 tanks were allocated to Barnwood shed for working the maze of lines around Gloucester Docks. In September 1962 both No. 41537 and No. 41535 could be seen at rest in the shed. Access to the docks and to the Gloucester Railway Carriage & Wagon Company's works was via an ungated crossing over Parkend Road adjacent to California Crossing on the ex-Midland route towards Bristol.

DASTARDLY DIESELS!

The first main line diesels in operational service on the GWR were the 38 AEC-engined streamlined diesel railcars first introduced in 1934. Nicknamed the 'Flying Banana', they were highly successful and remained in operation on cross-country services as Nos W1-W38 until the last examples were withdrawn in 1962. Although not diesel-powered, the next internal combustion locos to work on the Western Region were the gas turbine-electric prototypes Nos. 18000 and 18100. The former was built by Brown, Boveri in Switzerland and was in service on main line duty between 1949 and 1960. More expensive to operate, No. 18100 was built by Metropolitan-Vickers and was in service between 1951 and 1957.

An ex-GWR AEC-powered diesel railcar makes a fine sight as it trundles through an overgrown station. Known as 'Flying Bananas', a total of 38 of these highly successful vehicles were introduced between 1934 and 1942. Built in batches by Park Royal, Gloucester Railway Carriage & Wagon Company and the GWR (at Swindon) many of them remained in service until the late 1950s with the last being withdrawn in 1962.

Gas turbine prototype No. 18000 is seen here with a Bristol to Paddington express near Didcot on April 16, 1955. Ordered by the GWR in 1940, this pioneer loco was built by Brown, Boveri of Switzerland and delivered to British Railways in 1949. It was withdrawn in 1960 and subsequently returned to Europe as a test bed for the International Union of Railways.

'Warship' Class A1A-A1A diesel hydraulic D604 'Cossack' heads a Plymouth to Paddington express at Teignmouth in September 1959. Built by the North British Locomotive Company in 1958, D604 was one of five such locos that were all withdrawn at the end of 1967.

Resplendent in gleaming white livery, brand new prototype main line diesel D0260 'Lion' is seen here at Swindon in 1962 while taking part in trials for a new BR Type 4 fleet. Built by the Birmingham Railway Carriage & Wagon Company at Smethwick, the loco was withdrawn at the end of 1963 when BR ordered a fleet of the Brush Type 4 (class 47) diesels.

A classic 1965 period photo as the pride of the British motor industry waits for a Class 03 0-6-0 diesel shunter to cross Llanthony Road on the ex-GWR Gloucester Docks branch.

The 1955 Modernisation Plan called for the introduction of various types of non-standard main line diesels on British Railways. Despite the success with the standardisation of new BR steam locos this policy was not extended to diesels. Consequently numerous types of dubious quality were hurriedly introduced at great expense to the taxpayer. By far the worst offender was the autonomous Western Region who hurriedly introduced a range of unreliable, underpowered and short-lived diesel-hydraulics. Despite this, with their modern looks, they certainly added a certain amount of glitz to the early 1960s trainspotting scene. The first to arrive were the original five 'Warship' Class A1A-A1A diesels (D600-D604) which were built by the North British Loco Co and saw service from 1958 to 1967. These were followed by the Class 42/43 'Warship' Class B-B (D800-D870), Built in two batches by BR Swindon and NBL, they saw service on main line expresses out of Paddington from 1958 to 1972.

Next to arrive were the highly unreliable Class 22 B-B (D6300-D6357), also built by NBL, which were in service on secondary duties from 1958 until 1971 followed by the Class 35 B-B 'Hymek' (D7000-D7100). With their slick, contemporary looks, the latter were employed from 1961 on secondary passenger and freight duties and main line expresses to South Wales. More successful than their counterparts they remained in service until 1975. The final class of WR diesel-hydraulics were the sleek and powerful Class 52 'Western' C-C (D1000-D1073)

Resplendent in BR green livery, 'Warship' D825 'Intrepid' gets a quick hose-down at Kingswear before departing with the up 'Torbay Express' on May 31, 1961. Built at Swindon in 1960, this diesel hydraulic loco was less than a year old when pictured here and was one of the last few survivors of this class that were finally withdrawn in late 1972.

Rubbing shoulders with an 0-6-0 pannier tank on ECS duties, the South Wales Blue Pullman waits to depart from Paddington on July 30, 1964. Introduced in the summer of 1961 this train ran to Cardiff and Swansea until withdrawal in May 1973.

North British Locomotive Company Type 2 diesel hydraulic D6321 (Class 22) heads the Torrington to Exeter Riverside milk tankers near Cowley Bridge in May 1967. By this date this short-lived and unreliable class, introduced in 1959, had been relegated to more mundane duties and withdrawal was looming.

BR Sulzer Type 4 (Class 45) D41 halts at Gloucester Eastgate with a northbound express from Bristol in 1962. By the Autumn of 1961 ten of these powerful diesels had been allocated to Bath Road (82A) and had started to replace the once-familiar Barrow Road (82E) 'Jubilees' on the former Midland main line. D41 was later renumbered 45147 and was withdrawn in April 1985.

which were built in two batches at Swindon and Crewe. First introduced in 1962 they soon replaced the underpowered 'Warship' and 'Hymeks' on main line expresses out of Paddington and remained in service until 1977.

By the early 1970s BR had decided to move away from the non-standard WR diesel-hydraulics and they were soon replaced by more reliable standard types of diesel-electrics such as the English Electric Type 3 (Class 37), Brush Type 4 (Class 47), Brush Type 2 (Class 31) , BR Sulzer Type 4 (Class 45/46) and BR Sulzer Type 2 (Class 25). The introduction of the High Speed Train (Class 43) on main line services out of Paddington in the mid-1970s virtually ended locomotive-hauled passenger trains on the Western Region.

A surprisingly high number of fairly new 'Western' Class diesel hydraulics were noted on a visit to Swindon works on November 24, 1963. All, apart from D1014 and D1015, had been built at Crewe during the last 15 months and had been sent to Swindon for modification to their bogies following unsatisfactory ride problems. D1015 'Western Champion' was outshopped from Swindon in June 1963 finished in the unique desert sand (or golden ochre) livery. Although withdrawn in late 1976 this loco has since been preserved.

A total of 56 0-6-0 diesel hydraulic locos (Class 14) were built at Swindon between 1964 and 1965. One of nine such locos allocated to Bath Road (82A) at this time, D9502 heads a local freight towards Avonmouth at Redland in 1965. This class had an extremely short working life on BR with many subsequently sold to private users both at home and abroad. D9502 has since been preserved.

Resplendent in maroon livery, 'Western' Class diesel hydraulic D1052 'Western Viceroy', then allocated to Cardiff Canton, heads the 17.30 Paddington to Plymouth express at Blatchbridge Junction in June 1964. One of a batch of 44 such locos built at Crewe, D1052 was outshopped in early 1963 and was withdrawn from Plymouth Laira after a collision in the Autumn of 1975.

'Hymek' (Class 35) diesel hydraulics D7038 and D7002 look quite a picture as they pose for the photographer outside Swindon Works in March 1963. One of the more successful classes of diesel hydraulics, a total of 101 were built by Beyer Peacock between 1961 and 1964. Due to their non-standard design the entire class was withdrawn between 1971 and 1975. Four members of this class have since been preserved.

Diesel multiple units had begun to take over many of the local WR passenger services by the early 1960s. Pictured here at Cheltenham St James in 1965 are (left) a Swindon-built Cross-Country set and (right) a Gloucester R. C. & W. Co. three-car Cross-Country unit. St James station closed on November 1, 1966 with the last train, the 22.15 to Gloucester Central, hauled by Brush Type 4 D1901.

Headed by Brush Type 4 (Class 47) diesels D1636 and D1637, two special trains wait to leave Newbury Racecourse Station for Paddington on July 1, 1969. A total of 512 of these locos were built for BR between 1963 and 1968 and many of them saw service on the Western Region. Probably the most successful class of main line diesels ordered by BR, many have survived well into the 21st century.

Headed by 253 003, the first High Speed Train (HST) diesel service to Paddington departs from Bristol Temple Meads on October 4, 1976. Built at Crewe, these InterCity 125 units heralded a new age in rail travel and, despite their age, continue to provide sterling service on routes from Paddington to the West Country.

Bristol Temple Meads

A HISTORIC STATION, THE ORIGINAL PART OF TEMPLE MEADS WAS OPENED IN
1840 AS THE WESTERN TERMINUS OF BRUNEL'S GWR BROAD GAUGE ROUTE FROM
PADDINGTON. MORE ROUTES SOON OPENED TO THE MIDLANDS VIA GLOUCESTER
AND THE SOUTH WEST VIA EXETER AND PLYMOUTH LEADING TO AN EXPANSION OF
THE STATION, INCLUDING THE BUILDING OF THE OVERALL GLAZED ROOF, IN 1870.
THE GWR CARRIED OUT FURTHER IMPROVEMENTS TO THE STATION IN THE 1930S.

Fitted with double chimney and four row superheater, 'Castle' Class 4-6-0 No. 7018 'Drysllwyn Castle' of Bath Road shed (82A) gets ready to leave Temple Meads with the up non-stop 'Bristolian' to Paddington in the late 1950s. This particular train covered the 117.5-mile journey to London (via Badminton) in 102.5 minutes, arriving 2.5 minutes early at its destination. Occasionally completing this journey in under 94 minutes, the highly successful 'Castles' were replaced by 'Warship' diesel hydraulics in 1959.

Ex-LMS 'Jubilee' No. 45684 'Jutland' waits at Temple Meads with a stopping train to Gloucester and Birmingham on December 31, 1963. Named after the World War I sea battle it was built at Crewe in 1936 and withdrawn from Bank Hall shed (8K) at the end of 1965.

Bristol Temple Meads was pure joy for the trainspotter in the 50s and early 60s – with not only the continuous stream of passenger trains from north, south, east and west but also the comings and goings around the adjoining Bath Road engine shed. Services to and from the north and the Midlands were handled by Barrow Road's allocation of 'Jubilees', unrebuilt 'Patriots' and Standard Class 5s. Sightings of LMR locos from Saltley, Derby and Leeds Holbeck were also a common sight. It was at Temple Meads that named trains such as 'The Devonian' and 'The Cornishman' ('Castle'-hauled from Wolverhampton LL) had a change of engines. There were sleeping car services to Scotland and stopping trains to Gloucester, often in the charge of 2P 4-4-0s, and to Bath Green Park via Mangotsfield. Summer Saturdays saw a continuous stream of holiday trains from the north and Midlands to the holiday resorts of Devon and Cornwall – in the twilight of steam many hauled by filthy 'Britannias', 'Royal Scots' and 'Castles' and even the odd ER 'B1'.

The top link WR train was surely 'The Bristolian', but the last steam-hauled up service was hauled by 'Castle ' Class 4-6-0 No. 5085 'Evesham Abbey' on June 12, 1959. After that date it

'Blood and custard' heads south for the holidays! On a sunny summer Saturday in early BR days an ex-LMS Stanier 'Black Five' 4-6-0 departs from Temple Meads with a Birmingham to Paignton express. The station's overall roof was added during enlargements in 1870. Despite the disappearance of steam and some track rationalisation the scene remains little changed today.

was 'Warships' and downhill! The 'Bristol Pullman' to Paddington was operated by Blue Pullman diesel sets between 1960 and 1973. Temple Meads was also busy with services to Exeter and Plymouth and cross-country services to Cardiff, Westbury and Portsmouth. Local services to Portishead, Severn Beach and Frome via Radsotck added to the hustle and bustle. Bath Road closed to steam in September 1960 and a new diesel depot was built on the site to cater for the ever-increasing numbers of 'Warships', 'Westerns' and 'Hymeks' with the remaining steam locos moving to St Philip's Marsh shed. The latter closed in June 1964 and the remaining steam servicing was carried out at Barrow Road until November 1965 when that, too, was closed.

Opened in 1840 as the terminus of Brunel's broad gauge line from Paddington, the western part of Temple Meads station was usually the starting point for trains on the former Midland route to Gloucester and Birmingham. Here ex-LMS 'Black Five' 4-6-0 No. 44825 of Saltley shed (21A) blows off steam before drawing forward with a stopping train for Gloucester on 7 September 1963. All stopping train services on this route were withdrawn in January 1965.

By the early 1960s most services from Bristol to the north via the former Midland route were in the hands of the BR Sulzer Type 4 (Class 45/46) diesels. Here, Class 46 No. 46055 arrives at Temple Meads with the 12.23 from Manchester Piccadilly on April 22, 1975. The penultimate member of this class, No. 46055 (previously D192) was withdrawn from service in October 1982.

82 A Bristol Bath Road

A general view of Bath Road shed taken towards the end of the steam era, c. 1959. At its peak as a steam shed Bath Road had an allocation of around 20 'Castles' of which two, both 82A locos, can be seen here. On the left is No. 5090 'Neath Abbey' which was rebuilt from 'Star' Class 4-6-0 No. 4070 (also named 'Neath Abbey') in 1939. It was withdrawn in 1962. On the right, with train reporting number M96, is No. 5078 'Beaufort' which was built in 1939 and originally named 'Lamphey Castle'. Later fitted with a double chimney and four row superheater this loco was also withdrawn in 1962.

Another 82A 'Castle' and a 'Grange' get ready for their next turn of duty at Bath Road, c.1959. On the left No. 4075 'Cardiff Castle' was one of the original batch of these fine locos built back in 1924. It was withdrawn in late 1961. On the right is No. 6800 'Arlington Grange', then allocated to Penzance (83G). The first of 80 such locos built at Swindon between 1936 and 1939, this mixed-traffic loco was withdrawn in 1964.

Replacing an earlier shed originally opened by the Bristol & Exeter Railway in 1850, the large 10-road GWR shed at Bath Road was opened for locos in 1934.

Bath Road closed to steam in 1960 and its remaining allocation was moved to St Philip's Marsh (82B) until that, too, closed in 1964 and the remnants were moved to Barrow Road (82E) until closure of that shed in 1965. Bath Road steam shed was replaced by a modern diesel depot with an allocation of 'Warship', 'Western' and 'Hymek' diesel hydraulics, 'Peaks' and, later, Brush Type 4s. This too has closed and all loco servicing is carried out at Barton Hill.

Located on the east side of the south end of Temple Meads station, Bath Road was a difficult shed to visit without a permit but most of its movements could be easily observed from the station. Prior to closure it had an allocation

of around 80 locos, many of which were used on main line passenger services to Cardiff, Paddington and Exeter. Pride of the fleet were the 20 or so 'Castle' Class 4-6-0s which were kept in tip-top condition for working the crack expresses to Paddington. Star of the show in the late 1950s was No. 7018 'Drysllwyn Castle' – in 1956 the first 'Castle' to be fitted with a double-chimney – which put up electrifying 100 mph performances on the non-stop 'Bristolian'. A fleet of 'Counties' and 'Halls' worked many of the main line and cross-country stopping trains to destinations such as Westbury and Salisbury.

Bath Road's sub-sheds were Bath (closed in 1961), Wells (closed in 1963), Weston-super-Mare (closed in 1960) and Yatton (closed in 1960). Bath and Wells had come under the control of St Philip's Marsh in 1960.

With only just over two months before withdrawal and looking rather neglected without its nameplates, 'Warship' (Class 42) diesel hydraulic No. 829 'Magpie' is seen here at Bath Road on June 14, 1972. Built at Swindon in late 1960, 'Magpie' was withdrawn in August 1972 and cut-up at Swindon in early 1974.

Built by Pressed Steel Co. Ltd, single unit diesel railcar No.W55026 (Class 121) awaits attention at Bath Road in April 1975. At that time it had been working on the Severn Beach branch after transfer from Cardiff Canton and was later to move to Plymouth. Known as 'Bubble Cars', some examples of this class still remain in departmental service.

Exeter St Davids

DESIGNED BY BRUNEL AND OPENED IN 1844 BY THE BROAD GAUGE
BRISTOL & EXETER RAILWAY, EXETER ST DAVIDS STILL RETAINS MANY
OF ITS 19TH CENTURY FEATURES INCLUDING THE NEIGHBOURING GREAT
WESTERN HOTEL.

The majority of track ballast for the Southern Region came from Meldon Quarry near Okehampton. Here, on May 31, 1961, BR Standard Class 3 2-6-2 tank No. 82023 and 'N' Class 2-6-0 No. 31859 move forward from St Davids with a heavily loaded ballast train to tackle the short 1 in 37 gradient up to Central station. This train was banked in the rear by two of Exmouth Junction's 'Z' Class 0-8-0 tanks, Nos. 30956 and 30955.

Exeter St Davids is unique in the UK for having competing services to London departing in the opposite direction to each other – with trains on the former L&SWR route to Waterloo leaving in a southerly direction via Queen Street station (now renamed Central) while trains on the former GWR route to Paddington depart in a northerly direction. In the late 1950s this situation often led to SR 'West Country' or 'Battle of Britain' Pacifics on the 'Atlantic Coast Express' or other holiday trains destined for the 'Withered Arm' rubbing shoulders with WR 'Kings' or 'Castles' on expresses to Paddington or Plymouth and Penzance. In between all of this hustle and bustle were the diminutive WR 1400 Class 0-4-2 tanks on auto-train services up the Exe Valley to Tiverton and Dulverton and SR T9 4-4-0s and Class N 2-6-0s on local services to North Devon and North Cornwall.

Dieselisation of the WR West of England expresses had begun in earnest by 1960 and soon all of these trains were hauled by 'Warship' or 'Western' diesel-hydraulics. 'Hymeks' and the North British Type 2s were also employed on freight and local services. WR steam was ousted by 1963 with the ex-SR lingering on until 1965. Birmingham Railway Carriage & Wagon Co Class 33s were also later employed on the Meldon ballast trains. By 1966 Exeter had been totally dieselised.

A typical bi-regional scene at St Davids on May 25, 1960 as N Class 2-6-0 No. 31834 waits to tackle the incline up to Queen Street with a parcels train. Alongside, 'Warship' Class diesel hydraulic D811 'Daring' waits to depart with the down 'Torbay Express'.

Plymouth North Road

PLYMOUTH NORTH ROAD STATION WAS OPENED IN 1877 AND WAS USED BY BOTH THE GWR AND LSWR UNTIL 1891 WHEN THE LATTER OPENED ITS OWN TERMINUS AT PLYMOUTH FRIARY.

Dwarfed by the new Tamar road bridge, 'County' Class 4-6-0 No. 1006 'County of Cornwall' enters Saltash after crossing Brunel's famous Saltash Bridge with the 3.46pm Plymouth to Penzance local on September 7, 1962. No. 1006 was built at Swindon in 1945 and spent most of its life in Cornwall. It was withdrawn from Swindon shed (82C) in September 1963.

Plymouth Friary was used by LSWR and, later, SR trains to Exeter via Okehampton until 1958 when the station was closed to passengers and services reverted to using North Road. The latter was then renamed just Plymouth and was completely rebuilt in the early 1960s. Apart from the short section to Bere Alston for Gunnislake branch trains the remainder of the former LSWR route to Exeter via Okehampton was closed in 1966.

Summer Saturdays at North Road saw a succession of holiday trains from London, the Midlands and North bound for Cornwall, headed by 'Castles', Halls', 'Granges' and 'Counties'. Many changed engines at Plymouth. A steady stream of china-clay trains heading for the Potteries from St Austell and the famous St Erth to London milk trains were also a regular feature. Seasonal trains carrying potatoes and broccoli from Cornwall also ran, along with branch trains to Launceston via Yelverton usually headed by ex-GWR small 'Prairies'.

Dieselisation of trains on the WR routes started in the late 1950s with the introduction of the (D600) 'Warships' and by the early 1960s all main line trains to Penzance and Paddington were in the hands of the later 'Warships' and 'Westerns' hydraulics. Plymouth Laira closed to steam in April 1964 and dieselisation was complete. By then the dwindling freight services were being hauled by 'Hymeks' and North British Type 2 hydraulics.

Like Exeter St Davids, Plymouth North Road saw the comings and goings of both WR and SR locos. Here, unrebuilt 'Battle of Britain' Class 4-6-2 No. 34079 '141 Squadron' passes through with a milk train in the early 1960s. An Exmouth Junction (72A) loco, this loco was built by BR at Brighton in July 1948 and withdrawn from service in early 1966.

ON SHED

83 D Plymouth Laira

Opened by the GWR in 1901, Plymouth Laira was considerably enlarged in 1931. A new diesel depot was opened in 1961 but the steam shed continued to operate until closure in 1964. Located two miles to the east of North Road station, Laira was a 50-minute trek unless a No. 21 Plympton bus was caught from the city centre to Brandon Road. Here, it was but a short stroll to the end of this cul-de-sac and under the railway past the closed Laira Halt to the shed.

Once Laira's diesel depot had opened in 1960 it wasn't long before the shed's steam allocation was hauled off to pastures new or the scrapyard. By October 1961 it was down to a shadow of its former self with a total of only 46 including 2 'Counties', 6 'Castles', 5 'Halls', 1 'Modified Hall', 2 'Kings' and 6 'Granges' and these were all soon destined for withdrawal. The flip side of the coin at Laira included all five of the original North British 'Warships' (D600-D604), 46 of the new D800 'Warships', 26 of the useless North British Type 2 diesel-hydraulics and the new 'Western' Class hydraulics which were starting to appear from Crewe and Swindon Works.

Laira's only sub-shed was at Launceston (closed 1964) which normally housed a small 'Prairie' for working the branch service to Plymouth via Yelverton.

'Castle' Class 4-6-0 No. 5058 'Earl of Clancarty' stands over the ash pits at Laira shed on May 30, 1961. Built at Swindon in 1937, this loco was originally named 'Newport Castle'. Although allocated to 83D at the time of this photo, the 'Earl' was soon to move to Gloucester (85B) from where it was withdrawn in 1963.

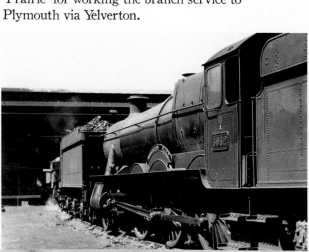

On May 27, 1962, 'Modified Hall' 4-6-0 No. 6962 'Soughton Hall' rests at Laira after a journey down from its home shed at Old Oak Common (81A). Built at Swindon in 1944 this loco became the first of its class to be withdrawn in early 1963.

On the right No. 6002 'King William IV' alongside North British Type 2 (Class 22) diesel hydraulic D6314. Built in 1927, the 'King' was withdrawn from Stafford Road shed (84A) in 1962. The unreliable Class 22 locos were extinct by 1972.

A diesel hydraulic trio at Laira on March 28, 1970. On the left is 'Warship' D817 'Foxhound' (built Swindon 1960, withdrawn 1971); on the right is another 'Warship' D834 'Pathfinder' (built by North British Loco Co in 1960 and withdrawn in 1971); at the rear is North British Type 2 D6318.

Six 'Western' (Class 52) diesel hydraulics at rest in the gloom of Laira's maintenance bay on April 23, 1974. By this date these fine-looking machines were only just over 10 years old but their non-standard design and unreliability led to their extinction by 1977. On the left is D1063 'Western Monitor' which was built at Crewe in 1963 and withdrawn from Laira in 1976.

Final Days

Alongside the introduction of new diesel-hydraulic locos emerging from Swindon, Crewe and north of the border, the early 1960s saw mass withdrawals of steam locos and the wholesale closure of many branch lines and cross-country routes throughout the Western Region.

Many stopping train services were also axed and the slow drip of freight from rail to road had become a torrent. By the end of 1965 steam had been ousted from many parts of the region but there were still a few exceptions, notable among them being the Somerset & Dorset route from Bath Green Park to Bournemouth which soldiered on with a restricted service until March 1966.

Any other pockets of steam still remaining were in former WR territories that had been transferred to the LMR in 1963. Notable steam sheds were Banbury (84C/2D, closed

(Left) Headed by the only 'Castle' Class 4-6-0 then in service, No. 7029 'Clun Castle', the final WR steam train from Paddington runs into Gloucester Eastgate after its second leg from Bristol on November 27, 1965. After continuing on to Cheltenham it returned to Gloucester Central (top) from where the 'Farewell to Steam' special is seen departing on its return trip to Paddington via Swindon. 'Clun Castle' has since been preserved.

SECOND CLASS

No. 134

LAST STEAM TRAIN FROM PADDINGTON
SATURDAY, 27 NOVEMBER, 1965
HAULED BY THE LAST CASTLE CLASS ENGINE
IN BRITISH RAILWAYS SERVICE

7029 "CLUN CASTLE"

ROUTE: PADDINGTON—SWINDON—BRISTOL—
GLOUCESTER—CHELTENHAM—GLOUCESTER—
SWINDON—PADDINGTON

DEPARTING PADDINGTON 09.18

COACH LETTER __H__   SEAT No. __30__

(W)   FACING / BACK TO ENGINE
             FOR CONDITIONS SEE OVER

to steam October 1966), Tyseley (84E/2A closed November 1966), Oxley (84B/2B, closed March 1967), Croes Newydd (89B/6C, closed June 1967) and Shrewsbury (89A/6D, closed November 1967). One of the last steam-hauled routes in the UK was the Cambrian main line from Shrewsbury to Aberystwyth and Pwllheli with the 'Cambrian Coast Express' being hauled by BR Standard Class 5 4-6-0s westwards from Shrewsbury until 1967.

Of course, as we all know, steam-haulage never really came to an end on BR in 1968. Out in the wilds of west Wales three diminutive narrow gauge 2-6-2 tanks (Nos 7, 8 and 9) continued to operate tourist trains on the state-owned Vale of Rheidol Railway until it was privatised in 1989.

'Castle' Class 4-6-0 No. 7005 'Sir Edward Elgar' waits to take over an LCGB special train to London at Cheltenham Lansdown on 12 October 1963. The special had been hauled by 'Jubilee' Class 4-6-0 No. 45552 'Silver Jubilee'.

Minus brass cabside numberplate, 'Castle' Class 4-6-0 No. 5055 'Earl of Eldon' was seen on station pilot duty at Hereford on April 18, 1964. Originally built as 'Lydford Castle', the 'Earl' was withdrawn from Gloucester Horton Road shed (85B) in October of that year.

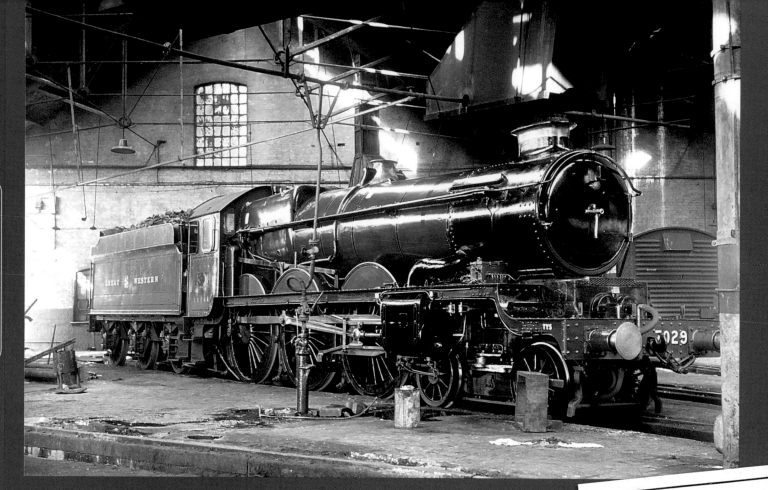

The Great Escape

THANKS TO DAI WOODHAM AND HIS BARRY SCRAPYARD, THE FORMER GREAT WESTERN RAILWAY AND ITS CONSTITUENT COMPANIES ARE REPRESENTED BY MORE PRESERVED STEAM LOCOS THAN ANY OTHER OF THE 'BIG FOUR' RAILWAY COMPANIES.

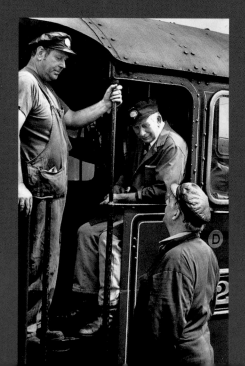

Of the 148 standard gauge locos preserved no less than 97 were rescued from Barry including all five of the '4200' Class 2-8-0 tanks and all 11 'Hall' 4-6-0s. Among the list of locos saved in the very early days of preservation, pre-Barry, are the sole surviving examples of the 'Dukedog' and 'City' Class 4-4-0s and a 'Star' 4-6-0. Apart from the 11 'Halls', other engines of note are eight 'Castle', three 'King', seven 'Modified Hall' and nine 'Manor' 4-6-0s. Additionally five former GWR narrow gauge locos (two from the Corris Railway and three from the Vale of Rheidol) and three ex-GWR standard gauge diesel railcars have also been saved from the cutter's torch.

Two major classes of ex-GWR locos were not saved and replicas of both of these, the 'County' Class and 'Grange' Class 4-6-0s, are currently being built from scratch apart from certain parts utilised from other locos.

Seen here on the Gloucestershire Warwickshire Railway on July 13, 1996 'Hall' Class 4-6-0 No. 4920 'Dumbleton Hall' was built at Swindon in 1929 and withdrawn from Bristol Barrow Road shed (82E) at the end of 1965. The loco was bought by Woodham's in 1966 and languished at Barry until 1976 when it was bought for preservation.

(Opposite) Seen here at Tyseley in 1967 shortly after being purchased for preservation, 'Castle' Class 4-6-0 No. 7029 'Clun Castle' was built at Swindon in 1950 and had the honour of hauling the last steam train out of Paddington in November 1965. It was withdrawn from Gloucester Horton Road shed (85B) at the end of that year and subsequently moved to Tyseley where it is still based. A total of eight 'Castle' Class locos have been preserved.

A feast for the eyes of any GWR enthusiast at Bishops Lydeard station on the West Somerset Railway in April 2000. Included in this lineup is '6400' Class 0-6-0 pannier tank No. 6412 and 'Manor' Class 4-6-0 No. 7820 'Dinmore Manor'. The 'Manor' was also saved from Woodham's where it spent 13 years before being purchased for preservation in 1979.

Supposedly the first steam locomotive in Europe to reach 100mph, '3700' Class 4-4-0 No. 3440 'City of Truro' was built at Swindon in 1903 and withdrawn in 1931. It was then bought by the LNER and exhibited at their railway museum in York until 1957 when it was restored by BR and returned to service. It eventually went back to the museum at York where it is now part of the National Collection.

The 2ft 6in-gauge Welshpool & Llanfair Railway opened in 1896 and was operated from the outset by Cambrian Railways. Becoming part of the GWR in 1923 the W&L lost its passenger service in 1931 but freight struggled on until 1956 when the railway was closed. A preservation group reopened part of the line in 1963 and has since extended it to a new terminus at Welshpool Raven Square. Both of the original steam locomotives, 0-6-0 tanks No. 822 'The Earl' and No. 823 'The Countess' have been preserved. The latter loco is seen here at the head of a small train at Castle Caereinion on 3 September 1966.

Railway Miscellany

'King' Class 4-6-0 No. 6000 'King George V' makes one of its last appearances in Swindon shed roundhouse (82C) on October 21, 1962. This famous loco was built at Swindon in 1927 and was soon shipped over the Atlantic to take part in the Baltimore & Ohio Railroad's centenary celebrations, While in the US the 'King' was fitted with a bell and cabside plaques (both visible in this photo) to record its visit. It was withdrawn in December 1962 and has since been preserved.

Ex-LNER locos occasionally strayed on to WR territory on summer Saturdays in the early 1960s. Here, Thomson 'B1' Class 4-6-0 No. 61051 of Sheffield Darnall shed (41A) heads the 12.05pm relief from Weston-super-Mare to Sheffield train near Standish Junction on August 22, 1964. The 'B1' survived until early 1966 when it was withdrawn from Langwith shed (41J).

WESTERN

BRITISH RAILWAYS LOCOMOTIVES

Awesome steam power at Newton Abbot in 1960. 'Castle' Class 4-6-0 No. 4095 'Harlech Castle' and Standard 9F 2-10-0 No. 92217 approach the station with an up parcels train on May 29. Not only the junction for the Moretonhampstead and Kingswear lines, Newton Abbot is also well-known to readers as the headquarters of David & Charles, the publishers of fine railway books for 50 years.

Built by Brush, the one-off experimental diesel loco D0280 'Falcon' was allocated for a time to Bath Road diesel depot, Bristol. This unique loco is seen heading west from Swindon with a Paddington to Bristol express on October 5, 1965. Built in 1961 this loco was eventually sold to BR for its scrap value and was subsequently rebuilt at Swindon as No. 1200. Due to its non-standard design it was withdrawn in 1975 and subsequently scrapped.

Apart from those saved at Woodham's in Barry, hundreds of other ex-GWR locomotives were cut up at scrapyards all over the region in the mid-1960s. This sad sight at a scrapyard in Sharpness, Gloucestershire, shows three once-mighty 'Castle' Class locos (No. 7015 'Carn Brea Castle', No. 7009 'Athelney Castle' and No, 7037 'Swindon') and '4700' Class 2-8-0 No. 4701 awaiting their fate on September 13, 1964.

BRITISH RAILWAYS

SCALE OF MILES

SOUTHERN REGION

35008

London Waterloo

THE PRINCIPAL TERMINUS FOR SUBURBAN ELECTRIC SERVICES TO SOUTH WEST LONDON AND MAIN LINE SERVICES TO PORTSMOUTH, SOUTHAMPTON, BOURNEMOUTH, WEYMOUTH, AND THE WEST OF ENGLAND VIA SALISBURY, WATERLOO WAS OPENED IN 1848 BY THE LONDON & SOUTH WESTERN RAILWAY.

This powerful image by Tom Heavyside depicts 'Merchant Navy' Class 4-6-2 No. 35008 (formerly named 'Orient Line' but now minus nameplates) at Waterloo on May 12, 1967 after arriving with the 17.30 train from Weymouth. This loco was built at Eastleigh in 1942 and withdrawn just two months after being seen here.

The station was greatly improved and enlarged during the early part of the 19th century, ending up with a total of 21 platforms. Despite third-rail electrification elsewhere on the Southern Region, Waterloo still retained main line steam operations until the summer of 1967 when the Southampton and Bournemouth route was finally 'switched on'.

For the trainspotter in the early 1960s, Waterloo – the last London terminus to see main line steam – was still a romantic place to be, with named trains such as the 'Channel Island Boat Express', 'The Royal Wessex', 'Bournemouth Belle' and the multi-destination 'Atlantic Coast Express' in the capable hands of Bulleid's rebuilt 'Merchant Navy' Class Pacifics. The 'ACE', in summer running in several portions, had through coaches for Ilfracombe, Torrington, Sidmouth, Exmouth, Bude, Padstow and Plymouth. Sadly, it last ran in September 1964 and reduced services between Waterloo, Salisbury and Exeter were gradually handed over to WR 'Warships' and, later, Class 50s, 33s and 47s. Steam, in the form of Bulleid's 'Merchant Navy', 'West Country' and 'Battle of Britain' Pacifics still held sway on Southampton, Bournemouth and Weymouth services until July 1967 when electric multiple units were introduced.

In addition to the named trains, Waterloo regularly witnessed 'Ocean Liner Specials' to and from Southampton Docks Terminus while 'Schools' 4-4-0s and 'H15', 'N15' ('King Arthurs'), 'Lord Nelson' and the named BR Standard Class 5 4-6-0s were also regularly seen hauling summer Saturday trains and local services to Basingstoke and Salisbury. Empty coaching stock was usually handled by Class M7 0-4-4 tanks until the twilight of steam when BR Standard Class 4 and Class 3 tanks were introduced.

Just arrived at Waterloo from Eastleigh, the first 'Merchant Navy' 4-6-2 to be rebuilt, No. 35018 'British India Line', is seen awaiting inspection from railway officials in February 1956. The remaining 29 'Merchant Navies' had all been rebuilt from their previous 'Spam Can' design by 1960. No. 35018 was originally built at Eastleigh in 1945 and withdrawn in August 1964. It was saved from Woodham's scrapyard at Barry in 1980 after languishing there for nearly 16 years and has since been preserved.

Two ex-LSWR Class 'M7' 0-4-4 tanks, Nos. 30123 and 30133 perform empty coaching stock movements at Waterloo in the late 1950s. Designed by Dugald Drummond, 105 of these locos were built between 1897 and 1911, the majority at the company's Nine Elms Works. Initially built to handle suburban services out of Waterloo many eventually found their way to branch line duties in the West Country for which they were fitted for push-pull operation. No. 30123 was built in 1903 and withdrawn from Eastleigh shed (71A) in 1959. No. 30133 was also built in 1903 but was withdrawn from Bournemouth shed (71B) in 1964.

On April 24, 1966, 'Battle of Britain' Class 4-6-2 No. 34064 'Fighter Command' and 'West Country' Class 4-6-2 No. 34032 'Camelford' wait to depart Waterloo with the 9.30am and 9.33am trains for Weymouth respectively.

Nine Elms 70A

Replacing a semi-circular roundhouse, the former LSWR loco shed at Nine Elms consisted of two adjacent sheds – the 'Old Shed' of 15 roads opened in 1885 and the 'New Shed' of 10 roads opened in 1910. Nine Elms, along with nearby Stewarts Lane (73A), which closed in 1963, was the Southern Region's main steam shed in London. The shed provided motive power for all main line services out of Waterloo – to Southampton, Bournemouth, Weymouth and West of England services via Salisbury.

By November 1961 empty coaching stock movements between Clapham and Waterloo were being handled by an allocation of eight M7 0-4-4 tanks and eight WR 0-6-0 pannier tanks. Main line services by then were in the hands of 19 of the very capable BR Standard Class 5 4-6-0s (all carrying names from the withdrawn N15 'King Arthur' Class locos), 12 'West Country' and eight 'Battle of Britain' Class light Pacifics and, to handle the heavyweight expresses such as 'The Bournemouth Belle' and 'Atlantic Coast Express', a total of 12 'Merchant Navy' Pacifics.

A scene that has disappeared forever. Three trainspotters – one with regulation duffel bag and another with impractical white trousers – have arrived from Wigan on May 13, 1967 to pay their last respects to Southern steam at Nine Elms. Less than two months later the shed had closed and steam had been eradicated from the region.

Despite the removal of its nameplate 'Merchant Navy' Class 4-6-2 No. 35008 ('Orient Line') looks in pretty good shape at Nine Elms on October 7, 1965. Originally built as No. 21C8 at Eastleigh in 1942, this loco was rebuilt in 1957 and withdrawn in July 1967.

This classic shot of steam at rest was taken at Nine Elms in 1966. Flanked by a BR Standard tank and a rebuilt 'West Country', rebuilt 'Battle of Britain' Class 4-6-2 No. 34077 '603 Squadron' awaits its next turn of duty. Built by BR at Brighton Works in 1948, this loco was rebuilt in 1960 and withdrawn in March 1967.

Ex-SR 'Remembrance' Class 4-6-0 No. 32328 'Hackworth' is seen here at Nine Elms in 1950. Designated Class 'N-15X' the seven engines of this class were rebuilds of LBSCR 4-6-4 'Baltic' tanks which were converted by Richard Maunsell in 1934 into 4-6-0 tender engines for hauling expresses on the Waterloo to Southampton line. 'Hackworth' was the first to be withdrawn in 1955 and by 1957 the class was extinct.

At the same time Nine Elms was still allocated eight of the 'Schools' Class 4-4-0s but these were soon victims of early withdrawal.

For the trainspotter, Nine Elms was located to the south of the main line between Vauxhall and Queens Road stations. Walking time from Wandsworth Road station was about 15 minutes.

Towards the end of its life both the shed and its allocation of steam locos were in a very shabby and rundown condition. It was the last main line steam shed to remain operational in London and, following electrification of the Waterloo to Southampton and Bournemouth lines, it was closed in July 1967. The new Covent Garden fruit and vegetable market was built on its site.

Basingstoke

NOT EXACTLY A DESTINATION ON MOST PEOPLE'S VISITING LIST, BUT BASINGSTOKE ON A SUMMER SATURDAY IN THE EARLY 1960S WAS A TRAINSPOTTER'S PARADISE.

Not only did we have the spine-tingling spectacle of Bulleid Pacifics thundering through with expresses between Waterloo and Bournemouth, Weymouth and the West Country, but also the slower north-south cross-country services between the Midlands and Bournemouth. Many of the latter worked through to and from Oxford with their SR loco and it was not uncommon to see other workings headed by WR locos such as 'Halls' and 'Granges'. To add to this rich tapestry were the numerous stopping trains, often headed by 'S15's, 'King Arthurs' and named BR Standard Class 5 4-6-0s that took on water at Basingstoke, together with the comings and goings from the nearby shed (70D).

Sadly, the steam-hauled West of England expresses such as the 'Atlantic Coast Express' were withdrawn in September 1964 and 'Warship' diesel-hydraulics – relegated from the WR main line by the new 'Western' diesel-hydraulics– were introduced to haul the much-reduced services. However, the Bournemouth and Weymouth trains continued with steam haulage until July 1967, when that line was electrified as far as Bournemouth Central.

More or less one year apart, two summer-Saturday trainspotting trips to Basingstoke show some interesting results and on both occasions a period of 5½ hours from about 10.30 to 16.00 was spent on the same platform.

On its way back to the Western Region via Reading and Oxford, ex-works 'Hall' Class 4-6-0 No. 6952 'Kimberley Hall' halts at Basingstoke with a Bournemouth to Wolverhampton LL train on August 22, 1964. No. 6952 was built at Swindon in 1943 and was withdrawn from Tyseley shed (2A) at the end of 1965.

'Merchant Navy' Class 4-6-2 No. No. 35024 'East Asiatic Company' takes on water at Basingstoke in August 1963 while heading a train for Salisbury. This loco was built at Eastleigh in 1948 and withdrawn at the beginning of 1965 after only 17 years' service.

August 31, 1963 – a total of 82 locos were recorded, of which ten were Birmingham R. C. & W. Co Type 3 diesels (later Class 33 and known as 'Cromptons'). Of the 72 steam locos seen, 23 were 'West Country', 12 'Battle of Britain', 11 'Merchant Navy' and 11 BR Standard Class 5. WR locos seen on cross-country services were four 'Halls', one 'Grange' and one 'Modified Hall'.

August 22, 1964 – a total of 80 locos were recorded, of which 13 were 'Crompton' diesels and one was a WR 'Warship' (the shape of things to come). Of the 66 steam locos seen, 14 were 'West Country', nine 'Battle of Britain', 14 'Merchant Navy' and 12 BR Standard Class 5. The WR locos seen on cross-country services were two 'Halls', two 'Granges' and two 'Modified Halls'.

In the space of 5½ hours on a sunny August 22, 1964 a total of 14 'Merchant Navy' Pacifics were spotted at Basingstoke. Here are ten of them. No. 35023 'Holland-Afrika Line' was seen heading through Basingstoke with the rerouted 'Pine Express' to Manchester as far as Oxford.

Closely watched by a couple of lineside enthusiasts, Brush Type 4 (Class 47) diesel D1690 heads the 10.08am York to Bournemouth train past Worting Junction on August 20, 1966. Located to the west of Basingstoke, Worting Junction was a popular spot for trainspotters and photographers on summer Saturdays.

Day Tripper

day 7

RAIL
ROVER
TICKETS

will take you anywhe

from KENT

to CORNWAL

SOUTHERN
BRITISH RAILWAYS

Gloucester to Lyme Regis 3/8/63

The family holiday in 1963 was a week in Lyme Regis. As home was in Gloucester, the trip involved many changes and each section was steam hauled, as follows: Gloucester Eastgate to Mangotsfield, BR Class 5 4-6-0 No. 73068; Mangotsfield to Bath Green Park, Ivatt Class 2 2-6-2T No. 41249; Bath Green Park to Templecombe, BR Class 5 4-6-0 No. 73054; Templecombe to Axminster, SR 'Merchant Navy' 4-6-2 No. 35016 'Elders Fyffes'; Axminster to Lyme Regis, Ivatt Class 2 2-6-2T No. 41307. What a great trip!

Apart from whistling the latest Top Ten hit '[You're the] Devil in Disguise' by Elvis Presley, most of the holiday was spent train spotting at Axminster station. Here, unrebuilt SR 'Battle of Britain' Class 4-6-2 No. 34078 '222 Squadron' pauses at Axminster on Bank Holiday Monday, August 5, 1963. It was a successful day with 10 'Battle of Britain', 4 'West Country' and 4 'Merchant Navy' seen in action.

With grindingly detailed observations, the notebook faithfully records the Gloucester to Lyme Regis train journey on August 3, 1963. There are some interesting observations about the weather and the number of passengers, and also the speeds recorded – a top speed of 87 mph behind No. 35016 between Templecombe and Yeovil Junction. It also lists the locomotives seen and photos taken at Axminster on Bank Holiday Monday, August 5, and the first part of a trip to Exeter on August 8.

Isle of Wight 1/10/65

Steam operations were due to end and most of the remaining lines on the Isle of Wight were to close in early 1966. On October 1, 1965, a final visit was made to the island and the notebook faithfully records the journey down from Gloucester to Ryde via Bristol, Salisbury, Eastleigh and Portsmouth.

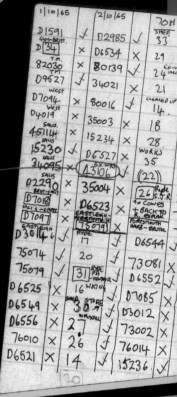

Albeit in much reduced numbers, steam locos were still seen at work in many locations at the beginning of October 1965. On the journey down they were recorded at Bristol Temple Meads, Salisbury, Eastleigh (including ex-works Ivatt Class 4 2-6-0 No. 43106) and Portsmouth. A total of ten Class 02 0-4-4 tanks were noted at Ryde (IOW) shed plus six other members of this class at work on the remaining lines to Ventnor and Cowes.

The journey southwards. On a damp and drizzly Saturday, August 3, 1963, BR Standard Class 5 4-6-0 No. 73054, running 10 minutes late, climbs towards the Mendips near Midford with a Bristol to Bournemouth West train. The train consisted of six coaches, of which three were in Southern Region livery.

The S&D signalbox and station at Midsomer Norton observed from the same train as No. 73054 pauses on its journey to Templecombe. The S&D finally succumbed to the conspiring of politicians and the powerful road transport lobby when it closed on March 7, 1966.

Class 02 0-4-4T No. 14 'Fishbourne' being lovingly cleaned at Ryde (IOW) shed on October 2, 1965 prior to hauling an enthusiasts special. This vintage scene was swept away a few months later and replaced by ex-London Underground third-rail electric trains as far as Shanklin. Mediocrity had won again – c'est la vie!

Bournemouth

THE TWO STATIONS IN BOURNEMOUTH, CENTRAL AND WEST, HAD TWO VERY DIFFERENT CHARACTERISTICS. CENTRAL, A THROUGH STATION, WAS ALWAYS THE BUSIEST WITH MAIN LINE SERVICES TO SOUTHAMPTON AND WATERLOO AND TO WEYMOUTH.

Rebuilt 'Battle of Britain' Class 4-6-2 No. 34077 '603 Squadron' arrives at Bournemouth Central with an express from Waterloo on September 3, 1961. Built by BR at Brighton in 1948 – the 1,000th loco to be built at the former LB&SCR works – No. 34077 was rebuilt in 1960 and withdrawn from Eastleigh shed (70D) in March 1967.

Bournemouth shed (71B) was located just to the west of the station and its allocation in the late 1950s and early '60s included such fine examples as 'N15' 'King Arthurs' and 'LN' 'Lord Nelsons' as well as a clutch of Bulleid Pacifics. By 1962, apart from two 'N15's, the shed was home to 47 other steam locos including 13 'M7' 0-4-4 tanks for working local services including the Swanage branch, 16 'West Countries', two 'Battle of Britains' and eight 'Merchant Navies'. The latter were employed hauling the crack 'Bournemouth Belle' Pullman train which originated at West station and 'The Royal Wessex', half of which originated at West and the other half at Weymouth; both trains united at Bournemouth and destined for Waterloo.

Steam-haulage on this route continued until July 1967 when third-rail electrification was 'switched on'. Electrification of the line to Weymouth was not completed until 1988 and in the intervening years Class 33/1 'Crompton' diesels operated a push-pull service with

4TC unpowered sets. The decrepit state of Central station was finally remedied in 2000 following a programme of extensive refurbishment.

Bournemouth West, a terminus and serviced by Branksome sub-shed, was not only the originating point for many of the Waterloo-bound expresses and local services to Brockenhurst and Salisbury via West Moors, but was also the southern terminus of the Somerset & Dorset Joint Railway services from Bath Green Park. Summer Saturdays were always busy here with 'The Pines Express' from Manchester and other through trains arriving from the north. Loco types on these trains ranged from S&D 7F 2-8-0s and Standard Class 5 4-6-0s to unrebuilt 'West Country' Pacifics and even BR Standard 9F 2-10-0s.

Sadly, through services on the S&D ended in 1962 and what remained, until closure in March 1966, could hardly be called a public service. Bournemouth West station closed for good in the previous October.

(opposite) Admired by two young trainspotters rebuilt 'Battle of Britain' Class 4-6-2 No. 34064 'Fighter Command' stands at Bournemouth West after arriving with a stopping train in May 1962. Built at Brighton in 1947, No. 34064 was later fitted with a Giesl Oblong Ejector before being withdrawn in 1966. Terminus of trains from London via Bournemouth Central and from Bath Green Park via the S&DJR, West station closed in October 1965.

While 'M7' Class 0-4-4 No. 30379 tank performs empty coaching stock duties, rebuilt 'West Country' Class 4-6-2 No. 34022 'Exmoor' approaches Bournemouth Central with a Weymouth to Waterloo train on September 8, 1961. 'Exmoor' was built at Brighton in 1946, rebuilt in 1957 and withdrawn in April 1965. On the West Somerset Railway in March 2004 preserved sister engine No. 34027 'Taw Valley' was fitted out with replica name and numberplates from No. 34022 and became 'Exmoor' for the day.

Ex-LSWR Class 'M7' 0-4-4 tank No. 30379 passes Bournemouth shed (71B) as it approaches Bournemouth Central with empty coaching stock. The 'M7' was built at Nine Elms Works in 1904 and was withdrawn from Three Bridges shed (75E) in October 1963. Bournemouth shed closed in July 1967 following completion of third-rail electrification from Waterloo.

SOUTHERN REGION

Salisbury was an important railway crossroads serving both trains on the SR and also to the WR. On September 7, 1961, far from its home shed of Neath (87A), ex-GWR 'Hall' Class 4-6-0 No. 4988 'Bulwell Hall' leaves Salisbury with a cross-country Portsmouth Harbour to Cardiff train. This loco was built at Swindon in 1931 and was withdrawn from Oxford shed (81F) in February 1964.

Salisbury

AN IMPORTANT JUNCTION, SALISBURY WAS A FASCINATING STATION FOR TRAINSPOTTERS WITH ALL SR WATERLOO TO WEST OF ENGLAND TRAINS STOPPING HERE FOR WATER AND A STEADY STREAM OF WR TRAINS ARRIVING FROM WESTBURY AND BRISTOL.

Ex-SR 'Lord Nelson' Class 4-6-0 No. 30862 'Lord Collingwood' enters Salisbury with a stopping train from Exeter on April 5, 1960. Designed by Richard Maunsell this class of loco was introduced in 1926 for express passenger work on the Waterloo to Exeter main line. 'Lord Collingwood' was built at Eastleigh in 1929 and withdrawn in October 1962. One member of this class, No. 30850 'Lord Nelson', has been preserved.

Some of these continued on to Portsmouth via Romsey and Eastleigh while Salisbury also saw local stopping services from Bournemouth West via West Moors and from Southampton via Redbridge. There were once two separate stations in Salisbury – one was a terminus served by the GWR (opened 1856) and the other adjacent station (opened 1859) was for L&SWR services between Waterloo and Exeter. The GWR station closed in 1932 and all services subsequently used the present layout.

The fierce competition between the GWR and L&SWR on their competing routes from London to Plymouth Docks in the early 20th century led to the derailment of the 'Ocean Mail' express as it attempted to negotiate Salisbury's curves at speed in 1906. After that date all steam trains, including the famous 'Atlantic Coast Express', were forced to halt at the station.

Steam continued to reign supreme well into the 1960s and in a few hours of trainspotting in September 1963 only two diesel shunters, one 'Hymek' and a three-car Eastleigh diesel-electric set were seen – not a 'Warship' in sight! Even at this late stage nearly all services were steam hauled with Bulleid Pacifics served up alongside 'Halls', 'Granges' and the occasional 'Castle'.

Sadly, with BR regional boundary changes, this was all to change and a year later the last 'ACE' ran and much-reduced services between Exeter and Waterloo were soon in the hands of demoted WR 'Warships'. Steam continued to struggle on until July 1967 when Salisbury shed finally closed.

The arrival of the up and down 'Atlantic Coast Express' always heralded a short but busy time at Salisbury station each day. Here, 'Merchant Navy' Class 4-6-2 No. 35013 'Blue Funnel' is serviced as it heads the up 'ACE' on April 18, 1964. Not only the last stop for this train before Waterloo, Salisbury also saw a change of enginemen, a water refill and the hard work of shovelling coal from the back of the tender to the front. Built at Eastleigh in 1945 'Blue Funnel' was rebuilt in 1956 and withdrawn in July 1967.

(below) Rebuilt 'West Country' Class 4-6-2 No. 34013 'Okehampton' draws out of the down bay platform at Salisbury with the 3.05pm local train to Exeter on April 18, 1964. On the right is station pilot 'M7' 0-4-4 tank No. 30025. Both local engines, 'Okehampton' was built at Brighton in 1945, rebuilt in 1957 and withdrawn in July 1967 while the 'M7' was built in 1899 and withdrawn only six weeks after this photo was taken.

ON SHED

Salisbury

Not an easy shed to access for the trainspotter unless you could sneak below the foreman's office window, Salisbury shed was located south of the main line west of the station. From here it was about a ten minute walk. The shed provided motive power for local services to Bournemouth, Eastleigh and Portsmouth as well as stopping services west to Exeter and east to Waterloo.

'Foreigners' from the WR via Westbury were also serviced at the shed. Opened by the London & South Western Railway in 1901, by November 1961 it still had 50 steam locos on its books with examples of 11 different classes represented. Some, the 'M7s', 'N15s' ('King Arthurs'), '700s' and 'H15s' were not long for this world, but others, such as its six 'West Countries', six 'Battle of Britains', three 'Merchant Navies' and nine BR Standard Class 3 2-6-0s held on until 1967.

Salisbury shed finally succumbed in July 1967 when the era of steam haulage on the Southern Region finally ended.

Unrebuilt 'Battle of Britain' Class 4-6-2 No. 34054 'Lord Beaverbrook' is prepared for its next turn of duty at Salisbury shed on September 6, 1963. Built at Brighton Works in 1947, 'Lord Beaverbrook' was withdrawn only a year after this photo was taken.

Along with a host of SR locos, eight WR steam locos were spotted at Salisbury on September 6, 1963. These included two 'Halls', one 'Modified Hall' and a 'Grange'. 'Castle' Class No. 5073 'Blenheim' was also noted on a train to Bristol.

The final year of steam at Salisbury – rebuilt 'West Country' 4-6-2 No. 34013 'Okehampton' is seen at rest inside the shed on August 21, 1966. Less than 12 months later it had been withdrawn and was heading for Cashmore's scrapyard in Newport.

Yeovil Town 72C

A scene that has disappeared forever - Yeovil Town station and engine shed as seen from the neighbouring farmland on August 17, 1963. In the shed yard is a seemingly motley collection of ex-SR locos including 'S15' 4-6-0s, 'U' 2-6-0s, an unrebuilt 'Battle of Britain' 4-6-2 and a BR Standard Class 4 2-6-4 tank. Also in view is the diminutive steam crane used for loading coal.

Located next to Yeovil Town station, access to this former LSWR shed was very easy through an entrance directly from the station platform. An ex-GWR shed, located at Pen Mill, was closed in 1959 when its allocation was transferred to Yeovil Town. Turntable and servicing facilities were provided at nearby Yeovil Junction which was reached from Town via a spur line. These facilities are used to this day by steam-hauled specials in the 21st century.

Although the shed's allocation was pretty humble, visiting Bulleid light Pacifics from the nearby main line were fairly common. In November 1961 a total of 17 steam locos were allocated to this bi-regional shed, including six WR 0-6-0 pannier tanks, two WR small 'Prairies', two ex-L&SWR M7 0-4-4 tanks and seven 'U' Class Moguls. The WR locos were employed on the local service to Taunton and on shuttle services between Town and Pen Mill station. Recoded 83E under new WR management in 1963, Town shed finally closed in the summer of 1965.

Looking battered but still clinging to life after 66 years' service, ex-LSWR Class '700' No. 30700, formerly of Exmouth Junction shed, was seen in steam at Town shed on December 31, 1963 - despite the fact that the loco had been officially withdrawn thirteen months earlier.

75

Trainspotting

Spotting book at the ready, duffle bag with crisps and pop in the grass alongside as these youngsters cop Gresley 'A3' Pacific No. 60062 'Minoru' at the head of a down train on the ECML at Welwyn on September 14, 1958.

COLLECTING TRAIN NUMBERS WAS A POPULAR PURSUIT FOR YOUNG MEN BEFORE WORLD WAR II, BUT THE PUBLICATION BY IAN ALLAN OF HIS FIRST LOCOSPOTTERS' GUIDE IN 1942 TRANSFORMED THE HOBBY.

Ian Allan (then an employee of the Southern Railway) published the *ABC of Southern Locomotives,* turning a minority interest into an all-consuming passion for thousands of men, young and old, across the country.

By the early 1950s a whole new publishing industry had grown up that documented every move of British Railways locomotives – magazines such as *Trains Illustrated, Railway Magazine* and *Railway World* fed the craze along with a plethora of books such as Ian Allan's regional *ABC Locospotter Books,* shed guides and directories.

By the 1960s steam haulage was doomed but the craze continued unabated, and there were still many diehard diesel enthusiasts out there who were prepared to stand on a draughty platform with their notebooks and cameras.

Sadly, the eradication of locomotive-hauled trains, the introduction of health and safety legislation and the fear of terrorism have all contributed to the downfall of this innocent and all-consuming passion. Those happy days are now but a fading memory for older people.

The Ian Allan *ABC Combined Volume* was essential for any serious trainspotter. The 264-page Summer 1961 edition shown here not only listed all steam locomotives by region but had separate sections listing diesel locos and multiple units and electric locomotives and multiple units.

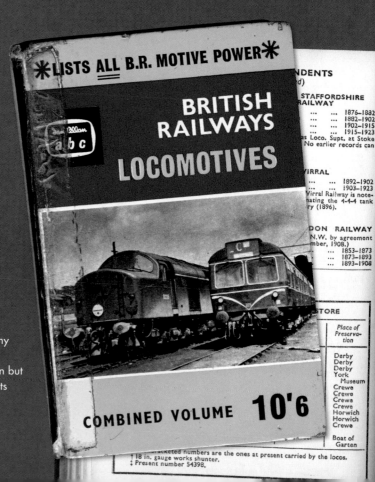

British Rail

Steam Locomotives

IAN ALLAN

3/-

MECCANO
MAGAZINE

VOL. XLII No.7   JULY

CITY DIESEL   1/-

MAY 1962

Modern Railways

2/6

formerly TRAINS ILLUSTRATED

An *Ian Allan* Periodical

SULZER

Sulzer-engined Type 3 Locomotive on the Southern Region of British Railw

(above) By 1966 steam locomotives still operating could be fitted into a 64-page guide. (above left) Ian Allan Locoshed Books were introduced twice a year detailing the shed allocation of each loco.

(above centre) Published for 'boys of all ages' between 1916 and 1963, *Meccano Magazine* also included interesting features on Britain's railways.

In 1962 Ian Allan replaced the ever-popular *Trains Illustrated* monthly magazine with *Modern Railways*. In its early years the cover usually featured an advert by a company supplying railway equipment.

RAILWAY WORLD

JANUARY, 1965

TRAINS
illustrated

incorporating
THE LOCOMOTIVE
Railway Carriage
and Wagon Review

· JANUARY
1961

Also published by Ian Allan, *Railway World* was a more learned monthly railway magazine which ceased publication in 2003. It was replaced by *Railways Illustrated*.

Until 1962, *Trains Illustrated* featured articles on loco performance accompanied by good photo features. Loco shed reallocations were included as were growing lists of withdrawn steam locomotives.

An *Ian Allan* Periodical

2/-

BRITISH RAILWAYS LOCOMOTIVES
Nos. 60001–69725

The code given in smaller bold type at the head of each class, e.g. " 4MT ", denotes its British Railways power classification.
The numbers of locomotives in service have been checked in E. & N.E.R. to January 20, 1962, L.M.R. to December 30, 1961, and Sc.R. to December 30, 1961.

4-6-2   8P6F   Class A4

Introduced 1935. Gresley streamlined design with corridor tender (except those marked †). All fitted with double chimney.
Inside cylinder reduced to 17".
Weight: Loco.   102 tons 19 cwt.
Tender { 64 tons 19 cwt.
{ 60 tons 7 cwt.†
Pressure: 250 lb. Su.
Cyls.: { (3) 18½″ × 26″.
{ (2) 18½″ × 26″ (1) 17″ × 26″.*
Driving Wheels: 6′ 8″.
T.E.: { 35,455 lb.
{ 33,616 lb.*
Walschaerts valve gear and derived motion. P.V.

60023†	Golden Eagle
60024	Kingfisher —
60025	Falcon
60026†	Miles Beevor —
60027	Merlin —
60028	Walter K. Whigham
60029	Woodcock
60030	Golden Fleece —
60031	Golden Plover —
60032	Gannet
60033	Seagull
60034	Lord Faringdon —

Total 34

60031
60011

4-6-2   7P6F   Class A3

Introduced 1927. Development of Gresley G.N. 180 lb. Pacific (introduced 1922, L.N.E.R. A1, later A10) with 220 lb. pressure (prototype and others rebuilt from A10). Some have G.N.-type tender with coal rails†, remainder L.N.E.R. pattern. All fitted with double chimney.
Weight: Loco.   96 tons 5 cwt.
Tender { 56 tons 6 cwt.†
{ 57 tons 18 cwt.
Pressure: 220 lb. Su.
Cyls.: (3) 19″ × 26″.
Driving Wheels: 6′ 8″.
T.E.: 32,910 lb.
Walschaerts valve gear and derived motion. P.V.

60001	Sir Ronald Matthews —
60002†	Sir Murrough Wilson —
60003	Andrew K. McCosh —
60004	William Whitelaw —
60005†	Sir Charles Newton —
60006†	Sir Ralph Wedgwood —
60007	Sir Nigel Gresley —
60008†	Dwight D. Eisenhower —
60009	Union of South Africa ✻
60010	Dominion of Canada —
60011	Empire of India —
60012*	Commonwealth of — Australia
60013	Dominion of New Zealand
60014	Silver Link —
60015	Quicksilver —
60016†	Silver King —
60017	Silver Fox —
60018†	Sparrow Hawk —
60019†	Bittern ✻
60020*†	Guillemot —
60021	Wild Swan —
60022	Mallard ⚑

60036	Colombo —
60037	Hyperion —
60038	Firdaussi —
60039	Sandwich —
60040	Cameronian —
60041	Salmon Trout —
60042	Singapore —
60043	Brown Jack —

Exeter Central

ORIGINALLY NAMED QUEEN STREET, CENTRAL STATION OPENED IN 1860 AS THE TERMINUS OF THE LSWR's MAIN LINE FROM WATERLOO AND SALISBURY.

The linking line to Exeter St Davids via a short tunnel and a 1 in 37 gradient was opened in 1862. This allowed LSWR trains to run through to the North Devon and North Cornwall resorts of Ilfracombe, Bude and Padstow and also to Plymouth via what became known as 'The Withered Arm'. Although St Davids was favoured by trainspotters, Central station in the early 60s was still full of interest. It was here that trains such as 'The Atlantic Coast Express' changed engines, with the larger 'Merchant Navy' coming off in favour of a lighter 'West Country' or 'Battle of Britain' for the rest of the journey west – nearby Exmouth Junction shed was allocated an impressive total of 39 Bulleid light Pacifics and seven 'Merchant Navies' in 1962.

BR Standard Class 4 2-6-4 tank No. 80064 makes easy going of the 1 in 37 incline up from St Davids station as it approaches Central station with a local passenger train in the 1960s. This loco was built at Brighton in 1953 and has since been preserved as a static display on the Bluebell Line. Note the handshunting of timber wagons on to their turntables on the right of the picture.

Ex-LSWR 'T9' 4-4-0 No. 30313 is seen here entering Central Station on August 31, 1960 with a train from Padstow after being banked up the 1 in 37 incline from St Davids by 'Z' Class 0-8-0 tank No. 30955. Known as 'Greyhounds' because of their excellent steaming abilities, 66 of the 'T9' Class were built between 1899 and 1901. No. 30313 was built at Nine Elms Works in 1901 and withdrawn from Exmouth Junction shed (72A) in July 1961.

Complete with eight-wheel tender Class 'S15' 4-6-0 No. 30829 arrives at Exeter Central with a train of empty ballast hoppers en route to Meldon Quarry on August 1, 1962. One of ten such locos then allocated to Salisbury (72B) these powerful goods locos were also employed on stopping passenger services. Although all had been withdrawn by 1966 seven have since been preserved.

Alongside this were the Exmouth branch trains usually hauled by 'M7' 0-4-4 tanks, stopping trains to Salisbury and Barnstaple usually hauled by light Pacifics, freight on the two central roads banked in the rear by a Z Class 0-8-0 tank engine from St Davids and usually hauled by an 'N' Class 2-6-0 with the more heavier ballast trains from Meldon and bulk cement trains in the charge of an 'S15' 4-6-0.

This glorious scene with the trains packed with holidaymakers all ended in September 1964 when the last 'ACE' ran. After that it was all downhill as WR 'Warships' and North British Type 2 diesel-hydraulics took over running of a much-reduced service with the nearby Exmouth Junction shed closing in June 1965.

Unrebuilt 'Battle of Britain' Class 4-6-2 No. 34076 '41 Squadron' and unrebuilt 'West Country' Class 4-6-2 No. 34034 'Honiton' stand at Exeter Central on September 11, 1959. The 'BB' was built by BR in 1948 and withdrawn in January 1966, the 'WC' was built in 1946 and withdrawn in July 1967.

A line-up of Bulleid unrebuilt Pacifics at Exmouth Junction shed in the early 1960s. All three were built at Brighton Works, from left to right: 'Battle of Britain' Class No. 34065 'Hurricane' (built 1947, withdrawn April 1964); 'West Country' Class No. 34023 'Blackmore Vale' (built 1946, withdrawn July 1967 and since preserved); 'Battle of Britain' Class No. 34073 '249 Squadron' (built by BR in 1948, withdrawn June 1964).

Exmouth Junction

72 A

Located over a mile to the east of Exeter Central station and north of the junction between the main line to Salisbury and the Exmouth branch, Exmouth Junction shed was best approached from Polsloe Bridge Halt from which it was about a ten minute walk. One of the largest on the Southern Region, the first shed here was opened by the LSWR in 1887. This was closed in 1927 when a new 12-road shed was opened on an adjacent site. With an allocation of over 100 locos, the shed provided motive power not only for top link duties such as the 'Atlantic Coast Express' and other main line services to Salisbury, North Devon and North Cornwall along the 'Withered Arm', but also for the many SR branch lines in the area. For years Exmouth Junction was also home to the entire class of 'Z' Class 0-8-0 tanks which were employed on banking duties between St Davids and Central station.

Far from its home at Aberdeen Ferryhill (61B), 'A4' Class 4-6-2 No. 60024 'Kingfisher' takes on water at Exmouth Junction on March 27, 1966. This much-travelled loco was heading the Locomotive Club of Great Britain (LCGB) 'A4 Commemorative Railtour' to the West Country. By this date the shed had already closed to steam but had obviously retained basic servicing facilities.

Unrebuilt 'West Country' Class 4-6-2 No. 34030 'Watersmeet' was seen outside Exmouth Junction shed on September 1, 1964. This loco was built at Brighton in 1946 and withdrawn shortly after being photographed here.

Unrebuilt 'Battle of Britain' Class 4-6-2 No. 34080 '74 Squadron' is seen here on Exmouth Junction's turntable shortly before withdrawal in 1964. By this date Southern steam at Exeter was on its way out and soon to be replaced by WR diesel-hydraulics. No. 34080 was built by BR at Brighton in 1948 and was withdrawn in September 1964.

Exmouth Junction shed still held on to a large allocation of SR locos in August 1963. Of the 40 locos seen on shed on the 8th of that month ten were Bulleid light Pacifics and five were 'Merchant Navies'. Ivatt Class 2 2-6-2 tanks, replacing the older 'M7' and Adams Radial tanks, were also common.

Even as late as November 1961 Exmouth Junction's allocation of steam locos totalled 123, but by then more modern ex-LMS and BR standard types had replaced many of the older LSWR engines such as the 'T9' 4-4-0s and Class '700' 0-6-0s. Only six of the 'M7' 0-4-4 tanks remained but there were 15 of the Ivatt Class 2 2-6-2 tanks and ten of the BR Standard Class 3 2-6-2 tanks, many of which were employed on branch lines such as Axminster to Lyme Regis. Freight trains and some local passenger services to North Devon and North Cornwall were mainly in the charge of 28 Class 'N' 2-6-0s, while freight towards Salisbury was handled by six 'S15' 4-6-0s. Primarily, Exmouth Junction had a massive allocation of 46 Bulleid Pacifics, nearly 50% more than Nine Elms. Of these 39 were the lighter 'West Country' and 'Battle of Britain'

classes which were ideally suited for both main line services to Salisbury and on the lines to North Devon and Plymouth and North Cornwall via Okehampton. Heavier expresses east of Exeter, such as 'The Atlantic Coast Express' were in the capable hands of seven 'Merchant Navies'.

The shed's code was changed to 83D in 1963 when the Western Region took responsibility for all former SR routes west of Salisbury and for a short time ex-GWR locos were also based at Exmouth Junction. Exmouth Junction's far-flung empire included sub-sheds at Bude (closed 1964), Callington (closed 1964), Exmouth (closed 1963), Lyme Regis (closed 1965), Okehampton (closed 1964) and Seaton (closed 1963). Exmouth Junction closed to steam in 1965 when most duties were taken over by relegated WR 'Warships' and North British Type 2 diesel hydraulics.

DASTARDLY DIESELS AND ELECTRICS!

Allocated to St Leonards depot (75D) E5020 heads the down 'Golden Arrow' at Victoria in April 1965. Later designated Class 71, these third-rail electric locos were also fitted with a pantograph for use in sidings. The class became extinct in 1977 but one member, E5001, has been preserved for the National Collection.

The Southern Railway were in the forefront of main line diesel development. Two prototype 1Co-Co1 main line diesel-electric locomotives, originally designed by Oliver Bulleid, were built at Ashford Works in 1950. With a power output of 1,750hp Nos 10201 and 10202 were assessed on main line services out of Waterloo to Exeter, Bournemouth and Weymouth and were joined for evaluation by the two LMR locos 10000 and 10001 in 1953. A third Bulleid loco in the series, No. 10203, was built at Brighton in 1954 with a power output of 2,000hp.

Because of the spread of 750 V DC third-rail electrification the Southern's requirement for main line diesels was much less than on other regions of BR. The only main line diesel type ordered specifically for the SR was the Birmingham Railway Carriage & Wagon Company's Type 3 Bo-Bo (D6500-D6597), later classified Class 33 and affectionately known as 'Cromptons'. Introduced in 1960 they first appeared in the South-Eastern Division where they soon replaced all steam workings. The last 12 locos were built with bodies that were seven inches narrower for working on the Hastings line. Following electrification of the line to Bournemouth 19 Class 33 locos were converted to push-pull operation for use on the Bournemouth to Weymouth non-electrified section. The highly successful 'Cromptons' (opposite) Two prototype 1Co-Co1 main line diesel-electric locomotives, originally designed by Oliver Bulleid for the Southern Railway, were built at Ashford Works in 1950. A third was built at Brighton in 1954. Here, No. 10201 is seen on an up train at Dorchester South in May 1952. All three SR locos were transferred to the London Midland Region in 1955 and were based at Willesden (1A) until they were withdrawn in 1963.

The two prototype LMS main line diesels were also evaluated on the Southern Region. Here, No. 10000 (forerunner of the Class 44 'Peak') is seen hauling a Bournemouth to Waterloo express on May 3, 1953. The train had been diverted via East Putney due to engineering work on the main line. This ground-breaking loco was withdrawn in 1962.

It's 1967 and the Bulleid Pacifics have gone and stretches of the Salisbury to Exeter line are being singled. Here 'Warship' diesel hydraulic D825 'Intrepid' approaches Gillingham on the old up line with the 13.00 Waterloo to Exeter St Davids on September 27, 1967. Built at Swindon in 1960, D825 was withdrawn in August 1972.

could be seen on all kinds of duties, including boat trains and cross-country services, throughout the region and stayed in service until well into the late 1990s.

Two classes of electro-diesels were also built for the SR. The Class 73 Bo-Bo electro-diesels (E6001-E6049) were built in two batches between 1962 and 1967 and, despite withdrawals, a few still remain in service with private operators. Introduced in 1967, ten locos of Class 74 were rebuilds of withdrawn Class 71 electric locos and remained in service until 1977.

Mention must be made of the Southern region's main line electric locos. Firstly, what later became known as Class 70, were three Co-Co locos (numbered 20001-20003), two of which were built by

at Doncaster between 1958 and 1960 and were numbered initially E5000-E5023. Although designed as mixed-traffic locos they were also employed hauling the 'Golden Arrow' and the 'Night Ferry'. The class became extinct in 1977.

Last but not least some mention must be made of the repercussions of the regional boundary changes in 1963 when all lines west of Salisbury came under the control of the Western Region. The last 'Merchant Navy'-hauled 'Atlantic Coast Express' ran in September 1964 and, from that date, the downgraded Waterloo to Exeter service was soon in the hands of downgraded WR 'Warship' diesel hydraulics. These were replaced by 'Cromptons' in 1971 which in turn were replaced by displaced Class 50s in 1980.

Final Days

During 1966 there was quite often disruption of services between Waterloo and Bournemouth during third-rail electrification work. On October 22, temporary single line working was in force on the Sway to New Milton section. Here rebuilt 'West Country' Class 4-6-2 No. 34040 'Crewkerne' halts at Sway with the 12.35 Waterloo to Bournemouth train while the signalman waits on the platform to retrieve the single line token from the fireman of rebuilt 'West Country' Class 4-6-2 No. 34013 'Okehampton' heading the 13.25 Weymouth to Waterloo.

31ST DECEMBER 1966 WAS NOT QUITE THE END OF STEAM ON THE SOUTHERN REGION, BUT IT WAS FOR THE UNIQUE STEAM-HAULED ISLE OF WIGHT RAIL SYSTEM.

With just over five months to go before the end of steam on the SR a quick visit to Waterloo on January 31, 1967 noted two Bulleid light Pacifics and two 'Merchant Navies' – No. 35023 'Holland-Afrika Line' and No. 35013 'Blue Funnel'. Both of these locos were withdrawn in July of that year.

As from that date the diminutive ex-LSWR '02' 0-4-4 tanks, suitably adorned with names of island villages and towns, ceased to haul their vintage carriages from Ryde to Ventnor and Cowes. They were replaced a few months later by ex-London Underground third-rail sets trundling between Ryde Pier Head and Shanklin! However, July 9, 1967, marked the absolute end of steam on the Southern Region. The writing had been on the wall for some years with the dieselisation and downgrading of the route west of Salisbury in 1964 and the ongoing third-rail electrification of the route from Waterloo to Southampton and Bournemouth. It wasn't a glorious ending either as the few remaining steam locos – Bulleid Pacifics and BR Standard locos – working out of Bournemouth or Nine Elms sheds

The last steam-hauled branch line operating on the Southern Region was between Brockenhurst and Lymington Pier. Here, BR Standard Class 4 2-6-4 tank No. 80019 is seen near Ampress Works Halt with a train from Lymington on January 21, 1967. Only 16 years old this fine loco was withdrawn from Bournemouth shed (70F) only two months later.

Down and out in Nine Elms - with less than two months to go before closure the depot looks a pretty depressing place. BR Standard Class 5 4-6-0 No. 73065 is seen leaving the coaling plant on May 13, 1967. Less than 13 years old this loco was withdrawn just over two months later.

were in a pretty decrepit state with the 'Merchant Navy', Battle of Britain' and 'West Country' Pacifics bereft of their handsome nameplates. The final steam sheds to close on the SR in July 1967 were Nine Elms (70A), Feltham (70B), Guildford (70C), Basingstoke (70D), Eastleigh (71A), Bournemouth (71B), Weymouth (71G), Southampton Docks (71I) and Salisbury (72B).

July 3, 1967 - only six days to go before the end of steam on the Southern Region. Driver Prior of Nine Elms shed is seen here at Bournemouth in charge of 'Merchant Navy' Class 4-6-2 No. 35023 'Holland-Afrika Line' with the 11.18am Weymouth to Waterloo express. This loco was built at Eastleigh in 1948, rebuilt in 1957 and withdrawn shortly after this photo was taken.

The Great Escape

SOUTHERN REGION

OLIVER BULLEID'S MAGNIFICENT STEAM LOCOS HAD A VERY SHORT WORKING LIFE. THE MAJORITY SAVED SPENT MANY YEARS AS RUSTING HULKS ON 'DEATH ROW' AT BARRY.

A surprising number of SR 'S15' Class 4-6-0 locos have been preserved – two of the original LSWR batch built between 1920 and 1921, and five of the SR batch built between 1927 and 1936. All of these locos were saved from Woodham's scrapyard at Barry. Here, No. 828 was seen at Bristol Temple Meads with an enthusiasts' special on October 8, 1994.

Lovers of ex-Southern Railway steam locos have much to thank Dai Woodham for, as out of a total of 84 ex-SR and its constituent companies' locos that have been preserved, no less than 41 were rescued from his scrapyard at Barry. What is staggering is that 18 out of the 20 'West Country'/'Battle of Britain' and 10 of the 11 'Merchant Navy' Pacifics since preserved all came from Barry. One example of an ex-SR loco, an LBSC Terrier Class 'A1X' 0-6-0 tank, is a static museum exhibit in Canada while a former Yugoslavian Railways 'USA' Class 0-6-0 tank, similar to those owned by the SR, has been restored to working order in the UK.

Ex-LBSCR Class A1X 0-6-0 tank No. 8 'Freshwater' (formerly BR No. 32646) waits to depart from Havenstreet with a train for Smallbrook Junction in August 2005. Built in 1877 this diminutive loco started life as LBSCR No. 46 'Newington', then sold to the LSWR in March 1903 and to the Freshwater, Yarmouth & Newport Railway in 1914. Under SR ownership the loco became No. W8 'Freshwater' until 1949 when it returned to the mainland to work the Hayling Island branch as BR No. 32646. It was withdrawn from Eastleigh shed (71A) in November 1963 and then spent some years on static display outside the Hayling Billy Pub on Hayling Island before returning to the Isle of Wight in 1979 where it has since been restored.

Also saved from Barry, 'Merchant Navy' Class 4-6-2 No. 35005 'Canadian Pacific' made a sensational return to main line operations in 1998 when it appeared in its early 1950s BR dark blue livery. Here it is seen heading an enthusiasts' special near Walmer, between Deal and Dover, on February 19, 2000.

Railway Miscellany

Rebuilt 'West Country' Class 4-6-2 No. 34013 'Okehampton' is seen here at Brighton terminus with a train from Southampton in the late 1950s. Third-rail electrification had come early to Brighton with steam being ousted on the main line to London Victoria in 1933. 'Okehampton' was built at Brighton Works in 1945, rebuilt in 1957 and withdrawn in July 1967.

Veteran ex-LBSCR Class 'A1X' 0-6-0 tank No. 32662 rumbles across the rickety-looking wooden structure of Langstone Bridge on the approach to North Hayling station with the 7.08pm train to Hayling Island. Due to weight restrictions on the bridge the line, from Havant, had been worked since Victorian times by these diminutive 'A1X' tanks (or 'Terriers' as they were known). This photo was taken on July 21, 1963, less than four months before closure of the line on November 3. No. 32662 was built at Brighton Works in 1875 and withdrawn from Eastleigh shed (71A) in November 1963.

In 1963 all former SR lines west of Salisbury came under the control of the Western Region. Soon former GWR locos were to be seen taking over many branch line duties including the push-pull service between Yeovil Town and Yeovil Junction. Here 0-6-0 pannier tank No. 5410, built at Swindon in 1932, is seen propelling its train to Junction station past neat rows of vegetables on August 17, 1963. The loco was withdrawn just over two months later.

Designed by Richard Maunsell for the South Eastern & Chatham Railway a total of 80 'N' Class 2-6-0 mixed traffic locos were built between 1917 and 1934. They were to be seen all over the Southern Region with the last withdrawals taking place in 1966. Only one member of this class, No. 31874, has been preserved. Here, No. 31854, built in 1925, awaits its fate along with withdrawn ex-GWR locos at Severn Tunnel Junction on October 20, 1964.

Watched by a young admirer and his friend, a rebuilt Bulleid Pacific thunders along the embankment east of Winchfield station with a train for Waterloo in 1966. A year later this scene had disappeared with the electrification of the line to Southampton and Bournemouth.

90484

36A

EASTERN REGION

London Liverpool Street

OPENED BY THE GREAT EASTERN RAILWAY AS ITS MAIN LONDON TERMINUS IN 1874, LIVERPOOL STREET HAD BECOME AN EARLY VICTIM OF DIESELISATION AND ELECTRIFICATION BY 1960.

Class 'B17/6' No. 61656 'Leeds United' arrives at Liverpool Street with an express from Yarmouth in April 1958. On the left 'Britannia' Class 4-6-2 No. 70003 'John Bunyan' waits to depart with an express for Norwich. The 'B17' (or 'Sandringham') was built in 1936 and withdrawn in January 1960. No. 70003 was built at Crewe in 1951 and spent the first half of its life working on the Great Eastern main line between Liverpool Street and Norwich. Displaced by English Electric Type 4 (Class 40) diesels this loco ended its days at Carlisle Kingmoor from where it was withdrawn in March 1967.

If it weren't for the then-modern diesel, this scene at Liverpool Street could have been taken in the 1930s. D5512, one of the first batch of Brush Type 2 diesels (Class 31) to be delivered to the ER from Loughborough in 1957–58, waits for laundry baskets to be loaded into a Gresley parcels van in March 1959.

A visitor from Norwich Thorpe shed (32A), 'B1' Class 4-6-0 No. 61043, waits to depart from Liverpool Street on August 29, 1959. Introduced in 1942 many of the 410 members of this widely-scattered class had relatively short working lives. No. 61043 was built by the North British Locomotive Company in 1946 and withdrawn from March shed (31B) in July 1962.

A portrait of contrasts under the wires – until the early dieselisation of the Great Eastern line out of Liverpool Street, Stratford shed always turned out their 'N7' 0-6-2 tanks in immaculate condition for both suburban and station pilot duties. Shortly before withdrawal in 1960, Class 'N7/4' No. 69614 makes a perfect contrast to the recently arrived Brush Type 2 (Class 31) D5571.

Prior to that and despite some early electrification of lines to Shenfield and Chelmsford, the station's 18 platforms were busy with the comings and goings of the numerous 'N7' 0-6-2 and 'J67' 0-6-0 tanks on the intensive suburban services. Main line services to Cambridgeshire, Essex, Suffolk and Norfolk were in the hands of Class 'B17' 'Sandringham' 4-6-0s (of which two were streamlined until 1951), Class 'B12' 4-6-0s, Class 'B1' 4-6-0s and, last but not least, the BR Standard Class 7MT 'Britannia' 4-6-2s which had started coming on stream in the early 1950s. These superb locos, of which 21 were allocated to Norwich by 1958, handled many of the top link services such as the 'Hook Continental' and 'The Norfolkman' out of Liverpool Street.

Other named trains leaving Liverpool Street in the early '60s included 'The Essex Coast Express', 'The East Anglian', and 'The Broadsman'. The introduction of English Electric Type 4 (Class 40) diesels in 1958 meant that there were only three 'Britannias' left on these services by 1961. Brush Type 2 (Class 31), soon joined by the English Electric Type 3 (Class 37) diesels, had already taken over many of the other steam-hauled services and by 1962 all main line services from Liverpool Street were diesel-hauled. The main steam shed for the area, Stratford (30A) had also closed by September of that year. A visit to Liverpool Street in August 1965 revealed all of the above diesel classes plus a number of Brush Type 4 (Class 47) diesels and empty coaching stock in the hands of short-lived BTH Type 1 (Class 15) diesels. The diesel picture was complete – but not for long, as by 1986 the electrified main line to Norwich was 'switched on', followed by the Cambridge line in 1987 and King's Lynn in 1992.

ON SHED

Stratford 30A

By far the shed with the biggest allocation in the UK, at one stage in the early 1950s Stratford boasted nearly 400 locos, nearly half of which were 'N7' 0-6-2 and 'J67' and 'J69' 0-6-0 tanks used for the intensive suburban service out of Liverpool Street. Dispersed over a wide area, the shed and the adjoining ex-GER works were a 10-minute walk from Stratford station. By 1960 a new diesel depot had been opened and the steam shed reduced in size. Following the early electrification of suburban lines and the dieselisation of other services the remaining steam locos at Stratford had become redundant by 1962. Once famous as the home to many ex-LNER 4-6-0 types employed on main line

The early dieselisation and suburban electrification of routes out of Liverpool Street led to the wholesale withdrawal of many steam classes. Here, a forlorn line-up of withdrawn engines await their fate at Stratford on May 2, 1959. From left to right: 'D16/3' Class 4-4-0 No. 65288 (a Gresley rebuild of an earlier GER 'D15' and withdrawn from Cambridge shed in October 1958); 'J39' Class 0-6-0 No. 64715 (built at Darlington in 1926 and withdrawn in May 1959); 'N7/2' 0-6-2 tank No. 69689 (built 1927, the first member of its class to be withdrawn in March 1957).

Seen here at Stratford shed c.1959, Thompson 'L1' Class 2-6-4 tank No. 67716 was one of 100 such locos that were introduced between 1945 and 1950. Sadly, the class was short-lived due to its poor steaming abilities and unreliability. Allocated to Stratford, No. 67716 was built at Darlington in 1948 and saw service on suburban passenger trains from Liverpool Street to Hertfordshire.

Away from the long lines of withdrawn steam locos, Stratford shed on September 4, 1962 was nearly 100% dieselised. The exceptions were a solitary 'B1' 4-6-0, two 'N7' 0-6-2 tanks a 'L1' 2-6-4 tank and a BR Standard Class 4 2-6-4 tank. Five of the original batch of English Electric Type 4 (Class 40) diesels, D200, D201, D203, D206 and D209, were also on shed.

services out of Liverpool Street including 'B1', B12/3' and B17' ('Sandringham') Classes, by November 1961 the steam allocation was reduced to a shadow of its former self with only 47 locos. This included 11 'B1' 4-6-0s, seven of the ancient 'J15' 0-6-0s, nine 'L1' 2-6-4 tanks, the remaining 11 members of the 'J69' 0-6-0 tanks and nine of the once numerous 'N7' 0-6-2 tanks. Departmental steam locos allocated to Stratford Works were two 'J69' tanks, a 'J66' 0-6-0 tank and a 'Y4' 0-4-0 saddle tank.

By 1962 Stratford was growing from strength to strength with an allocation of 171 diesel locos. These included the first ten of the English Electric Type 4 (Class 40), 29 of the English Electric Type 3 (Class 37), 56 of the Brush Type 2 (Class 31) and two types of very unsuccessful locos – the entire class of ten of the North British Type 1 (Class 16) and 16 of the British Thomson-Houston Class 1 (Class 15). Even this impressive line-up has since been dispatched to the breaker's yard, and the diesel shed and the railway works have all gone.

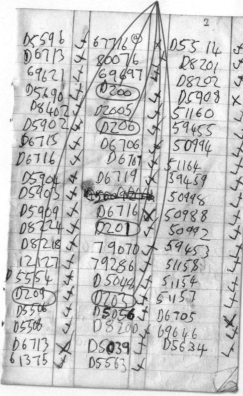

London King's Cross

DESIGNED BY LEWIS CUBITT, KING'S CROSS STATION WAS OPENED IN 1852 AS THE LONDON TERMINUS OF THE GREAT NORTHERN RAILWAY.

This panoramic view of King's Cross station shows Peppercorn 'A1' Class 4-6-2 No. 60127 'Wilson Worsdell' leaving with a train of 'blood and custard' coaches for Newcastle in June 1957. On the left 'N2' Class 0-6-2 tank waits its next call of duty on this gloriously sunny day.

In addition to handling the intensive north London suburban services the station was also the starting point for expresses up the East Coast Main Line via York and Newcastle to Edinburgh and Aberdeen. The most famous of these were the 'Flying Scotsman' and the pre-war 'Silver Jubilee', but others during BR days included the 'Elizabethan', 'Aberdonian', 'Queen of Scots', 'Talisman' and the 'Tyne-Tees Pullman'.

Haulage of these top link trains was in the capable hands of King's Cross shed's (34A) allocation of Class 'A3' and 'A4' Gresley Pacifics, but regular 'foreign' locos included Peppercorn Class 'A1' Pacifics and, towards the end of steam, Immingham-based 'Britannia' Pacifics. Gresley Class 'V2' 2-6-2s and Thompson Class 'B1' 4-6-0s were also often employed on passenger duties during peak holiday periods.

Suburban services including those to Moorgate were handled by King's Cross shed's large

The inaugural up 'Elizabethan' of the 1960 summer season arrives at King's Cross on June 13, 1960 behind 'A4' Class 4-6-2 No. 60027 'Merlin' of Haymarket shed (64B). Built in 1937, this loco ended its days at St Margarets shed (64A) from where it was withdrawn in September 1965. On the right is newly-built Brush Type 2 (Class 31) D5605 of Finsbury Park depot (34G).

(above) 'V2' Class 2-6-2 No. 60854 and 'A3' Class 4-6-2 No. 60065 'Knight of Thistle' simmer at the buffer stops on May 4, 1963 after arriving with trains from the north. The 'A3', fitted with a round dome and German-style smoke deflectors, was built as an LNER 'A1' Class at Doncaster in 1924, rebuilt as an 'A3' in 1947 and withdrawn in June 1964.

allocation of Class 'L1' 2-6-4 and 'N2' 0-6-2 tanks. By 1962 diesel multiple units, 'Baby Deltics' (Class 23) and Brush Type 2s (Class 31) had taken over suburban services. However, in April of that year – only just over a year before the end of steam at King's Cross – the station was still a great place for the trainspotter with, in the space of a few hours, Classes 'A1', 'A3', 'A4', 'V2' and 'Britannia' all being spotted.

Steam was in about equal numbers to the diesels seen, these coming mainly from Finsbury Park shed (34G) and including English Electric Type 4 (Class 40), 'Deltic' (Class 55), Brush Type 2 (Class 31), BR Sulzer Type 2 (Class 24) and the short-lived 'Baby Deltics' (Class 23). Steam operations ended in June 1963 when King's Cross shed was closed and diesels continued to reign until electrification of the ex-GNR line between 1976 and 1991.

(above) A classic scene of Gresley Pacifics at King's Cross bufferstops in 1962 – 'A3' Class No. 60109 'Hermit' and record-breaking 'A4' No. 60022 'Mallard' have just arrived with trains from the north. Both King's Cross shed (34A) locos, No. 60109 was built in 1923 as an LNER 'A1' Class, rebuilt as an 'A3' in 1943 and withdrawn in November 1962. No. 60022, holder of the world speed record for steam locos of 126 mph, was built in 1938 and withdrawn in April 1963. It has since been preserved as part of the National Collection.

London King's Cross

A powerful line-up at King's Cross shed in 1959 - Peppercorn 'A1' 4-6-2 No. 60153 'Flamboyant' (built Doncaster 1949, withdrawn November 1962) and 'A4' No. 60034 'Lord Faringdon' (built Doncaster 1938, originally named 'Peregrine', withdrawn August 1966). The 'A1' was one of five of this class fitted with Timken roller bearings which totally transformed their performance, reliability and mileage between general overhauls.

Home, until the end of steam, to such famous locos as 'Flying Scotsman' and 'Mallard', King's Cross shed was originally opened by the Great Northern Railway in 1851 and under both LNER and BR ownership went through several changes before finally succumbing to the diesel invasion when it closed in June 1963.

Located in King's Cross goods yard, the shed was about 15 minutes' walk north from King's Cross station. As the Eastern region's top link shed, King's Cross provided motive power for many of the East Coast Main Line expresses and for the intensive suburban services to north London and Hertfordshire. With the new diesel depot at Finsbury Park coming on stream in 1960, by November 1961 King's Cross shed's allocation was down to 53 steam locos, having already lost most of its 'L1' and 'N2' suburban tanks due to the early dieselisation of the suburban services.

However, even at this late stage and with the 'Deltic' onslaught already underway the shed could still muster an impressive line-up of 19 'A4' and 11 'A3' Gresley Pacifics, plus seven 'B1' 4-6-0s and eight 'V2' 2-6-2s. At the same time Finsbury Park was allocated 99 main line diesels including six 'Deltics' (Class 55), 40 Brush Type 2 (Class 31) and 25 BR Sulzer Type 2 (Class 24).

The shed yard at King's Cross in the days when engine shed security was somewhat more lax than today and spotters could get closer to the engines they so admired. The object of the boy photographer's attention on 27 July 1960 appears to be the appearance of Edinburgh Haymarket Class 'A3' No. 60037 'Hyperion', a rare sight at Kings Cross if ever there was one. Also in attendance is 'A3' No. 60059 'Tracery', 'A4' No. 60025, 'Falcon' bearing 'The Elizabethan' headboard, 'A4' No. 60014 'Silver Link', complete with 'Flying Scotsman' headboard and another, unidentified A4. What a line up!

A steamy line-up of Pacifics at King's Cross shed in 1960. From left to right: 'A4' No. 60014 'Silver Link' (the first 'A4', built 1935, withdrawn end of 1962); 'A2/3' No. 60519 'Honeyway' (built 1947, withdrawn end of 1962); 'A4' No. 60003 'Andrew K. McCosh' (originally named 'Osprey', built 1937, withdrawn end of 1962); 'A2/3' No. 60512 'Steady Aim' (built 1946, withdrawn June 1965) and an unidentified Peppercorn 'A1'.

Looking in good fettle, Class 'A3' 4-6-2 No. 60055 'Woolwinder' is coaled up in readiness for its next turn of duty from its home shed, c.1960. Built as an LNER 'A1' in 1924 and named after the 1907 St Leger winner, 'Woolwinder' spent much of its life on the Great Central main line. Here it is seen fitted with a double Kylchap exhaust system and experimental smoke-deflecting 'fins', shortly before withdrawal in September 1961.

Day Trippei

East Anglia, August '65

August 9, 1965 dawned bright and clear and the dream of a railway holiday in East Anglia had become a reality. The journey started at Birmingham where the train to Rugby was doubleheaded by D369 and D300. Departure was at 9.50am and a brisk run ensued with a maximum of 82mph being recorded through Hampton-in-Arden. Steam was in short supply but BR Standard Class 5 No. 73119 'Elaine' was seen heading a parcel train on the Great Central line at Rugby. The next stage to Peterborough saw D5012 at the head of the train – en route Ivatt Class 2 2-6-2 tank No. 41212 was spotted at Seaton with a train for Stamford Town. Changing trains at Peterborough East and March my destination of King's Lynn was finally reached. The week was happily spent travelling over many country byways including those to Hunstanton, Norwich to Sheringham and Grimsby to Peterborough via Louth and Boston. The return home was via Cambridge, Bletchley and Oxford. My diesel tally had increased significantly!

August 11, 1965 and not a steam engine in sight. The day out included a trip from King's Lynn to Hunstanton, followed by King's Lynn to March, via Wisbech, and to Cambridge via St Ives, all by dmu. A brisk return to Ely behind D6723 was faithfully recorded in the notebook. The final leg was by dmu from Ely to King's Lynn via March and Wisbech.

Once a popular destination for holidaymakers served by through trains from Liverpool Street, Hunstanton station (seen here on August 11, 1965) was the terminus of the branch line from King's Lynn. Although not listed for closure in the Beeching Report, all passenger services were withdrawn on May 3, 1969.

Seen here in August 1965, the neat forecourt and single storey building of Hunstanton station is now a car park. Gone are the days when holidaymakers thronged to this seaside resort by train.

March was once an important railway junction with lines to Ely, Wisbech, Spalding and Peterborough. Together with Whitemoor marshalling yard and locomotive depot (31B) it made an ideal trainspotting destination. By 1965 steam had disappeared and most trains were in the hands of Brush Type 2 diesels such as D5522 which was seen leaving March at the head of a passenger train on August 11.

Also spotted at March on August 11, 1965 was BR Sulzer Type 2 diesel D5038 at the head of a fitted van train. The two-tone green livery, grey roof and yellow front warning panel made these early diesels a colourful sight.

Along with all of the diesels seen the notebook faithfully records the meandering journey from King's Lynn to Norwich via Swaffham and Dereham on August 18, 1965. The scene at Swaffham looked particularly interesting on that day with weeding of the goods yard in progress and the rusty line to Thetford still intact.

Doncaster

DONCASTER WAS A FABULOUS SPOT FOR TRAINSPOTTERS IN THE 1950S AND EARLY 60S. NOT ONLY DID IT SIT ASTRIDE THE EAST COAST MAIN LINE AND WAS THE LOCATION OF THE FAMOUS DONCASTER WORKS, BUT WAS ALSO A MAJOR JUNCTION FOR HUMBERSIDE, NORTH LINCOLNSHIRE AND THE INDUSTRIAL HEART OF YORKSHIRE.

A surprise visitor to Doncaster on June 9, 1963 was ex-LMS 'Coronation' Class 4-6-2 No. 46245 'City of London' at the head of an enthusiasts' special to Doncaster Works, organised by the Home Counties Railway Society. Seen here immaculately turned out in BR maroon livery, the 'Semi' was built with streamlined casing at Crewe in 1943 (casing removed in 1947) and withdrawn from Crewe North shed (5A) in October 1964.

Gresley 'V2' Class 2-6-2 No. 60983 passes through Doncaster's middle road with an up empty coaching stock train in August 1961. One of 184 powerful and versatile 'V2' locos introduced between 1936 and 1944, this loco was built at Darlington in 1944 and withdrawn from Grantham shed (34F) in September 1962.

Watched by a gaggle of spotters, ex-LNER 'J39' Class No. 64840 waits to leave Doncaster with a local stopping train in June 1954. Although one of Gresley's less handsome locos, the 'J39' Class was the most numerous with 289 being built between 1926 and 1941. No. 64840 was built at Darlington in 1932 and withdrawn from Ardsley shed (56B) in November 1962.

(below) Fairly reliable maids of all work, the Brush Type 2 (Class 31) diesels were a common sight all over the Eastern Region from the late 1950s through to privatisation of BR. Here, in ex-works condition, No. 5622 is seen on empty coaching stock duties at Doncaster on July 23, 1971.

Until dieselisation of the East Coast Main Line the station was alive with the comings and goings of 'A1s', 'A2s', 'A3s' and 'A4s' heading south to King's Cross or north to Leeds, York, Newcastle and Edinburgh with their important expresses. However, by 1963 the arrival of the English Electric Type 4 (Class 40), BR Sulzer Type 4 (Class 46) and 'Deltic' (Class 55) diesels had brought about the demise of steam on these services. Despite this, steam locos – albeit in ever-decreasing numbers – continued to be used for a few more years on the heavy goods trains from the Yorkshire coalfields and the massive steel works at Scunthorpe. Dieselisation was complete in May 1966 when Doncaster shed (36A) closed – the last to do so on the Eastern Region.

Even as late as August 1965 a short stay (arrived 11.19, departed 13.50) on the platforms at Doncaster station revealed in just that time three 'B1' 4-6-0s, one 'O4/8' 2-8-0, eight 'exWD 2-8-0s and two BR 9F 2-10-0s in action on freight trains.

(above) Photographed in the original BR livery soon after delivery from Darlington Works in 1949, Peppercorn Class 'A1' 4-6-2 No. 60144 pauses at Doncaster with an up train. A local engine (36A) for most of its life, No. 60144 was later named 'King's Courier' and was withdrawn from Doncaster shed in April 1963.

Doncaster Works

OPENED BY THE GREAT NORTHERN RAILWAY IN 1853, DONCASTER WORKS
WENT ON TO BUILD SOME OF THE WORLD'S FINEST STEAM LOCOMOTIVES.

DONCASTER WORKS & SHED

ALSO **YORK** SHED & MUSEUM

SUNDAY 11th OCTOBER

MERCHANT NAVY PACIFIC

From
BIRMINGHAM (New St.)
BURTON-ON-TRENT   } **FARE**
DERBY (Midland)   **45/-**

BUFFET CAR

OUTWARD via SHEFFIELD,
DONCASTER & SELBY
RETURN   via CHURCH FENTON
& SHEFFIELD

Tickets

Under the GNR's Chief Mechanical Engineers, firstly Patrick Stirling then Henry Ivatt (from 1896) and Nigel Gresley (from 1911), Doncaster Works produced, among others, the famous Stirling Singles, Ivatt Atlantics and Gresley Pacifics. The first two of the original 'A1' Class Pacifics were introduced in 1922 and a year later the GNR was absorbed into the LNER.

A total of 52 of these locos were built before being rebuilt as 'A3' Pacifics, with another 27 of the latter being built from new. These were followed by 35 of the world-famous 'A4' Pacifics, including the holder of the world steam record, 'Mallard', and batches of the highly successful 'V2' 2-6-2 mixed traffic locos. Thompson's A2/2 and Peppercorn's A2 and a batch of A1 Pacifics followed, with many of the latter built after Nationalisation under the new British Railways management.

Under BR the Works (nicknamed the 'Plant') went on to build 42 of the BR Standard Class 5 4-6-0s, 70 of the Class 4 2-6-0s (of which No. 76114 was the last steam loco to be built at Doncaster

(opposite) 'A4' Class 4-6-2 No. 60031 'Golden Plover' is undergoing overhaul at the 'Plant' (the loco's birthplace in 1937), photographed during a visit organised by the Home Counties Railway Society on September 9, 1963. Although steam locomotive construction ended at Doncaster in October 1957, the overhaul of main line steam continued into the 1960s. 'Golden Plover', allocated to St Rollox (65B), was undergoing its last overhaul before withdrawal in November 1965.

(right) Peppercorn 'A1' Class 4-6-2 No. 60123 'H. A. Ivatt' at Doncaster Works on September 29, 1962. The loco had been involved in an accident at Offord on the ECML south of Huntingdon earlier that month, and in October it became the first 'A1' to be withdrawn from service. When only eight months old, No. 60123 was also involved in an accident at Lincoln.

when completed on 31 October 1957) and ten of the Class 4 2-6-4 tanks. By 1957 Doncaster had produced over 2,000 steam locos. Diesel loco construction followed with batches of Classes 03, 08 and 10 diesel-shunters, 84 of the Class 56 and 50 of Class 58 diesels.

Doncaster had also built the prototype Class EM1 electric locomotive (later Class 76) for the 1.5 kV DC Woodhead line back in 1941. Production of electric locos was resumed in 1958 with 24 of the 750 V DC third rail Class 71 (E5000-E5023) for the Southern Region and, starting in 1961, 40 of the Class 85 and 60 of Class 86 25kV Ac locos for the West Coast Main Line. The 'Plant' celebrated its 150th anniversary in July 2003.

(above) Doncaster Works, Crimsal Erecting Shop, on June 19, 1947 - not quite British Railways but only just over six months to go before Nationalisation. A Thompson 'B1' 4-6-0 and a Gresley 'A3' 4-6-2 receive heavy-duty attention as the sun streams through the soot-stained windows. This famous building was demolished in 2008 and replaced by a modern housing development.

(below) The end of the road for two Gresley Class 'N2' 0-6-2 tanks. Nos. 69557 and 69566 were on Doncaster's scrap line in 1957. Introduced by the GNR in 1920 many of these sturdy locos could be found hard at work on King's Cross suburban trains until withdrawal in the late 1950s.

ON SHED

Doncaster

36 A

This view of the south end of Doncaster shed was taken on June 9, 1963. Along with ex-WD 2-8-0, BR '9F' 2-10-0, 'B1' 4-6-0 and a Brush Type 4 (class 47) diesel are Peppercorn 'A1' Class 4-6-2 No. 60124 'Kenilworth' (built Doncaster 1949, withdrawn March 1966) on the left and, left of centre 'A1' Class No. 60149 'Amadis' (built Darlington 1949, withdrawn June 1964). BR Standard 'Britannia' 4-6-2 No. 70008 'Black Prince' (built Crewe 1951, withdrawn January 1967) was visiting from March shed (31B).

Not only one of the largest sheds in the Eastern Region, Doncaster was also one of the last to close to steam. In addition to providing top link motive power for the East Coast Main Line, Doncaster shed also provided heavy freight locos for the local coal and steel traffic in this heavily industrial area of south Yorkshire.

About a 20-minute walk south from Doncaster Station, the shed was originally opened by the Great Northern Railway in 1876. By the late 1950s its allocation was just under 200 locos but, even with the increasing dieselisation of main line services, by November 1961 it was still home to a staggering 155 steam locos plus 19 0-6-0 diesel shunters. Twelve different classes were represented including 13 'A1' and three 'A2' Pacifics, 22 'V2' 2-6-2s, 25 'B1' 4-6-0s, 16 'K1'/'K3' 2-6-0s and for heavy freight 20 '02/04' 2-8-0s, 30 ex-WD 2-8-0s and 16 BR Standard '9F' 2-10-0s.

The shed finally closed to steam in May 1966 but continued to serve as a diesel depot.

Contrasting giants at Doncaster Motive Power Depot in 1964 featuring (left) ex-GCR Robinson '04' Class 2-8-0 No. 63613 rebuilt with a 'B1' type round-topped boiler and a pair of ex-WD 'Austerity' 2-8-0s, including No. 90305. These two classes alone originally totalled 1,254 engines – an indication of the vast freight traffic once handled by Britain's railways.

The surrounding coalfields gave rise to Doncaster having a large allocation of ex-WD 'Austerity' 2-8-0s. This scene, taken on a Sunday afternoon in 1964, shows six of these classic heavy freight machines waiting to resume their diagrams the following morning.

A smoky scene in Doncaster shed in 1963 depicting 'War Department' 2-8-0 No. 90484 – one of 33 still allocated there in May 1965. After World War II the 'dub-dee' spent its life working in the Doncaster area and was withdrawn from that shed in May 1966. On the left is a former Great Central '04' Class 2-8-0 rebuilt with a round-top boiler.

Every trainspotter worth his salt had a small library of Ian Allan locomotive and shed guides. From early beginnings in 1942 when he published his first locospotters' guide, the *ABC of Southern Locomotives*, Ian Allan went on to build a small publishing empire catering for the trainspotting craze in the 1950s and 1960s. Essential titles were the *ABC Regional Guides*, the *ABC Combined Volume*, *Locoshed Book* and the *British Locomotive Shed Directory*.

All the gear

ESSENTIAL GEAR FOR A DAY OUT TRAINSPOTTING INCLUDED NOTEBOOK, BIRO, LOCOMOTIVE SHED DIRECTORY, *ABC COMBINED VOLUME*, CHEAP CAMERA, DUFFEL BAG AND PACKED LUNCH. OPTIONAL EXTRAS COULD INCLUDE A PACKET OF FIVE WOODBINES!

Half-term February 25, 1963. Alarm goes off at 5.30am, hurriedly get dressed, have a quick bowl of cereal and a cup of tea and then, with duffel bag hitched over my shoulder, I was off on my Dawes racing bike down to Central station to catch the early morning train to Cardiff – local 'Hall' Class No. 4929 'Goytrey Hall' was at the head of our train. This was the first leg of a day's 'shed bashing' to Port Talbot Duffryn Yard (87B), Neath (87A), Llanelly (87F) and Carmarthen (87G). The object of the exercise was to cop the last 'Castle' needed to complete the underlining of this class in my Ian Allan ABC of British Railways Locomotives Combined Volume. Late that afternoon the object of my desires, No. 4081 'Warwick Castle', was found tucked away out of use behind Carmarthen shed. Mission accomplished!

The above story illustrates the dedication and, some would say, fanaticism that some trainspotters possessed to catch that last elusive number. Trainspotting books had been around before World War II but these were published by each of the Big Four railway companies. In 1942 a young Southern Railway clerk by the name of Ian Allan published his first book – the *ABC of Southern Locomotives*. Selling

start train snapping with a coronet CAMERA

It's so much more exciting to make a permanent pictorial record of your train spotting activities. Taking wonderful shots of fast moving trains and impressive pictures of standing engines raising steam — adds so much more to your hobby.

Money saver —16 pictures on any 120 roll film. Optical viewfinder, two stops — one for colour, one for black & white and flash synchronised.

Rapier

With only a small amount of pocket money and the earnings from a newspaper round it was quite a struggle to save up enough for even the cheapest camera. Cameras such as the Coronet and Brownie Box were favourite accessories for any trainspotter but, unless the sun was shining and the train was stationary, the results could often be dire!

(above) In the 1950s and 1960s special trains to railway works and locomotive sheds were organised for trainspotters by Ian Allan and various railway societies. Here 'A4' Class 4-6-2 No. 60014 'Silver Link' is at the head of a 1950s Ian Allan excursion.

(left) Ian Allan's shed directory was an essential tool for locating engine sheds. This 1962 edition also provided itineraries for shed bashes around the country.

THE BRITISH LOCOMOTIVE SHED DIRECTORY

A COMPLETE GUIDE TO ALL MAIN LINE LOCOMOTIVE SHEDS & WORKS IN GREAT BRITAIN

LOCOMOTIVES of the LMS

OFFICIAL ILLUSTRATED LIST OF ALL LMS LOCOMOTIVES SPECIALLY ARRANGED FOR ENGINE SPOTTERS

2'6

(below) The result of a day's trainspotting in Hereford and Shrewsbury on April 18, 1964. The neat underlining was carried out after returning home.

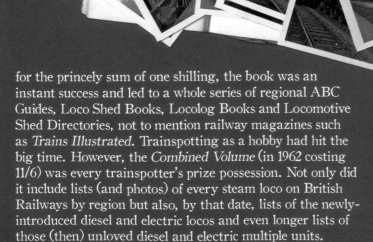

(above) Prior to Ian Allan's publishing enterprise the 'Big Four' railway companies issued books with lists of their own locomotives 'specially arranged for engine spotters'. This LMS guide was published in 1947.

for the princely sum of one shilling, the book was an instant success and led to a whole series of regional ABC Guides, Loco Shed Books, Locolog Books and Locomotive Shed Directories, not to mention railway magazines such as *Trains Illustrated*. Trainspotting as a hobby had hit the big time. However, the *Combined Volume* (in 1962 costing 11/6) was every trainspotter's prize possession. Not only did it include lists (and photos) of every steam loco on British Railways by region but also, by that date, lists of the newly-introduced diesel and electric locos and even longer lists of those (then) unloved diesel and electric multiple units.

Of course, the *Combined Volume* wasn't the only item required for a day of trainspotting. Also packed in the duffel bag was the latest edition of Ian Allan's *Trains*

Illustrated magazine, a notebook and pen for writing in the numbers of each loco spotted, a cheap camera (if you were lucky) like a Brownie Box or Coronet, a supply of Mum's wholemeal bread and Marmite sandwiches, an apple and a couple of cartons of Kia-Ora orange squash. Naturally, the neat underlining of loco numbers spotted was done back at home in the evening while listening to the latest Top 10 hit on Fabulous 208 Radio Luxembourg!

By February 25, 1963 the days were numbered for steam-haulage on passenger trains in South Wales. Apart from the solitary 'Hall' on the Gloucester to Cardiff stage, all of the other trains to Carmarthen and back on that day were hauled by 'Hymeks' or 'Westerns'.

Norwich (Thorpe)

EASTERN REGION

Photographed on August 29, 1959, exactly one month before withdrawal, Class 'B17/6' 4-6-0 No. 61612 'Houghton Hall' of Ipswich shed (32B) was still alive and kicking at Norwich shed. Built at Darlington as a 'B17' in 1930, No. 61612 was rebuilt as a 'B17/6' in 1950. In total 73 locos of this class were built and all were named, either after English country houses or football clubs. In 1937 two members of this class (No. 61659 'East Anglian' and No. 61670 'City of London') were given streamlined casings similar in appearance to the 'A4'. The casing was removed in 1951.

Located about a 10-minute walk east of Norwich Thorpe station, this shed was opened by the Yarmouth & Norwich Railway in 1844. Further improvements were carried out by the LNER in the 1930s but the early dieselisation of services in East Anglia had brought about the end of steam by the early 1960s. The shed's heyday was in the 1950s when around 80 steam locos were allocated here including the classic 'D16' 4-4-0s, 'B12', 'B17' ('Sandringhams') and 'B1' 4-6-0s.

However, pride of place must go to the 21 BR Standard Class 7MT 'Britannia' Pacifics (including 70000 herself) which did such sterling service on expresses to London Liverpool Street. Sadly, with the onslaught of the Brush Type 2 (Class 31) and English Electric Type 4 (Class 40) diesels, by November 1961 there were only three 'Britannias' left, with the rest having been reallocated to March (31B). In fact, on closure to steam in April of that year, Norwich Thorpe's allocation of steam locos had dwindled to only 16, of which seven were ex-GER 'J17' and 'J19' 0-6-0s.

Sub-sheds of Norwich Thorpe were Cromer Beach (closed 1959), Dereham (closed 1955) and Wymondham (closed 1958).

Norwich Thorpe shed was famous for its allocation of 'Britannia' Pacifics. By 1960, when this photo was taken, with the introduction of English Electric Type 4 (Class 40) diesels on the GEML the writing was on the wall for these fine locos. Here, 'K3' Class 2-6-0 No. 61957 (built by NBL Co in 1935 and withdrawn from Colwick shed in September 1962) and BR Standard 'Britannia' Class 4-6-2 No. 70038 'Robin Hood' (built at Crewe in 1953, withdrawn from Carlisle Kingmoor in August 1967) are seen at rest inside Norwich shed.

40E Colwick

This former Great Northern Railway shed was located on the main line to Grantham and Sleaford a few miles east of Nottingham. Its enormous allocation of freight locos reflected its importance in providing motive power for the heavy traffic from the Nottinghamshire coalfields. Colwick was recoded 16B when it came under LMR control only a few months prior to its closure to steam at the end of 1966.

The shed was about a 10-minute walk from Netherfield & Colwick station but its impregnable cordon made it virtually inaccessible to would-be trainspotters! By November 1961 Colwick's allocation had shrunk considerably to a total of 93 steam locos comprising 20 'O4' 2-8-0s, 27 ex-WD 2-8-0s, 18 'B1' 4-6-0s, 15 'K3' 2-6-0s, 11 'L1' 2-6-4 tanks, one 'J50' and 2 'J94' 0-6-0 tanks and five ex-LMS Ivatt Class 4 2-6-0s.

Introduced in 1911 by the Great Central Railway, the Class 'O4' 2-8-0 heavy freight loco went on to become the standard loco built for the Railway Operating Division (ROD) of the Royal Engineers during World War I. A total of 131 were built by the GCR, with an additional 521 being built for ROD. Of the latter 273 found their way on to the LNER's books during the 1920s. Even by May 2, 1965, with the end of steam on the ER in sight, Colwick shed was still allocated nine of these long-lived locos, including No. 63707 seen here.

A shed bash to Derby, Colwick, Kirkby-in-Ashfield, Barrow Hill and Staveley (GC) was organised for September 7, 1965. However, the visit to Colwick was cut short by an irate shed foreman but not before ten locos had been seen, including two 'B1' 4-6-0s Nos. 61070 and 61141.

41528

41 E

By 1965 Barrow Hill had quite a collection of veteran steam locos - built in 1907, diminutive ex-MR Deeley '0F' 0-4-0 tank No. 41528 was seen inside the roundhouse on 7 February 1965. A total of 10 of these locos were built for shunting in docks, breweries and industrial sites where their short wheelbase enabled them to traverse sharp curves. In addition to No. 41528, Barrow Hill was also allocated sister engine No. 41533 at this time and the remaining five of the veteran Johnson '1F' 0-6-0 half-cab tank locos introduced in 1878.

Staveley (Barrow Hill)

This former Midland Railway roundhouse was opened in 1870, but in 1958 came under the control of the Eastern Region and the shed's code was altered from 18D to 41E. Amongst the shed's allocation were ancient ex-Midland Railway tank locos used as shunters around the adjoining Staveley steel works. In late 1961 its allocation totalled 47 steam locos, including three of the diminutive ex-MR Deeley '0F' 0-4-0 and seven of the ancient ex-MR Johnson '1F' 0-6-0 'half-cab' tanks, plus a selection of Ivatt Class 4 2-6-0s, Fowler '4F' 0-6-0s and Stanier '8F' 2-8-0s.

The shed was best reached either by taking a No. 99 bus from Sheffield or Chesterfield, or a 15-minute walk from Staveley Works station. Barrow Hill closed to steam in October 1965 and was then used as a diesel depot (recoded BH) for some years until the rundown and closure of the steel works. Fortunately, following closure in 1991, Barrow Hill was saved two days before it was due to be demolished and has since been preserved and reopened as a centre for the railway heritage movement.

Compared to Colwick, the visits to Kirkby-in-Ashfield and Barrow Hill sheds on September 7, 1965 were highly successful. Both sheds still housed many steam locos – of the 23 seen at Kirkby 19 were Stanier 8F 2-8-0s. Barrow Hill was still home to some ancient ex-MR locos used for working around the Staveley steel works, including Deeley 0-4-0 tank No. 41528 and Johnson half-cabs Nos. 41835, 41804, 41763 and 41708. To complete this spectacle was ex-LMS 0-4-0 saddle tank No. 47001.

48222	92075	47001
48303	48342	90084
48105	BARROW HILL 4E	41804
48272	D8606	41763
D5294	90730	90509
48156	D4072	41708
D1808	43089	D1886
48614	D4092	D2904
D1630	41528	STAVELEY G.C.
48225	90340	90474
48096	D8608	90266
48102	90573	63590
D1821	41835	63913
D1831	92172	63646
48694	90377	D4063
48094	48695	D5826
48201	48162	DN45
92093	90258	D85
48304	D5813	D1693
	D5698	

Taken on June 16, 1956, Gresley 'V2' Class 2-6-2 No. 60817 arrives at Staveley (Central) station on the Great Central main line. The grey, wet day makes the smoke cloud from the approaching engine particularly impressive. The trainspotter on the left takes up a gallant pose, eager to identify the emerging loco. The 'V2' was built at Darlington in 1937 and withdrawn from New England shed (34E) in June 1963.

Staveley (GC)

Opened by the Manchester, Sheffield & Lincolnshire Railway in 1892, Staveley (Great Central) was located on the east side of the Great Central main line a few minutes' walk from Staveley (Central) station. The shed's allocation in November 1961 was only 25 steam freight locos, of which 22 were ex-GCR Class '04' 2-8-0s – a reflection of the deliberate running down of freight services on the former GCR main line. Through freight services were totally withdrawn in June 1965 and the shed was closed. A quick trip to the desolate shed in September revealed the sorry sight of five stored locos, including two ex-WD 2-8-0s and three '04' 2-8-0s. The end came for the rest of the Great Central in September 1966.

Class '04/7' 2-8-0 No. 63630 was one of 13 such Great Central workhorses still allocated to Staveley (GC) shed in May 1965. Closure came in June 1965.

DASTARDLY DIESELS!

Although many main line diesels working out of King's Cross were allocated to Finsbury Park depot (34G/FP), a diesel refuelling point was required closer to the terminus. Here, Class 55, 47 and 31 diesels are seen at the refuelling point on February 6, 1971.

The Eastern Region became the first region on British Railways to replace steam locos with main line diesels. Apart from a few locations such as Peterborough and Doncaster, steam had been ousted from East Anglia and most of the ECML by 1963.

Designed initially for use on the Eastern Region, one of the first main line diesel types on BR was the Brush Type 2 A1A-A1A (Class 31) (D5500-D5699 and D5800-D5862). Built between 1957 and 1962 these machines were highly successful when later re-engined and were soon to be seen at work throughout the region. In later years they also became common on the Western and London Midland regions. Although underpowered, the English Electric Type 4 1Co-Co1 (Class 40) main line diesels (D200-D399) saw early service on the ER, with D200 making its debut on the Liverpool Street to Norwich line in April 1958 and soon replaced the 'Britannias' on that route. Along with the Class 45 'Peaks' they also saw service on the East Coast Main Line until the introduction of the 'Deltic' Co-Co (Class 55) (D9000-D9021) in 1961. The most powerful main line diesel in Britain, these handsome machines dominated ECML services until 1981 when they were ousted by HST sets.

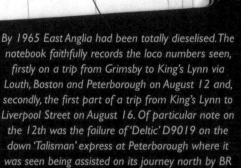

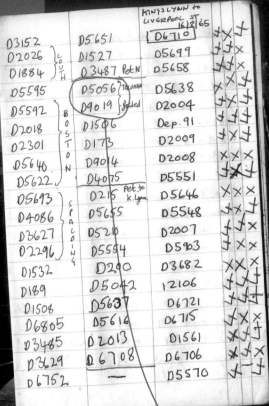

By 1965 East Anglia had been totally dieselised. The notebook faithfully records the loco numbers seen, firstly on a trip from Grimsby to King's Lynn via Louth, Boston and Peterborough on August 12 and, secondly, the first part of a trip from King's Lynn to Liverpool Street on August 16. Of particular note on the 12th was the failure of 'Deltic' D9019 on the down 'Talisman' express at Peterborough where it was seen being assisted on its journey north by BR Sulzer Type 2 D5056.

Seen here at the head of a parcel train at Liverpool Street in 1961, D8208 was one of ten BTH/Clayton Type 1 (Class 15) diesels introduced in 1957/58. First allocated to Devons Road (Bow) (1D), they were soon reallocated to the Eastern Region along with 34 more of this class which were introduced between 1959 and 1961. Their unreliability and non-standard design led to their withdrawal by 1971. Four were converted to train-heating units for use at Finsbury Park carriage depot but these, too, had been withdrawn by 1982. One example, D8233, was saved for preservation.

Introduced in 1957 the Brush Type 2 (Class 31) was one of the more successful early diesels on the Eastern Region. Here, No. 31160 is seen shunting at the Bishop's Stortford Coal Concentration depot on July 23, 1980.

Ten of the English Electric Type 2 (Class 23) 'Baby Deltic' diesels were introduced for King's Cross outer suburban services in 1959. By 1963, owing to continuing engine problems, they had all been placed into store at Finsbury Park. The locos were later modified which improved reliability but, because of their non-standard design, they had all been withdrawn by 1971. Here, D5909 is pictured leaving King's Cross station with a suburban train in August 1960.

The introduction of the Class 47 Brush Type 4 Co-Co (D1500-D1999 and D1100-D1111) in 1963 soon saw many of these highly successful machines at work throughout the region, taking over many of the Liverpool Street to Norwich services until electrification of that route in 1986. Some of these aged workhorses are still at work on the national rail network. Introduced between 1960 and 1965, the Class 37 English Electric Type 3 Co-Co (D6700-D6999 and D6600-D6608) took over many of the main line passenger and freight duties in East Anglia allowing many Class 31 locos to be transferred to other regions. Over 40 years later a few of these machines can still be seen at work on the national rail system.

Despite the success of many of the Eastern Region's main line diesels there were a few duffers. Notable among these is the Class 23 English Electric Type 2 Bo-Bo 'Baby Deltic' (D5900–D5909) introduced in 1959 which were employed on outer suburban trains from King's Cross. They soon succumbed to severe engine failure and, despite modifications, had all been withdrawn by 1971. Two other unreliable classes in the 'black book' were the Class 15 BTH/Clayton Type 1 Bo-Bo (D8200-D8243) introduced in 1957 and all withdrawn by 1971 and Class 16 North British Locomotive Company Type 1 Bo-Bo (D8400-D8409) introduced in 1958 and all withdrawn by 1968.

Introduced in 1961, the English Electric Type 5 (Class 55) 'Deltic' diesels (D9000-D9021) transformed services on the ECML and spelled doom for Gresley's Pacifics. At the time they were the most powerful main line diesels in the UK and these handsome machines dominated ECML services until 1981 when they were ousted by HST sets. Here, D9010 'The King's Own Scottish Borderer' is about to depart from King's Cross with the down 'Flying Scotsman' in the early '60s. Allocated to Haymarket shed (64B), this loco was eventually withdrawn in December 1981.

Despite the ending of steam haulage on BR in August 1968, the railway fraternity, young and old, continued their passion for trainspotting and photography. Here, a young railway photographer lines up the nameplate of 'Deltic' No. 9000 'Royal Scots Grey' at King's Cross in February 1969. The 'D' prefix has gone but the TOPS renumbering to 55 010 was yet to come. The 'Deltic' was withdrawn in January 1982 and has since been preserved.

King's Cross in the last years of steam – watched by a few young spotters, Peppercorn 'A1' 4-6-2 No. 60136 'Alcazar' arrives with an express from Edinburgh in May 1962. Then allocated to Doncaster (36A), this fine loco was less than 15 years old when it was withdrawn in May 1963.

Final Days

ALTHOUGH EAST ANGLIA WAS AN EARLY CASUALTY OF DIESELISATION, THE INDUSTRIAL REGION IN SOUTH YORKSHIRE CLUNG ON TO STEAM UNTIL 1966.

By August 1965 the Doncaster area was the last outpost of steam in the Eastern Region. A circuitous trip from King's Lynn via Peterborough and the ECML on August 13th included a one-hour stopover at Doncaster before returning via Scunthorpe, Grimsby, Louth and Boston. A total of 26 steam freight locos were seen in action in the Doncaster and Scunthorpe area including 14 ex-WD 2-8-0, six 'B1' 4-6-0, two '04' 2-8-0, two BR Standard '9F' 2-10-0. Two 'K1' 2-6-0 Nos 62035 and 62067 were seen in action between Scunthorpe and Grimsby.

The mass closure under the Beeching 'Axe' of rural branch lines and cross-country routes (the affectionately-remembered Midland & Great Northern Joint Railway went in 1959) and the early introduction of diesel multiple units and main line diesels had seen the end of steam throughout most of East Anglia by 1962.

The East Coast Main Line was the next to follow and King's Cross shed with its handsome 'A4' Pacifics was closed a year later. New England, Peterborough, (34E) lasted until 1965 and by early 1966 the last remaining outposts of steam left operating on the ER were centred on the industrial areas of south

The end of the line for Thompson 'B1' 4-6-0 No. 61056 as it is dismantled at Central Wagon Works, Ince, Wigan on July 1, 1965. Built by the North British Locomotive Co. in 1946 this loco was withdrawn from Immingham shed in April 1964.

Steam-hauled express passenger workings on the GEML ceased on the last day of the 1961 summer timetable. Here, in June 1961, Norwich shed's immaculate No. 70010 'Owen Glendower' backs on to its train at Norwich, the 10.45am to Liverpool Street.

Yorkshire and north Lincolnshire, around Doncaster and Colwick and at former Great Central Railway sheds at Frodingham (36C), Immingham (40B), and Langwith (41J).

All of the former GCR sheds were closed in February 1966 with the former Great Northern shed at Doncaster (36A) holding on until May. The final ER steam outpost was at Colwick (40E), but even this once-important GNR freight shed had shut by the end of the year.

February 28, 1959 was a sad day in railway history as it heralded the end of the M&GN Joint Railway system. Here, on the last day, Ivatt 2-6-0 No. 43161, allocated to Yarmouth Beach shed (32F), is seen approaching Weston with the 9.02am train from Yarmouth. Weston was located on one of the 'lines west', i.e. between Sutton Bridge and Bourne, two miles east of Spalding. Note the scribbled 'That's Yer Lot' headboard carried by the locomotive which had, apparently, been attached by local drivers as an epitaph. No. 43161, built at Doncaster in 1952, went on to live for another six years until it was withdrawn from Barrow Hill shed (41E) in June 1965.

The Great Escape

THE FLYING SCOTSMAN ... a new role

ONLY 50 FORMER LNER STEAM LOCOS
HAVE BEEN SAVED FOR PRESERVATION,
FAR FEWER THAN ANY OF THE OTHER
'BIG FOUR' RAILWAY COMPANIES.

Sadly not very many ex-LNER locos were bought by Dai Woodham and only one, 'B1' Class 4-6-0 No. 61264, was subsequently saved from Barry for preservation.

Consequently there are only 50 locos from the LNER and its constituent companies that have been saved for preservation – much less than from any other of the 'Big Four' railway companies. Stars of the show are no doubt the six 'A4', one 'A3' (No. 60103 'Flying Scotsman') and one 'A2' (No. 60532 'Blue Peter') Pacifics and one 'V2' 2-6-2 (No. 60800 'Green Arrow'). Of the six Gresley 'A4' Pacifics saved one is world steam record-breaker No. 60022 'Mallard', while No. 60008 'Dwight D. Eisenhower' is a static museum exhibit in the USA, and No. 60010 'Dominion of Canada' is in a Canadian museum.

Some of the older pre-Grouping locos from the former Scottish railways and the Great Northern Railway are in British museums. A glaring omission from the ex-LNER preserved loco stud is of course the Peppercorn 'A1' Class. This has now been rectified with the building of brand-new locomotive No. 60163 'Tornado'.

Celebrity 'A3' Class 4-6-2 No. 4472 (BR No. 60103) 'Flying Scotsman' paid a visit to Tyseley shed open day where it was the star attraction on September 29, 1969. Designed by Nigel Gresley for the GNR, 'Flying Scotsman' emerged from Doncaster Works as an LNER 'A1' in 1923. It was rebuilt as an 'A3' in 1947 and withdrawn from King's Cross shed (34A) early in 1963. The loco was purchased and restored by Alan Pegler and, in 1969, travelled to the USA where it toured the country. While the loco was in North America Pegler went bankrupt and it did not return to the UK until 1973 when it was saved by William McAlpine. This famous loco was eventually bought (after several more changes of ownership) by the National Railway Museum in York where it is currently being given a major overhaul.

Designed by T W Worsdell, 289 'J15' Class 0-6-0 locos were built for the Great Eastern Railway between 1883 and 1913, and could be seen at work on East Anglian branchlines until the late 1950s. The last withdrawal took place in 1962 and No. 65462 was preserved. It is seen here with its Lowestoft Central (32C) shed plate on December 1, 2008 while visiting the Gloucestershire & Warwickshire Railway.

Introduced in 1936, Gresley's 'V2' 2-6-2 loco was probably one of the most successful mixed traffic locos built in Britain. A total of 184 had been built by 1944, and the last members of this class were withdrawn in 1966. The first loco of this class to be built, No. 4771 (BR No. 60800) 'Green Arrow', seen here at York on September 29, 1979, has been preserved for the National Collection and restored in LNER apple green livery. The loco is currently awaiting major repairs before returning to main line service.

Gresley's 'A4' Pacific was probably the most exciting steam locomotive class ever built in Britain. Introduced in 1935 a total of 35 of these streamlined locos were built at Doncaster by the LNER. No. 4468 (BR No. 60022) 'Mallard' went on to set a world speed record for steam of 126mph on July 3, 1938. Displaced from the ECML by 'Deltic' diesels, many of these fine locos ended their days hauling the Aberdeen to Glasgow expresses until 1966. Six have been preserved, including 'Mallard' and No. 4498 (BR No. 60007) 'Sir Nigel Gresley', here seen at Dinting in June 1968.

Railway Miscellany

A scene that has disappeared forever – ex-LNER 'B17/6' 4-6-0 No. 61620 'Clumber' is seen here at Sheffield Victoria in September 1958 with a boat train for Harwich. Named after English country houses and football clubs, the class was known collectively as 'Sandringhams' after the first 'B17' which bore this name. No. 61620 was built at Darlington in 1930, rebuilt as a 'B17/6' in 1951 and withdrawn from Kings Lynn shed (31C) in January 1960. Note 'B1' 4-6-0 No. 61181 on the left and the gaggle of trainspotters on the right.

To celebrate the 100th anniversary of Doncaster Works a special train was run over two weekends in September 1953 from King's Cross to Doncaster. Here, hundreds of enthusiasts watch ex-GNR Class 'C1' 4-4-2 No. 990 'Henry Oakley' (built 1898) and sister engine No. 251 (built 1902) as they prepare to depart on one of their historic trips. Both engines are now preserved as part of the National Collection.

BR Standard 'Britannia' Class 4-6-2 No. 70010 'Owen Glendower' pulls out of Norwich Thorpe with the 10.45am to Liverpool Street in June 1961. By this date the English Electric Type 4 (Class 40) diesels were handling most of the trains on the GE main line. Built at Crewe in 1951, No. 70010 was one of 21 of these locos originally allocated to the GE main line. It was reallocated to March shed (31B) in 1961 and to Carlisle Kingmoor (12A) in 1965, from where it was withdrawn in September 1967.

Diversions of trains from the East Coast Main Line were common on Sundays during engineering work. Accidents also happened and, following one that occurred at Sandy on July 23, 1969, all trains were diverted on to the GEML at Cambridge via Royston and Shepreth Junction. Here, 'Deltic' (Class 55) D9013 'The Black Watch' heads the down Flying Scotsman' at Shepreth Junction on July 24.

Until 1960 the Great Central main line from Sheffield to Marylebone was operated by the Eastern Region. In that year it was transferred to the London Midland Region and the die was then cast for the eventual closure of the whole route in September 1966. Ex-LNER 'A3' 4-6-2 No. 60052 'Prince Palatine' is seen heading out of Marylebone in the happier days of July 1952 with the down 'Master Cutler' express to Sheffield. No. 60052 was built as an LNER 'A1' in 1924, rebuilt as an 'A3' in 1941 and, in January 1966 on allocation to St Margarets shed (64A), became one of the last surviving members of its class to be withdrawn.

abc LOCOS BOOK

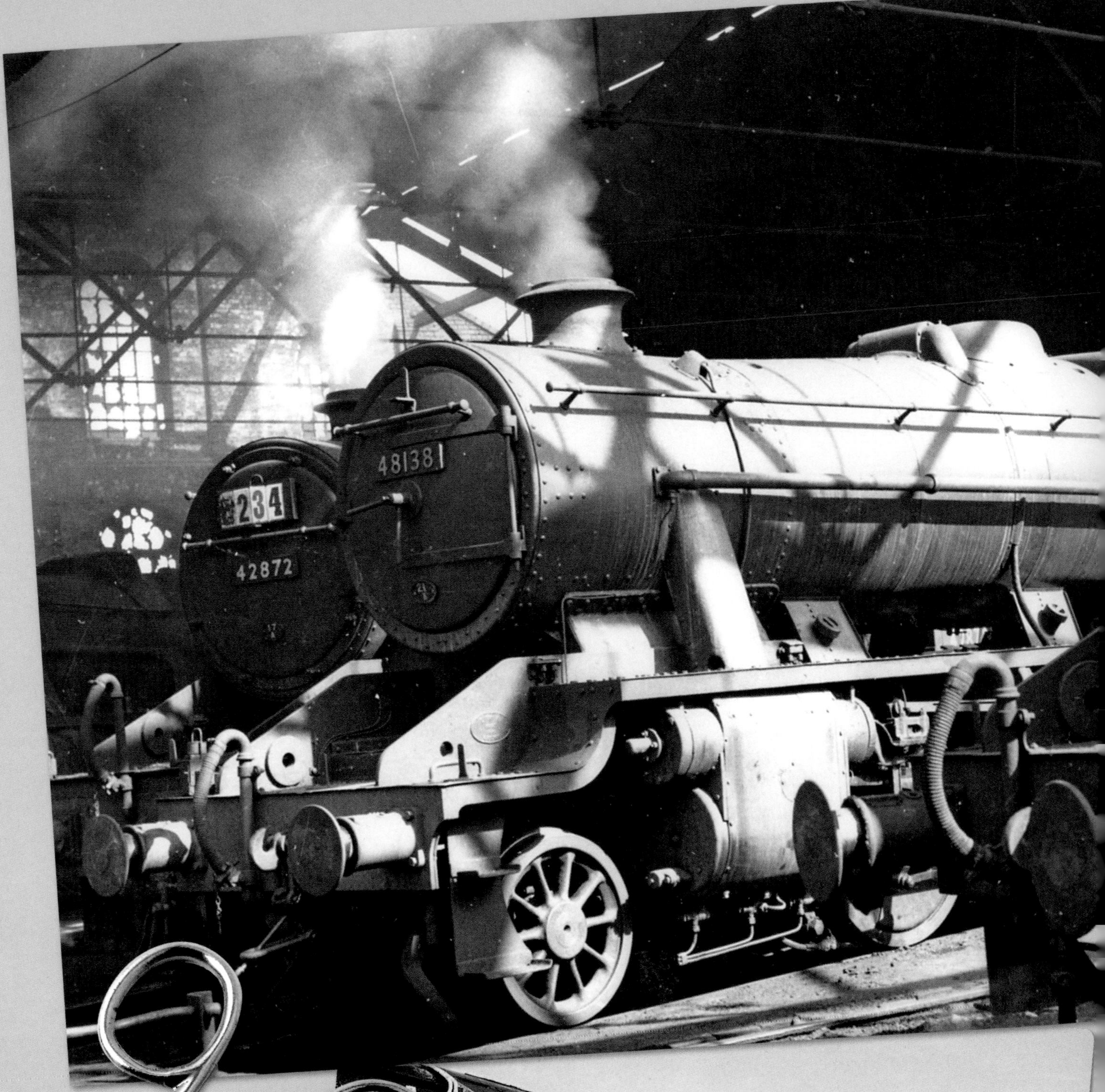
48138
234
42872

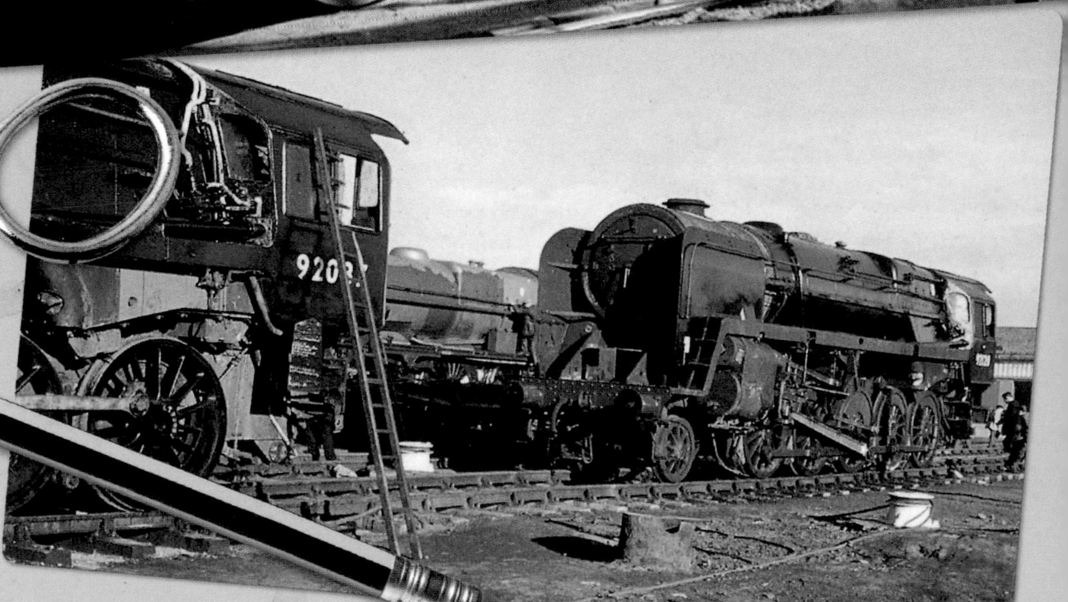

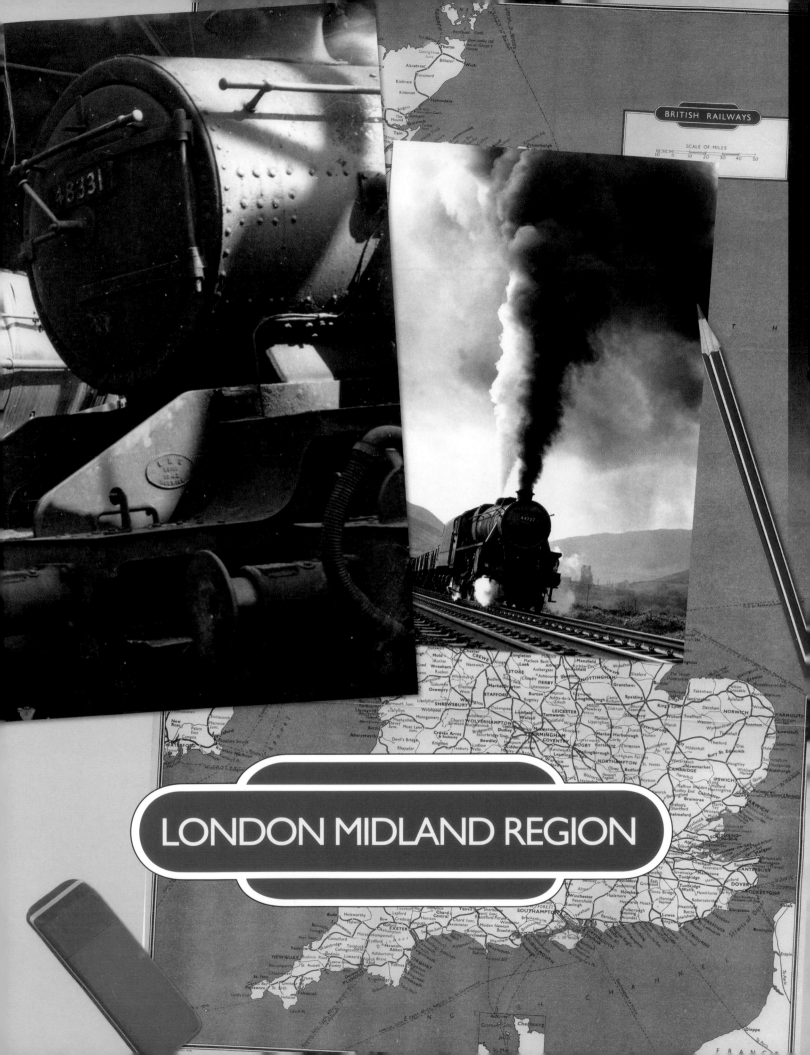

LONDON MIDLAND REGION

London Euston

OPENED IN 1837 AS THE LONDON TERMINUS OF THE LONDON & BIRMINGHAM RAILWAY, EUSTON STATION BECAME THE GATEWAY FOR LONG-DISTANCE TRAINS TO THE MIDLANDS, NORTHWEST ENGLAND AND SCOTLAND.

Then allocated to Warrington (8B), unrebuilt 'Patriot' Class 4-6-0 No. 45518 'Bradshaw' is seen here at Euston in 1960 after arriving with a special from the north. Based on the LNWR 'Claughton' Class and designed by Henry Fowler for the LMS, a total of 52 were built at Crewe and Derby between 1930 and 1934. After World War II 18 locos were rebuilt with a new taper boiler, cab, tender and smoke deflectors. All were withdrawn by 1965. 'Bradshaw' was built at Crewe in 1933 and withdrawn from Lancaster shed (24J) in October 1962.

By the 1930s it also became the starting point for many famous express trains such as the 'Royal Scot' and the streamlined 'Coronation Scot', both destined for Glasgow. By the 1950s the list of romantically-named trains departing from Euston was impressive and included the 'Caledonian', the 'Emerald Isle Express', the 'Lakes Express', the 'Merseyside Express', the 'Midday Scot' and, of course, the 'Royal Scot'. At the same time Euston had become a great place for the locospotter to see LMR top link locos such as 'Jubilee', 'Royal Scot' and 'Patriot' 4-6-0s and the classic 'Princess' and 'Coronation' Class Pacifics,

Apart from the regular appearances of the two LMS Co-Co diesels (Nos 10000 and 10001) and the three SR main line diesels (Nos.

Stanier 'Coronation' Class 4-6-2 No. 46252 'City of Leicester', seen here at Euston in 1960, has just arrived with a train from the north. By that date the English Electric Type 4 (Class 40) diesels, seen on the right, were already usurping steam haulage on the WCML. Then allocated to Carlisle Kingmoor (12A), 'City of Leicester' was built at Crewe without streamlined casing (but with a streamlined tender) in 1944 and was withdrawn from Camden (1B) in June 1963.

Then allocated to Willesden (1A) Stanier 'Black Five' 4-6-0 No. 44916 is seen here carrying out carriage shunting duties at Euston in April 1961. One of 842 such locos built between 1934 and 1951, No. 44916 was built at Crewe in 1945 and was withdrawn from Stockport Edgeley (9B) in December 1963.

10201-10203), steam held sway until the introduction of the first English Electric Type 4 (Class 40) and BR Sulzer Type 4 (Class 44) diesels in 1960, but even their reign was short-lived with electrification of the West Coast Main Line proceeding apace, and by the early 1960s steam and diesel traction and Euston's days as a historic station building were all coming to an end. The station and its famous Euston Arch were demolished and, amidst much public outcry, replaced by the current modern bland building which opened in 1968. The end for diesels came so quickly that on a short visit to Euston in May 1966 only one was spotted – the rest were all 25kV AC electric locos. Now, even they are gone and tilting 'Pendolino' trains cover the journey to Glasgow in around 4½ hours.

Introduced in 1958, the English Electric Type 4 (Class 40) was the mainstay of diesel haulage out of Euston until electrification of the WCML to Crewe in April 1966. Only one year old, D380 waits to depart from Euston with an express for Liverpool in August 1963. It was withdrawn 20 years later.

ON SHED

Camden was justly famous for its allocation of 'Coronation' Pacifics, but by 1963 their days were numbered due to the increasing availability of Type 4 diesels. Here, on April 28, green-liveried No. 46239 'City of Chester' awaits transfer to Crewe North shed from where it was withdrawn in September 1964.

London Camden

This brass tally or pay token was issued to driver or fireman No. 52 of Camden shed by the London & North Western Railway.

The first engine shed at Camden, 1½ miles north of Euston station, was opened in 1837 to the east of the newly-built London & Birmingham Railway. At that time trains out of Euston were hauled uphill to Camden Town by cables until 1847 when more powerful steam locos were introduced. A new roundhouse was built on the site by the L&BR but, although closed in 1871, this famous building has been preserved and is now in use as an arts and concert venue. The Camden shed known and beloved by trainspotters – a five minute walk from Chalk Farm underground station - was opened on the west side of the main line in 1847 and modernised and enlarged in turn by both the L&NWR and the LMS. Under both companies it became the main shed for the top link West Coast Main Line Expresses from

Euston and consequently had an allocation of locos that were definitely in the celebrity status! During the early BR era, Camden, with its allocation of Stanier 'Princess' and 'Coronation' Pacifics, supplied motive power for famous trains such as the 'Royal Scot' and 'The Caledonian'. 1960 saw the introduction of English Electric Type 4 (Class 40) and BR Sulzer Type 4 (Class 44) diesels on many of these services and by November 1961 Camden had lost all of its 'Royal Scot' and 'Jubilee' 4-6-0s and its 'Princess' Pacifics – all that was left were four 'Coronation' Pacifics and these were soon to go. At the same time, on the diesel side, the shed had 19 of the English Electric Type 4 diesels (including eight named members) and four of the early named 'Peak' (Class 44) diesels. Camden officially closed to steam in September 1963, but carried on as a diesel depot until 1966 when it succumbed to the electrification of the WCML and was finally closed.

A visit to Camden was made during a 'shed bash' around London on September 4, 1962. Despite the high numbers of English Electric Type 4 seen on shed that day there were still five 'Coronation' Pacifics (Nos. 46227, 46240, 46239, 46236 and 46229) and one 'Princess Royal' Pacific (No. 46206) to be seen. The shed closed to steam a year later.

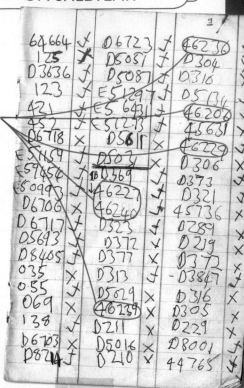

Despite being a top link shed, Camden also had a small allocation of 'Jinty' 0-6-0 tanks which were used on local duties. Here, on August 1, 1959 No. 47307 rubs shoulders with its main line shed mates including, on the far right, 'Royal Scot' Class 4-6-0 No. 46106 'Gordon Highlander'. The latter was unique in its class as it was fitted with BR style straight smoke deflectors. The 'Scot' was built by the NBL Co. in 1927, rebuilt in 1949 and withdrawn from Leicester Central (15E) in December 1962. However, due to the arctic winter conditions existing at that time it was reinstated until April 1963. No. 47307 was built by Hunslet in 1925 and withdrawn in August 1966.

Fitted with a red-background shedplate, 'Royal Scot' Class 4-6-0 No. 46156 'The South Wales Borderer' was seen on shed in April 1963 – only five months before Camden closed to steam. Built at Derby in 1930 the 'Scot' was rebuilt in 1954 and withdrawn from Annesley shed (16B) in October 1964. This loco should not be confused with ex-GWR 'Castle' Class 4-6-0 No. 4037 which carried a very similar name – 'The South Wales Borderers'.

ON SHED

London Willesden

Originally opened by the L&NWR in 1873, Willesden depot went through various rebuildings and additions under the LMS until it ended up as a roundhouse and adjacent straight shed. The principal LMR shed for freight locos in London, by November 1961 its allocation was a very mixed bag that totalled 131 locos, of which 48 were diesels. Included in the latter were the two ex-LMS 1947/48-built Co-Co diesels and the three later Southern Region Ashford-built 1Co-Co1 diesels, 21 BR Sulzer Type 2 (Class 24), seven English Electric Type 2 (class 20) and 15 diesel shunters.

On the steam side 13 different classes were represented including two 'Princess Royal' Class Pacifics (relegated from 1B Camden), three rebuilt 'Patriot' and four 'Royal Scot' 4-6-0s, 21 Stanier 8F 2-8-0s, and five 'Britannia' Pacifics. Willesden shed was located on the west side of the main line out of Euston, just north of Willesden Junction station, from which it was just a five minute walk. A trainspotting visit to the shed in September 1962 ended with a tally of 33 diesels and 88 steam locos.

Following electrification of the West Coast Main Line the shed closed completely in August 1965.

Early diesel days at Willesden - seen here inside the roundhouse on May 9, 1962, ex-LMS main line diesel No. 10001 and ex-SR main line diesel No. 10102 were among the earliest diesels allocated to Willesden. The precursors to the first-generation diesels ordered in the 1955 Modernisation Plan, No. 10001 was withdrawn in 1962 and No. 10202 was withdrawn at the end of 1963.

With the fatal sack over its chimney after a snowfall, 'Coronation' class 4-6-2 No. 46234 'Duchess of Abercorn' awaits the cutter's torch at Willesden on February 3, 1963. Built at Crewe in 1938 the 'Duchess' had been withdrawn only three days before being photographed here and was disposed of at Crewe in June.

'Coronation' Class 4-6-2 No. 46235 'City of Birmingham' of Crewe North was seen at Willesden in immaculate condition on May 11, 1963. It was built with a streamlined casing at Crewe in 1939, de-streamlined in 1946 and withdrawn from Crewe North (5A) in September 1964. It has since been preserved as a static exhibit in Birmingham.

WS1379	45240	75030
D7027	46472	46154
5041	47307	45288
6165	45623	73067
9440	D5079	45528
9405	45287	44805
D1005	44910	45287
D1002	44805	44910
5979	45379	03016
WS1380	42161	D5030
8430	46146	45494
7928	48012	D5144
D1037	92111	D5075
6133	48686	(10000)
8459	D5082	45535
9411	92077	75031
WS1338	D5035	48136
D5073	46168	42071
D5035	45655	42218
D5078	44747	08008

Willesden-allocated rebuilt 'Patriot' class 4-6-0 No. 45530 'Sir Frank Ree' waits its next turn of duty on May 11, 1963. Built with a parallel-boiler at Crewe in 1930 this loco received its name after it was transferred from No. 5501 in 1937. Rebuilt with a taper boiler in 1947 it was withdrawn from Carlisle Kingmoor shed (12A) at the end of 1965.

A visit to Willesden on September 4, 1962 revealed 33 diesels and 88 steam locos. The LMS Ivatt-designed main line diesel No. 10000 was spotted in among numerous 'Royal Scot', 'Jubilee', rebuilt 'Patriot' and 'Black Five' 4-6-0s.

131

London St Pancras

DESIGNED BY WILLIAM BARLOW, ST PANCRAS STATION WITH ITS VICTORIAN GOTHIC FRONTAGE AND ENORMOUS CAST IRON TRAIN SHED WAS OPENED IN 1868 AS THE LONDON TERMINUS OF THE MIDLAND RAILWAY.

Allocated to Leeds Holbeck, ex-LMS 'Jubilee' Class 4-6-0 No. 45651 'Shovell' is here seen at St Pancras in January 1952 at the head of a train to Derby. A widely travelled engine, it was later transferred to Bristol (Barrow Road) shed (82E) until ending its days at Shrewsbury (89A) in 1961 where it often headed trains over the Central Wales Line to Swansea. It was built at Crewe in 1935 and withdrawn in November 1962.

At the time of its opening the station was considered one of the wonders of the Victorian Age. Built on cast iron piers, the space below the station was used to store beer barrels carried by MR trains from Burton-upon-Trent. On the formation of the Big Four in 1923 the former L&NWR terminus at Euston was chosen by the newly-formed LMS as its main London terminus and St Pancras was then relegated to playing second fiddle with services for the Midlands and the North.

By Nationalisation the principal services from St Pancras continued to serve Nottingham, Manchester, Sheffield and Carlisle with named trains

One of five such locos then allocated to Kentish Town (14B) ex-LMS Fowler Class '4' 2-6-4 tank No. 42334 is seen on station pilot duties at St Pancras on February 28, 1962. A total of 125 of these locos were built at Derby between 1927 and 1934, the final 26 being fitted with side-window cabs. No. 42334 was built in 1929 and withdrawn from Trafford Park shed (9E) at the end of 1965.

When rebuilt, the 'Royal Scot' 4-6-0s were fairly handsome engines. Allocated to Kentish Town (14B) and watched by two young trainspotters, No. 46133 'The Green Howards' waits to depart with the 5.25pm 'Robin Hood' restaurant car express to Nottingham in 1961. Built by the North British Locomotive Co. in 1927 and rebuilt in 1944, this loco was soon to move to Newton Heath (26A) from where it was withdrawn in February 1963.

Introduced between 1960 and 1962 the BR Sulzer Type 4 (Class 45) diesels, nicknamed 'Peaks' after the earlier Class 44 named locos, were soon displacing steam on the Midland main line out of St Pancras. D133 is seen at St Pancras with a down express on May 23, 1964. This loco was withdrawn with the TOPS No. 45003 at the end of 1985. 12 members of this class have survived in preservation.

such as 'The Palatine' (to Manchester), 'The Waverley' (to Edinburgh via the Settle & Carlisle and Waverley routes) and the 'Thames-Clyde Express' (to Glasgow St Enoch via the Settle & Carlisle route and Dumfries). Prior to dieselisation in the early 1960s these trains were usually drawn by Kentish Town (14B) 'Jubilee' or 'Royal Scot' 4-6-0s. However, steam soon gave way to diesel in the shape of the 'Peak' Class (Class 45) of which some 16 had been allocated to Cricklewood diesel depot by November 1961 along with a number of BR Sulzer Type 2s (Class 24).

Between 1960 and 1966 'The Midland Pullman', operated by Blue Pullman diesel units, ran between St Pancras and Manchester Central. 'The Palatine' made its last run in 1964, 'The Waverley' ceased to run in 1968 when the line between Carlisle and Edinburgh via Hawick was closed and the 'Thames-Clyde Express' ended in 1975. HST sets took over remaining services to Leicester and Nottingham in 1983 and, since 2007, St Pancras has taken on a new lease of life as the London terminus of Eurostar services to Paris and Brussels.

ON SHED

Cricklewood

14 A

A contrast in motive power at Cricklewood on October 21, 1962. 'Peak' Class diesel (Class 45) D123 stands next to rebuilt 'Patriot' class 4-6-0 No. 45532 'Illustrious'. The 'Peak' was built at Crewe in 1961, withdrawn as TOPS No. 45125 in May 1987 and has since been preserved. The 'Patriot' was built with a Fowler parallel boiler at Crewe in 1933, rebuilt in 1948 and withdrawn from Carlisle Upperby shed in February 1964.

Consisting of two adjoining ex-Midland Railway roundhouses, the steam shed at Cricklewood was located on the west side of the main line about a 15 minute walk north of Cricklewood station and provided motive power for freight services on the Midland main line. With the opening of a diesel shed on the east side of the main line in 1960, Cricklewood's steam allocation was rapidly dwindling and by November 1961 totalled only 43 locos made up of six Ivatt Class 4 2-6-0s, eight Fowler 4F 0-6-0s, seven 'Black Five' 4-6-0s, six 'Jinty' 0-6-0 tanks and 16 Stanier 8F 2-8-0s. On the diesel shed by that date were 16 'Peak' Class (Class 45), 10 BR Sulzer Type 2 (Class 24) and 11 shunters. The steam shed closed in December 1964.

A foreigner from Yorkshire visits Cricklewood - Gresley 'V2' 2-6-2 No. 60925 from York (50A) was seen on shed in October 1962. Note the Standard Eight parked by the shed entrance. Built at Darlington in 1941, the 'V2' spent most of its life allocated to 50A and was withdrawn from that shed in May 1964.

134

A visitor from Leeds – ex-LMS 'Jubilee' Class 4-6-0 No. 45605 'Cyprus' from Holbeck shed (55A) receives an inspection at Cricklewood on May 11, 1963. Built by the North British Locomotive Co. in 1935, 'Cyprus' was withdrawn from Burton shed (16F) in February 1964.

A visitor from Royston shed (55D) – the penultimate member of its class, BR Standard Class 5 4-6-0 No. 73170 was seen at Cricklewood on December 16, 1962. Built at Doncaster in 1957 this loco was only nine years old when withdrawn from Eastleigh (70D) in June 1966.

Day Tripper

Birmingham & Crewe shed tour, January 1965

Organised like a military operation a major 'shed bash' from Glasgow to Warrington, the West Midlands and Crewe at the end of January 1965 brought a tally of 550 cops. This was some trip with visits to Tyseley, Saltley, Bescot, Oxley, Bushbury, Warrington Dallam, Crewe South and Crewe North engine sheds and Crewe Works. Although the former WR sheds at Tyseley and Oxley were now part of the LMR they still featured a good selection of ex-GWR locos – at Tyseley there were six 'Castles' (Nos 7014, 5014, 7014, 7026, 7029 and 7034) while at Oxley there were seven (Nos. 5026, 5056, 5089, 7011, 7012, 7019 and 7024). There were nine 'Jubilees' at Warrington Dallam while at Crewe South we found four ex-GWR locos – 'Hall' No. 5955, 'Granges' Nos 6817 and 6870 and 'Manor' No. 7819.

...while another five were seen at Crewe W...

By 1965 'Britannia' Pacifics, many displaced from the Eastern Region a few years earlier, had become commonplace up and down the WCML north of Crewe. An amazing total of 27 – nearly 50% of the class - were seen during the two-day 'shed bash' at the end of January 1965.

After the closure of Crewe North in May 1965, Crewe South shed

Birmingham and Derby, 7/9/1965

It was the end of the 1965 school summer holidays and a final 'shed bash' from Gloucester was organised on September 7 to visit Derby, Nottingham, Colwick, Kirkby-in-Ashfield, Barrow Hill and Staveley (GC). The trip up to Birmingham New St was behind 'Peak' D37 followed by a run to Derby behind D1693. The most numerous type of steam loco seen on that day were the 49 Stanier '8F' 2-8-0s that were spotted. Diesel traction, in the shape of newly outshopped BR Sulzer Type 2s (Class 25), was also increasingly taking over their duties at the head of freight trains. Brush Type 4 (Class 47) diesels also featured strongly with D1597 making a spirited run back from Derby to Gloucester at the end of the day.

'Who said that diesels were cleaner than steam'? 'Peak' D66 (Class 45) emits a voluminous cloud of exhaust at Derby Midland station on September 7, 1965 while Brush Type 4 (Class 47) D1693 waits to leave with a southbound train. The 'Peak' was withdrawn as No. 45146 in April 1987.

46526	48755	90237
BRUM - DERBY	44057	48662
D24	12061	D4149
D116	92452	D3570
D341	12044	D3572
D324	90529	48345
D1693	D8	12652
48522	D130	92159
D3107	D3974	D4137
D1719	60145	48367
44859	B770	44839
D.1611	D5281	D3586
12043	90491	12050
48375	D1635	92211
46448	46358	48098
D5223	90501	D5297
D5243	48393	45191
D5236	48286	D1798
D.1639	48279	D7580
43149	90686	D7549
	90439	

While passenger services were virtually all diesel-hauled steam haulage of freight trains still featured strongly during a trip to the Derby area on September 7, 1965. Our train from Birmingham New St. to Derby was hauled by Brush Type 4 D1693 while en route we spotted an interesting foreigner – Peppercorn 'A1' Class Pacific No. 60145 'Saint Mungo' of York shed (50A).

Carlisle Upperby July 29, 1964

Carlisle Upperby was one of the sheds visited during a circular trip from Glasgow via the WCML to Carlisle and return via the Waverley Route and Edinburgh on July 29, 1964. Despite many of its locos being withdrawn or stored out-of-use, Upperby shed still had some crackers to spot on that day including five rebuilt 'Patriot', four 'Jubilee' and two 'Royal Scot' 4-6-0s, 'Princess Royal' Class Pacific No. 46200 and 'Coronation' Class Pacifics Nos. 46228, 46226, 46238 and 46241. Another member of this class, No. 46225, was later seen at Citadel station at the head of a parcels train.

Withdrawn from service two months earlier, rebuilt 'Patriot' Class 4-6-0 No. 45545 'Planet' was seen stored at the back of Upperby shed on July 29, 1965.

Various withdrawn locos were seen in storage on a visit to Upperby on July 29, 1964 including red-liveried 'Princess Royal' Class 4-6-2 No. 46200 (minus 'The Princess Royal' nameplates). The loco had been withdrawn 20 months earlier, but was finally scrapped in October 1964.

12B	44689	46200 P
46118	46226	47614
45545	45736	44009
44452	45512	45230
45531	45526 P	46241 P
46228	46238 P	46225
45665	42783	44671 B
47415	90348	43027
43625	46434	45012
45093	44461	47667
47345	D291	D5185
45583	D308	47326
44673 B	D267	D374
46488	D313	D291
44911 B	45640	D299
46426	45532	D297
44484	46110	D343
44802 B	44027	D233
44761 B	46458	CARLISLE to EDINBURGH
45371 B	45106 B	D24
1ST 32M		5D

Birmingham New Street

Despite its dingy surroundings, New Street attracted its fair share of trainspotters – BR Standard 'Britannia' Class 4-6-2 No. 70021 'Morning Star' attracts a group of admirers at New Street some time in the early 1960s. Built at Crewe in 1951, 'Morning Star' was withdrawn from Carlisle Kingmoor shed (12A) at the end of 1967.

ONE OF THE BUSIEST STATIONS IN THE UK, THE ORIGINAL SUBTERRANEAN NEW STREET STATION WAS BUILT JOINTLY BY THE LONDON & NORTH WESTERN RAILWAY AND THE MIDLAND RAILWAY AND OPENED IN 1854.

Immaculately restored, preserved ex-Midland Railway Compound 4-4-0 No. 1000 attracts many young admirers at New Street before departing with an SLS enthusiasts special to York and Doncaster on August 30, 1959.

Congestion soon led to the building of a separate adjacent station by the Midland Railway and this, along with major track improvements, was completed by 1885. Following severe damage to the station during World War II, the overall roof was removed in the early 1950s. However, despite New Street being one of the most depressing and grimy stations on the BR network, it still attracted its fair share of trainspotters during the 1950s and early '60s.

The obvious attraction was that the station served through services on two main lines – a loop of the West Coast Main Line and the ex-MR route from Derby to Bristol. Consequently they were treated to a wide range of ex-LMS and BR steam classes burrowing through the tunnels into the gloomy depths of the station on their journeys to the north and south. In addition to the 'Coronations' and 'Britannia'

'Black Five' 4-6-0 No. 45272 (built by Armstrong Whitworth in 1936 and withdrawn from Oxley shed in October 1965) attracts interest at New Street as it departs with a northbound train on August 10, 1963. The lad nearest to the camera appears rather bored – he's probably seen this Saltley (21A) loco hundreds of times before!

Pacifics and 'Jubilee', 'Patriot', 'Royal Scot', 'Black Five' and BR Standard Class 5 4-6-0s, the station was also alive with the comings and goings of the more humble 2P 4-4-0s on local trains to the south and on station pilot duty.

The early 1960s witnessed the arrival of the new English Electric Type 4 (Class 40) diesels on WCML duties and 'Peaks' (Class 45 and 46), newly-outshopped from Derby and Crewe, on the former Midland route. By 1964, with electrification of the WCML in progress, change was in the air for New Street. The old station was demolished and the current modern structure was opened in 1967. All services on the WCML were now in the hands of electric locos but, until the introduction of HST services, diesel locos continued to reign for some years on the Midland route.

A group of drivers and firemen await their next turn of duty as ex-LMS 'Jubilee' Class 4-6-0 No. 45579 'Punjab' blows-off before departing from the cramped confines of New Street with a Pembroke Dock to Derby train on August 10, 1963. 'Punjab' was built by the North British Locomotive Co. in 1934 and withdrawn from Derby (16C) in August 1964.

All main line services between Paddington and Shrewsbury via Birmingham Snow Hill were diverted in 1967 through New Street. Diesel hydraulic No 1037 'Western Empress' departs with the 12.25pm train to Paddington on October 12, 1974. The loco was built at Crewe in 1962 and withdrawn in May 1976.

Saltley

Located a 10-minute walk south from Saltley station, Saltley shed was partially visible to the east of the ex-Midland Railway main line from Birmingham New Street to Derby. This large shed consisted of three adjoining roundhouse sheds, the earliest of which was opened by the MR in 1868. It was the most important Midland shed in Birmingham and supplied motive power for both freight and passenger duties on services south to Gloucester and Bristol and north to Derby and beyond. By the end of 1961, while being allocated 23 0-6-0 diesel shunters, the shed still had 140 steam locomotives on its books despite increasing dieselisation of passenger services on the main line between Derby and Bristol. By this time Saltley's allocation was a motley mix of 12 different classes of loco, ranging from 12 of the ancient ex-MR Johnson 3F 0-6-0s (soon to be scrapped), 35 4F 0-6-0s, 42 'Black Five', two rebuilt 'Patriot' and three 'Jubilee' 4-6-0s to nine Stanier 8F 2-8-0s and 13 BR 9F 2-10-0s. Saltley was recoded 2E in 1963 and finally closed to steam in March 1967.

BR Standard Class 5 4-6-0 No. 73069 receives attention from the welder at Saltley on November 22, 1964. In the background, complete with yellow diagonal cabside warning sign, is withdrawn 'Jubilee' class 4-6-0 No. 45674 'Duncan' (minus nameplates) awaiting its fate at Draper's scrapyard in Hull.

Giants at rest inside Saltley roundhouse on January 31, 1965 – from left to right: 'Black Five' 4-6-0 No. 45369 (built by Armstrong Whitworth in 1937, withdrawn from Chester (6A) in March 1967); BR Standard '9F' 2-10-0 No. 92125 (built at Crewe in 1957 and withdrawn from Carlisle Kingmoor (12A) at the end of 1967); ex-GWR 'Grange' Class 4-6-0 No. 6817 'Gwenddwr Grange' visiting from Worcester (built at Swindon in 1936 and withdrawn from Worcester (85A) in April 1965).

Stanier 'Black Five' 4-6-0 No. 44691 and BR Standard '9F' 2-10-0 No. 92138 in Saltley's roundhouse in November 1964. The 'Black Five' was built at Horwich in 1950 and withdrawn from Workington shed (12D) in April 1967; the '9F' was built at Crewe in 1957 and was withdrawn from Speke Junction shed (8C) in July 1967.

Saltley was renowned for its large allocation of ancient ex-MR Johnson '3F' 0-6-0 freight locos. Over 900 of these locos were built for the Midland Railway between 1882 and 1908 and many lasted through to Nationalisation. Seven were also built in 1896 for the Somerset & Dorset Joint Railway. The final withdrawals took place in 1964 but none of this class has been preserved. A typical line-up is seen here at Saltley in 1955 – the foremost loco, No. 43374, was built in 1892 and was withdrawn in 1961.

Despite closure to steam in 1967, Saltley continued to operate as a diesel depot. Here, Class 31 No. 31125 of Stratford shed was seen visiting Saltley on November 8, 1980. Built by Brush, these first-generation diesels were introduced between 1957 and 1962 and some have survived Privatisation into the 21st Century. 33 have been preserved.

"What's the Answer to this one Mate?"

24 PAGES CONTAINING
80 Questions and Answers
DIRECTLY AFFECTING ALL FOOTPLATE STAFF
TAKEN FROM THE
1950 BRITISH RAILWAYS RULE BOOK
ON

Protection, Wrong Line Orders, Detonator Explosions and their different meanings, Single Line Working over Double Lines, Block Failures, etc.

By INS. T. A. WOOD,
Motive Power Dept.
Saltley.

April, 1950.

PRICE 9d.

...will at once proceed
...(a).

...signal box if there i...
...ere telephone commu...
...enable earlier intima...
...alman of the obstruct...
...e 181 (g).

...been carried out and...
..., what must the man...
...rmation do?

...of the Signalman or St...
...Rule 181 (a).

...en stopped in the secti...
...ain. What is the duty...

...while the Guard will ta...
...ty of the passengers. Ru...

18.
...t is a freight train that b...

19.
...with the burning vehicles...

...of those on fire must be d...
...s drawn forward at least 3...
...d left properly secured, th...
...effort m... ...made to extinguish the fire. Ru...

8

Interior view of Derby Works Erecting Shop in the early 1950s showing a line up headed by two ex Midland Railway stalwarts in the form of Class 3F 'Jinty' 0-6-0T No. 47249 and Class 4F 0-6-0 No. 43887, both undergoing a general overhaul.

Derby Works

REACHED VIA A FOOTBRIDGE FROM DERBY MIDLAND STATION, THE RAILWAY WORKS AT DERBY WAS A POPULAR DESTINATION FOR TRAINSPOTTERS IN THE 1950S AND EARLY '60S.

Derby had become the headquarters of the Midland Railway on that company's formation in 1844 and all of its locomotive building was concentrated here. Under its Chief Mechanical Engineers Matthew Kirtley (1844-1873), Samuel Johnson (1873-1903), Richard Deeley (1903-1907) and Henry Fowler (1907-1922) Derby produced vast numbers of highly successful locomotive types ranging from the graceful 4-2-2 'Midland Spinners', the handsome 4-4-0 'Midland Compounds' and hundreds of rugged 0-6-0 freight locos – many of the latter class managed to continue in service until the early 1960s.

The Midland Railway had always had a small engine policy so that double-heading on heavily loaded trains was usually the order of the day. The only exceptions to this were the eleven 7F 2-8-0 freight locos built for the Somerset & Dorset Railway between 1914 and 1925 and the solitary 0-10-0, nicknamed 'Big Bertha', designed by James Clayton and built in 1919 for banking duties on the Lickey Incline. Despite this nothing much changed at Derby after the 1923 Big Four Grouping - 98 2P 4-4-0s and 70 2-6-2 tanks were turned out between 1928 and 1932 - until the final 20 of Fowler's 'Royal Scot' Class 4-6-0 which were built here in 1930.

General Information

Area of Works	47 acres
Area occupied by workshops and offices	13 acres
Total staff employed	up to 4,000
Number of apprentices (included in the above figure)	449
Total number of machines	1,600
Total number of locomotives maintained:—	
Steam	1,743
Diesel	391
Number of classified locomotive repairs effected during 1959:—	
Steam	507
Diesel	54
Number of diesel railcar engines re-conditioned during 1959	535
Number of locomotives built during 1959:—	
Diesel electric main line locomotives	
Type 2 1,160 h.p.	29
Type 4 2,300 h.p.	9
Diesel electric shunting locomotives	
0-6-0 400 h.p.	40

Fuel and Power used in the Works per annum

Total solid fuel used	22,000 tons
Fuel used for steam production	19,500 tons
Steam	209,000,000 lbs.
Gas	86,000,000 cu. ft.
Electricity	9,000,000 units
Heavy fuel oil	178,000 gals.
Petrol	8,250 gals.
Diesel fuel oil	154,000 gals.

Derby Locomotive Works

inside information

BRITISH RAILWAYS

LONDON MIDLAND REGION

Visitors to Derby Works in the early 1960s were handed a useful information leaflet. Apparently Derby repaired 507 steam and 54 diesel locos during 1959. The Works also built 9 'Peak' Class Type 4 diesels and 29 Type 2 diesels during that year.

Everything changed in 1932 when William Stanier was appointed CME. Under his big engine policy the majority of the LMS main line express locomotives were built at Crewe although Derby did build ten of his 'Jubilee' Class 4-6-0s and went on to build other Stanier locos including ten 0-4-4 tanks, 114 2-6-2 tanks, 113 4-cylinder 2-6-4 tanks, 37 3-cylinder 2-6-4 tanks and, during World War II, a large batch of 'Black Five' 4-6-0s.

After the War the Works was kept busy constructing 220 Fairburn 2-6-4 tanks, some of which were built after Nationalisation. In addition to building ten Ivatt push-pull fitted 2-6-2 tanks in 1952, Derby was heavily involved in the building of BR Standard locos including 130 of the highly successful Class 5 4-6-0 between 1951 and 1957, and 15 Class 4 2-6-4 tanks. In June 1957 Class 5 4-6-0 No. 73154 became the 2,941st and last steam loco to be built at Derby.

With an ear-splitting noise, stays are driven into a locomotive's firebox at Derby Works in the early 1950s.

Then allocated to Stafford (5C), Fowler 2-6-4 tank No. 42347 undergoes a major overhaul at its birthplace in the early 1950s. Built in 1929, this loco was withdrawn from Barrow shed (12E) in September 1962.

Derby was also involved in the building of Britain's first main line diesels including the Ivatt-designed LMS Co-Co locos Nos 10000 and 10001 (built 1947-48), the unique experimental Fell loco No. 10100 (built 1952) and a batch of the early (Class 11) diesel shunters. From 1958 to 1962 the Works went on to build a batch of the Class 08 diesel shunters, several batches of BR Sulzer Type 2 (Class 24/25), all ten of the early 'Peak' Class (Class 44 D1-D10), a batch of the later Class 45 Peaks and the full complement of Class 46 Peaks (D138-D193). Last but not least, Derby Carriage & Wagon Works in Litchurch Lane had turned out some of the first diesel multiple units to be made in Britain, including the famous 'Derby Lightweights' of 1953.

While Derby Works has now closed, production of passenger rolling stock including new sets for London Underground continues under private ownership at Litchurch Lane.

Part of the National Collection, restored Johnson-designed Midland Railway 'Spinner' 4-2-2 No. 673 was on display at Litchurch Lane on the Derby Works Centenary Open Day on August 14, 1976. This graceful loco was built at Derby in 1897, rebuilt in 1910 and withdrawn in 1928.

ON SHED

Derby

17 A

Derby in 1953 with ubiquitous '8F' 2-8-0 No. 48138 in the centre and ex-LMS 'Crab' 2-6-0 No. 42872 – a Crewe engine – in the background and carrying a 'Special' reporting number. These highly capable and adaptable Moguls were used extensively on specials, both passenger and freight. 245 members of the class were built and allocated to depots nationwide. They could be seen in many parts of Britain and, as such, represented a great challenge to trainspotters.

The Midland Railway was the first large scale amalgamation of several small railway concerns into one larger company. The earliest engine shed at Derby, centre of the new company's operations from 1844, had been opened by the Midland Counties Railway in 1839 and the final double roundhouse shed was opened in 1890 by the Midland itself.

Located at the south side of Derby Midland station to the east of the main line to St Pancras it was a popular destination for trainspotters who were usually able to take in a tour of both the shed and adjacent works.

Once home to the elegant '4P' Compound and '2P' 4-4-0s, by late 1961, with brand new 'Peaks' emerging from the neighbouring Works and the dieselisation of the Midland lines, the shed's steam allocation had fallen to 65 with 11 different classes represented. The seven 'Jubilee' and six BR standard Class 5 4-6-0s had pride of place but there were still some home grown vintage characters around, including four ex-MR Johnson 3F 0-6-0s (dating from 1885) and three ex-MR Johnson 3F 0-6-0 tanks (built in 1899).

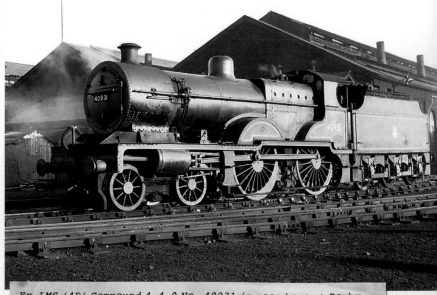

Ex-LMS '4P' Compound 4-4-0 No. 40931 is seen here at Derby, presumably ex works, in 1953. Far away from its natural haunts, being allocated to Llandudno Junction (6G), the loco used to work stopping passenger trains along the North Wales Main Line. Built at the Vulcan Foundry in 1927 this loco was withdrawn in October 1958.

A foreign visitor to Derby in September 1956 was ex-GER 'D16' Class 4-4-0 No. 62564 which had just completed a turn from Lincoln via Nottingham. Built at Stratford Works in 1908 this elegant Edwardian machine was withdrawn from Lincoln (40A) in March 1958. Behind it Fowler 2-6-4 tank No. 42358 has just emerged from the neighbouring works in a fresh coat of paint.

On the diesel side the invasion had well and truly begun and by late 1961 Derby shed had an allocation of no less that 50 'Peaks' (class 45/46) which had recently arrived shining and new from the adjacent Works.

At the same time Derby had been allocated the entire class (D5700-D5719) of the unreliable Co-Bo 'Metrovick' (Class 28) diesels which had been introduced in 1958 and had been returned to their manufacturers, Metropolitan-Vickers, for urgent remedial work. Originally used on the 'Condor' express freight service, for their sins, they all finally ended up in Barrow-in-Furness (12E) and were withdrawn by 1969.

From 1963 until closure to steam in Spring 1967, when it was replaced by a diesel maintenance depot, Derby shed carried the code of 16C. Derby's only sub-shed was at the former Great Northern Railway terminus station of Friargate. This was closed in 1955.

'Peak' Class diesel (Class 45) D82, at Derby during a visit in the early '60s, was withdrawn as TOPS No. 45141 in August 1988.

Toton (Stapleford and Sandiacre)

Located midway between Derby and Nottingham, Toton motive power depot was the principal freight engine shed in the heart of the Derby/Nottingham coalfield and supplied motive power for shunting and freight trains at the adjacent marshalling yard.

By the early 1950s Toton Marshalling Yard was one of the busiest and largest mechanised marshalling yards in Europe and was capable of handling over 3,000 wagonloads each day. Although not a glamorous destination for the trainspotter, Toton – especially on a Sunday - could yield vast numbers of freight locos to cross off in the ABC book.

It was located on the west side of the former Midland main line between Long Eaton and Stapleford & Sandiacre stations, being about a 15-minute walk from the latter. There had been a shed at Toton since the Midland Railway opened one here in the mid-19th century but with later alterations and additions by both the MR and BR the depot had grown to three adjacent roundhouses by 1948. Many of the ex-LMS Beyer Garratt 2-6-0+0-6-2 articulated locos – first introduced in 1927 - were also stationed at Toton to haul heavy coal trains. Numbered by BR 47967-47999, the 33 members of this class were withdrawn over the period between 1955 and 1958.

Apart from the addition of 12 diesel shunters used in the adjoining marshalling yard, Toton was still an all-steam shed even in November 1961 with an allocation of 86 locos. This not only included 52 Stanier 8F 2-8-0s, 13 BR Standard 9F 2-10-0s and 16 4F 0-6-0s but also an ancient Johnson 3F 0-6-0 tank and two Johnson 2F 0-6-0s. The latter were soon to go to the great scrapyard in the sky, but Toton clung on until the end of 1965 when it closed to steam. It retained its importance with a 16-road diesel depot and was later a major centre for spotting many diesel classes including 20, 31, 37, 44, 45. 46, 47, 56, 58 and, more recently, 60 and 66.

Toton is still used today for the heavy maintenance of EWS diesel locos.

Seen here at Toton in September 1958, ex-LMS Class '3F' 'Jinty' 0-6-0 tank No. 47551 was built by Hunslet Engineering in 1928 and spent many years shunting at Toton. It was withdrawn in February 1963. On the right is ex-London, Tilbury & Southend Railway 4-4-2 tank No. 41947 which was built at Derby in 1927 and was usually seen at work on the Fenchurch Street to Tilbury and Southend lines. No. 41947 eventually found its way to Toton and, as the last member of its class, was withdrawn at the end of 1960. No. 41966 is preserved as LTSR No. 80 'Thundersley'.

Toton, seen here in 1962, provided motive power for heavy freight trains in the area. Chief among these were the Beyer Garratt 2-6-0+0-6-2 articulated locos (withdrawn by 1958) and large numbers of Stanier 8F 2-8-0s. This latter class was slowly replaced during the 1960s by main line diesel power such as the Class 44 'Peaks'.

After closure to steam, Toton continued to be a magnet for trainspotters with its wide variety of diesel types. Here a pair of Class 20 locos, 20077 and 20071, pass Toton Sidings on June 7, 1975 with a southbound train of cement 'Presflos'.

Manchester

APART FROM LONDON, MANCHESTER AND ITS SUBURBS IN THE LATE 1950S AND EARLY '60S PROBABLY BOASTED MORE ATTRACTIONS FOR TRAINSPOTTERS THAN ANYWHERE ELSE IN THE UK. IT NOT ONLY HAD FOUR MAJOR RAILWAY STATIONS BUT SEVEN ENGINE SHEDS AND TWO RAILWAY WORKS.

Pure nostalgia - this wonderfully detailed photo taken at London Road station in 1960 surely sums up the joy of trainspotting. With electrification gathering pace in the background and watched by an excited group of spotters, red-liveried 'Coronation' Class 4-6-2 No. 46243 'City of Lancaster' (built Crewe 1940, withdrawn from Edge Hill (8A) in September 1964) enters the station with an express from Euston. Beyond the LNWR signals and water tower, English Electric Type 4 (Class 40) D220 (built 1959, named 'Franconia' in 1963 and withdrawn in 1982) waits to depart with an up express.

Manchester London Road (now Piccadilly)

The station, opened in 1842 by the Manchester & Birmingham Railway, was considerably enlarged by the L&NWR and also used as the terminus of the Great Central Railway line from Sheffield. The latter route via Woodhead Tunnel and Penistone was electrified at 1,500V DC in 1954 and, until closure in 1970, brought EM1 (Class 76) and EM2 (Class 77) electric locos (based at 9C Reddish) into one side of London Road station. The rest of the station served main line services to the south via the West Coast Main Line to London Euston, including named trains such as 'The Lancastrian', 'The Comet' and 'The Mancunian'. Prior to electrification of this route in the early 1960s motive power for these trains was supplied by Longsight (9A) shed's allocation of 'Jubilee' and 'Royal Scot' 4-6-0s and 'Britannia' Pacifics. A short diesel interregnum saw the early named English Electric Type 4s (Class 40) only to be followed shortly by Class 83 25kv electric locos. To coincide with the electrification of the WCML, London Road station was rebuilt and renamed Piccadilly in 1960.

'Black Five' 4-6-0 No. 44735 of Newton Heath shed (9D) exits Victoria station with a parcels train in early 1968. Less than 20 years old, this loco was built at Crewe in 1949 and withdrawn from Carnforth shed (10A) in August 1968.

Manchester Victoria and Exchange

Originally opened in 1844 by the Manchester & Leeds Railway, Victoria station was considerably enlarged by the Lancashire & Yorkshire Railway in 1909. A through platform at the adjacent Exchange station (opened by the L&NWR in 1884, closed 1969) was linked to one of Victoria's platforms making it the longest in Europe. Destinations from Victoria ranged across the wide spectrum of former L&Y routes from Liverpool and Southport in the west to Huddersfield, Leeds, York, Goole and Hull in the east. Motive power for many of these trains came from Newton Heath shed (26A) which, in the 1950s and early '60s would have supplied 'Black Fives', 'Jubilees' or the occasional 'Patriot'. In the summer of 1968, it was still common to see 'Black Fives' or the occasional BR Standard Class 5 at work in the station on pilot duties, empty coaching stock or parcels trains – making Victoria one of the last city centre stations in the UK to see steam operations.

The end is nigh – Manchester Victoria station early in 1968 with only months to go before the end of steam on BR. From left to right 'Black Five' 4-6-0s Nos 45269 (built by Armstrong Whitworth in 1936, withdrawn from Lostock Hall shed (10D) August 1968) and 45268 (built by AW in 1936, withdrawn from Carnforth shed (10A) August 1968) blow off as they await their next turn of duty.

Bereft of nameplate and with yellow cabside diagonal warning sign, ex-LMS 'Jubilee' Class 4-6-0 No. 45705 'Seahorse', allocated to Newton Heath (9D), waits to depart from a litter-strewn Manchester Central station with the 17.22 train to Buxton on June 29, 1965. Built at Crewe in 1936, 'Seahorse' was withdrawn from Newton Heath shed in November 1965.

Manchester Central

Opened by the Cheshire Lines Committee in 1880, Central station was crowned with an enormous wrought-iron single span arched roof which can still be seen, in a different guise, today. It was used by the Midland Railway, and later the LMS, as its Manchester terminus for services to London St Pancras via Derby. Until 1964 the main express of the day was 'The Palatine' which ran to St Pancras via Millers Dale, Matlock, Derby and Leicester and until the introduction of the 'Peak' diesels was usually hauled by a 'Royal Scot', 'Jubilee' or 'Britannia'. A diesel Blue Pullman service from Central to St Pancras was introduced in July 1960 but was withdrawn in March 1967 following completion of the electrification of the WCML between Manchester and London Euston. Central station was closed in 1969 but has since been converted into a conference centre.

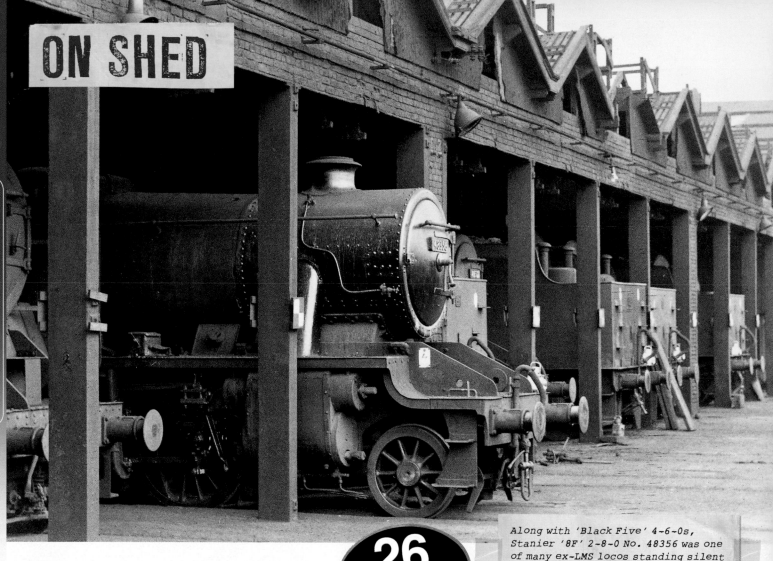

ON SHED

Newton Heath

26A

Opened by the Lancashire & Yorkshire Railway in 1876, Newton Heath was a large 24-road engine shed that serviced steam locos for freight duties on former L&Y routes and passenger services operating out of Manchester's Victoria station until the last few months of steam on BR.

Altered by the LMS in the 1930s, Newton Heath was reduced in size in the late 1950s to make way for a new diesel depot. Located in the fork of the Miles Platting to Dean Lane, and Miles Platting to Newton Heath lines, the shed was quickly accessed on foot from either Newton Heath or Dean Lane stations.

Despite the reduction in its size and the onset of dieselisation the shed still had an allocation of 119 steam locos in November 1961. This comprised 15 different classes and included 30 'Black Five' (including two of the four named engines of this class, 45154 and 45156), one unrebuilt 'Patriot', one rebuilt 'Patriot', 11 'Jubilee' and four 'Royal Scot' 4-6-0s, 12 2-6-4 tanks, 11 'Crab' 2-6-0s, 20 ex-WD 2-8-0s and six BR 9F 2-10-0s.

The shed's code was changed to 9D in 1963 and it was closed to steam in 1968.

By 1968 Newton Heath was one of the last steam sheds still operating on BR. This photo taken from the footplate of 'Black Five' 4-6-0 No. 45096 on June 8, shows the shed yard in terminal decline. Built at Vulcan Foundry in 1935 the 'Black Five' only had two months more active service until being withdrawn from Rose Grove shed (10F) in August.

The famous ex L&YR Newton Heath Locomotive Shed on the Oldham Road, from where Manchester United football club began, was a true place of legend. Steam traction survived there almost until the end as witnessed in this scene featuring a Stanier '8F' 2-8-0 and two 'Black Five' 4-6-0 (Nos 45134 and 45312) in a grimy rundown condition in 1967.

On the same day, No. 45025 was seen in action at Newton Heath moving a 'dead' 'Black Five' around the yard. It is now one of 18 such locos preserved and is currently awaiting overhaul at Aviemore on the Strathspey Railway.

Allocated to Carnforth (10A), 'Black Five' 4-6-0 No. 45025 was seen on Newton Heath's turntable in 1968. Built at Vulcan Foundry in 1934, this loco was withdrawn from Carnforth in August of that year.

151

One of the last three BR steam sheds to close in August 1968 was Lostock Hall (10D). Here, one of its locos, 'Black Five' 4-6-0 No. 45353, is seen on shed during the night of February 10, 1968. It was built by Armstrong Whitworth in May 1937 and was withdrawn in July 1968.

Final Days

BY THE DAWN OF 1968, THE LMR HAD BECOME THE LAST REGION ON BR TO OPERATE MAIN LINE STEAM LOCOS.

Centred around Manchester and Liverpool, the last months of steam drew thousands of enthusiasts from all over the UK eager to witness the end of an era in the history of rail transport.

Starting with Kingmoor (12A), Workington (12D) and Tebay (12H), between January 1 and May 6 all but three LMR steam sheds had been closed. These last three, Carnforth (10A), Rose Grove (24B) and Lostock Hall were closed at midnight on August 4. Prior to this date many 'final' steam specials were run across the northwest of England. However, with a total ban on steam coming into operation the following day, the famous '15 Guinea Special' of August 11 was the absolutely final steam train to be operated by BR.

The route taken was from Liverpool Lime Street, Manchester Victoria and over the Settle & Carlisle to Carlisle and return and was hauled at various stages by 'Black Five' 4-6-0s Nos. 44781, 44871 and 45110 and 'Britannia' Class Pacific No. 70013 'Oliver Cromwell'. Despite the ban on steam the latter engine had the last laugh on BR as it was driven under its own steam during August 12/13 to its former home at Norwich and then on to Diss, from where it was carried on road by low-loader to its destination, Bressingham Steam Museum.

Fortunately, three of the locos involved in this historic occasion have since been preserved.

Thought to be Mr C W Thorp, the driver and his fireman of 'Black Five' 4-6-0 No. 45156 'Ayrshire Yeomanry' ponder their future on BR less than two months before the end of steam. Seen here as Manchester Victoria station pilot on June 15, 1968 this loco was built by Armstrong Whitworth in 1935 and withdrawn from Rose Grove shed (10F) in August.

Steam stalwarts to the very end, the 'Black Fives' must have been one of the most photographed locos on BR. Here, No. 45420 has its photo taken while acting as Manchester Victoria's station pilot on March 30, 1968. Built by Armstrong Whitworth in 1937 this loco was withdrawn from Newton Heath shed (9D) at the end of June.

The last working 'Britannia' 4-6-2 No. 70013 'Oliver Cromwell' was in great demand to haul specials during the summer of 1968. Admired by two young enthusiasts and complete with its original home shed plate of 32A but with a painted name, it is seen passing westbound through Manchester Victoria station on June 10.

The final standard gauge steam train on BR was run on August 11, 1968. 'The Special' is seen here at Carlisle headed by No. 70013 'Oliver Cromwell' after hauling train 1T57 from Manchester Victoria via the Settle & Carlisle line. For the whole of the nostalgic round trip to Liverpool, hauled at various stages by four different steam locomotives, the route was lined with tens of thousands of photographers and enthusiasts intent on paying their last respects.

Liverpool

THE FIRST LIVERPOOL TERMINUS OF THE LIVERPOOL & MANCHESTER RAILWAY WAS LOCATED AT EDGE HILL IN 1830. THE LINE WAS LATER EXTENDED THROUGH A TUNNEL AND DOWN AN INCLINE TO A NEW STATION AT LIME STREET WHICH OPENED IN 1836. A ROOF WAS BUILT OVER THE STATION IN 1849 AND WAS FURTHER EXTENDED IN THE 1880S.

The very last day – to mark the end of steam haulage on British Railways a fair number of special trains were run in 1968. However, the very last train was the famous '15 Guinea Special' of August 11. The route taken was from Liverpool Lime Street, Manchester Victoria and over the Settle & Carlisle to Carlisle and return and was hauled at various stages by 'Black Five' 4-6-0s Nos. 44781, 44871 and 45110 and 'Britannia' Class Pacific No. 70013 'Oliver Cromwell'. Here, watched by a throng of enthusiasts and a couple of British Transport policemen, the train is seen waiting to depart from Lime Street at 9.10am on the first leg of its journey to Manchester Victoria behind 'Black Five' 4-6-0 No. 45110. This famous loco was built at the Vulcan foundry in 1935 and was withdrawn from Lostock Hall shed (10D) after hauling the special but has since been preserved.

Before the onset of diesels (in the shape of English Electric Type 4s) on long-distance trains and the creeping WCML electrification (to Crewe in 1959 and to Euston in 1966), Lime Street offered a good choice of glamorous steam locos for the spotter. The station had its fair share of named trains to London including 'The Red Rose', 'The Merseyside Express', 'The Shamrock' and 'The Manxman'. Many of the locos for these trains came from Liverpool's main steam shed at Edge Hill (8A) and on a good day would include examples of 'Patriot', 'Jubilee' and 'Royal Scot 4-6-0s and 'Princess Royal' and 'Coronation' Pacifics. However, with the influx of 14 of the English Electric Type 4s, by November 1961 Edge Hill's steam allocation was down to 95 locos of which 34 were 'Black Five', seven unrebuilt 'Patriot', two rebuilt 'Patriot' and five 'Royal Scot' 4-6-0s along with one 'Princess' and four

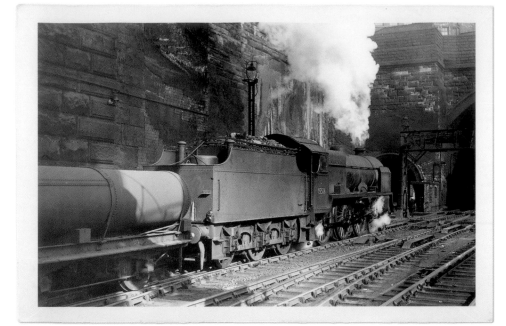

Unrebuilt 'Patriot' Class 4-6-0 No. 45516 'The Bedfordshire and Hertfordshire Regiment' fills in time with odd jobs while acting as standby engine at Lime Street on March 31, 1956. Carrying the largest nameplate of its class, No. 45516 was built at Crewe in 1932 and withdrawn from Warrington Dallam (8B) in August 1961.

Modern traction at Lime Street – BR-built E3092 waits to depart with the up 'Manxman' to Euston in June 1964. The last part of the train's journey south would have been diesel-hauled as electrification through to Euston hadn't been completed by this date. E3092 was one of 40 'AL5' Bo-Bo main line electric locos built at Doncaster between 1961 and 1964. Later classified Class 85, this loco was withdrawn as No. 85037 in 1990.

'Coronation' Pacifics. Interestingly, Edge Hill was also home to one of the Fowler 2F 0-6-0 dock tanks and 16 of the ex-L&NWR 0-8-0 heavy freight locos. The shed finally closed to steam in May 1968 and the diesel depot closed in 1986.

The other major stations in Liverpool were Central and Exchange. Central was opened in 1874 by the Cheshire Lines Committee and provided services to Manchester Central, London St Pancras, Hull and Harwich. In 1966 most of its services were diverted to Lime Street and it was finally closed in 1972. Liverpool Central Low Level station was opened by the Mersey Railway in 1892 and the site is now used by Merseyrail Northern Line trains.

Exchange station became the Liverpool terminus of the Lancashire & Yorkshire Railway in 1886 and provided services to Manchester Victoria, Blackpool, Cumbria and Glasgow. It became the last city termini in the UK to see regular steam-hauled trains until the very end of steam on BR in August 1968. It closed in 1977.

Looking extremely handsome and carrying the original British Railways motif on its tender, Edge Hill (8A) rebuilt 'Patriot' Class 4-6-0 No. 45527 'Southport' receives last minute attention before departing from Lime Street with an express for Newcastle in the early 1950s. 'Southport' was built at Derby in 1933, rebuilt in 1948 and withdrawn from Carlisle Kingmoor (12A) shed in December 1964.

155

Crewe

ONE OF BRITAIN'S MAJOR RAILWAY JUNCTIONS, CREWE STATION WAS OPENED IN 1837 BY THE GRAND JUNCTION RAILWAY. ITS IMPORTANCE STEADILY GREW, ESPECIALLY WHEN THE GRAND JUNCTION MOVED ITS LOCOMOTIVE WORKS FROM EDGE HILL TO CREWE IN 1843.

Catching a few admiring glances, Edge Hill (8A) 'Princess Royal' Class 4-6-2 No. 46204 'Princess Louise' waits to depart from Crewe on November 25, 1960. Built at Crewe in 1935, this loco was one of the first four of its class to be withdrawn in October 1961.

Two years later the London & North Western Railway was formed by the merger of the Grand Junction with the London & Birmingham Railway and Liverpool & Manchester Railway and Crewe Works grew from strength to strength. So did Crewe station and by the 1890s it had reached the limits of its capacity necessitating the building of a deviation line for through freight traffic.

With its major railway works and two large engine sheds Crewe retained its importance under the LMS and, later, in BR days. These attractions together with a multitude of services not only on the West Coast Main Line, but also to Manchester, Liverpool, Chester and North Wales, Shrewsbury and the Potteries brought trainspotters to bustling Crewe station in their droves. Even with the onset of WCML electrification in 1959, steam locos still could be seen in large numbers for a few more years.

Ex-LMS prototype main line diesel No. 10000 and 'Coronation' Class 4-6-2 No. 46251 'City of Nottingham' meet under the wires at Crewe c.1960. Built at Derby in 1947 No. 10000 was withdrawn from Willesden shed (1A) in 1962. Built at Crewe without streamlined casing in 1944, No. 46251 had a slightly longer life and was withdrawn from Crewe North shed (5A) in October 1964.

Despite the creeping electrification of the WCML, Crewe still managed to retain its magic for trainspotters in the early 60s. Oblivious to the new electric loco on the next platform, this trainspotter gives his undivided attention to 'Royal Scot' Class 4-6-0 No. 46154 'The Hussar'. Built at Derby in 1930 and rebuilt in 1948, this loco was withdrawn from Willesden (1A) in November 1962.

By 1960, the diesel invasion had started and many of the WCML expresses were soon in the hands of English Electric Type 4 (Class 40) diesels, displacing the Stanier 'Princess Royal' and 'Coronation' Pacifics. In their twilight years these magnificent machines, along with the remaining 'Royal Scots' and 'Jubilees', were adorned with diagonal yellow stripes on the side of their cabs denoting that they weren't allowed to work 'under the wires' south of Crewe. Crewe North (5A) had closed by 1965 and the end came for steam in November 1967 when Crewe South (5B) was closed. Electrification proceeded apace until 1974 when the entire route from Euston to Glasgow was completed.

Pre-electrification days at Crewe - the usual gaggle of trainspotters at the north end of the station watch rebuilt 'Patriot' Class 4-6-0 No. 45522 'Prestatyn' arrive with a Llandudno to Euston train on July 20, 1957. Built at Derby in 1933 and rebuilt in 1949, 'Prestatyn' was withdrawn from Longsight shed (9A) in September 1964.

Under the wires - 'Royal Scot' Class 4-6-0 No. 46121 'Highland Light Infantry, City of Glasgow Regiment' of Polmadie shed (66A) at the head of a train from Glasgow on November 25, 1960. Bearing one of the two longest names of any 'Royal Scot' (the other was No. 46137 'The Prince of Wales's Volunteers (South Lancashire)') No. 46121 was built by the North British Locomotive Co in 1927, rebuilt in 1946 and withdrawn from Polmadie shed at the end of 1962.

Crewe Works

The scene outside Crewe Works erecting shop on August 30, 1961 with two 'Black Fives' in undercoat and two Stanier 8Fs, Nos 48642 and 48735, and 'Britannia' Class 4-6-2 No. 70032 'Tennyson' awaiting their tenders.

TOGETHER WITH ITS IMPORTANT JUNCTION STATION AND TWO MAJOR STEAM SHEDS, CREWE WORKS HAD TO BE ONE OF THE 'MUST VISIT' RAIL CENTRES FOR TRAINSPOTTERS IN THE 1950s AND EARLY '60s.

THE HOME COUNTIES RAILWAY SOCIETY
(FORMERLY HOME COUNTIES RAILWAY CLUB)
are pleased to announce their next special train to
CREWE WORKS & SHEDS
on
Sunday, 10th February, 1963
FARES: 37/6 (adult)   20/- (under 16)
Depart Marylebone, 9.00 a.m. (approx)   Return Marylebone, 9.00 p.m. (approx)
Outward Journey:- via High Wycombe, Wolverhampton & Wellington.
Return Journey:- via Burton, Leicester & G.C. Main line to Marylebone.
Motive Power:- An Un-Rebuilt "WEST COUNTRY" Class.
_facilities are available.

All non-members ar_   _companied by an adult. Full_

Mr. R. WALKD
Cheques and postal ord_

B.R. 9790/1

BRITISH TRANSPORT COMMISSION
British Railways
Locomotive Works
CREWE

Nº 47369

OFFICIAL PERMIT (Juvenile 6d.)

Admit one JUVENILE into the Works on

30 APR 1962

AT 2.00 P.M., EATON STREET ENTRANCE.

(Proceeds for the Crewe Railway Charity Fund)

Built by the Grand Junction Railway on a green field site in 1843, Crewe Works grew to be the largest railway works in the UK. Within three years the merger of the GJR with the London & Birmingham and the Manchester & Birmingham Railways created the London & North Western Railway.

The LNWR eventually concentrated all of its loco building at Crewe and under its Chief Mechanical Engineers (John Ramsbottom 1857-1871; Francis Webb 1871-1903; George Whale 1903-1909; Charles Bowen-Cooke 1909-1920; H. P. M. Beames 1920-1922 and George Hughes 1922) produced over 6,000 new and rebuilt locos by the time of the Big Four Grouping in 1923.

Under the LMS Crewe went on to build 175 of Hughes' 2-6-0 'Crabs' and, from 1932, under its new CME William Stanier, went on to build some of the most successful steam locos in the UK. These included 25 2-6-2 tanks, 40 Moguls, a large batch of the 8F 2-8-0s, 142 Class 5 ('Black Five') 4-6-0s and 131 'Jubilee' 4-6-0s. By far the most famous of Stanier's locos built at Crewe were the 13 'Princess Royal' and 38 'Princess Coronation' Class Pacifics. These were followed by 65 of Ivatt's Class 2 2-6-0s and 120 of his 2-6-2 tanks - construction of both these classes started under the LMS but continued in production under BR until 1953.

Crewe Works built 198 BR Standard Class '9F' 2-10-0s between 1954 and 1958. Here, two examples await being reunited with their tenders after receiving overhaul at Crewe in February 1961. In 1958 No. 92250 became the 7,331st and last steam engine to be built at Crewe.

Heavy overhauls in the last years of steam as 'Britannia' 4-6-2 No. 70022 'Tornado' is seen here in the famous erecting shop at Crewe Works in the early 1960s. Little could it be imagined at that time that this loco's name would be bestowed on a new 'A1' Pacific half a century later. Built at Crewe in 1951, No. 70022 spent the 1950s on the WR before moving to the LMR where it was withdrawn from Carlisle Kingmoor shed (12A) at the end of 1967.

Despite the end of steam on BR in 1968 Crewe Works continued to overhaul diesel locos for many more years. Seen undergoing overhaul inside the erecting shop on Open Day on September 18, 1971 were Class 50s Nos. 416 and 442 and Class 47 No. 1864.

Under BR Crewe Works went from strength to strength and went on to produce 55 Class 7 'Britannia' Pacifics between 1951 and 1954, ten Class 6 'Clan' Pacifics in 1952 and the unique Class 8 No. 71000 'Duke of Gloucester' Pacific in 1954. The final batch of steam locomotives built at Crewe were 198 of the Standard Class 9F 2-10-0s built between 1954 and 1958.

The Works went on to build large numbers of diesel locos: a batch of the numerous Class 08 diesel shunters, a batch of the BR Sulzer Type 2 (Class 24 and 25), the two power-cars of the prototype HST, 197 HST (Class 43) power-cars, a batch of the 'Peak' (Class 45), 202 Brush Type 4 (Class 47), 39 'Western' (Class 52) diesel-hydraulics for the Western Region and 20 Class 56. Crewe also built 36 Class 87 25kV AC electric locos for the West Coast Main Line, the prototype Class 89 No. 89001 'Avocet', 50 Class 90 and 31 Class 91 electric locos. By 1990 over 8,000 locos (steam, diesel and electric) had been built at Crewe. Now nothing much remains of what was once an industry that, at its peak, employed over 20,000 people.

By 1962 Crewe was not only repairing steam locos but also building batches of the 'Western' Class diesel hydraulics for the Western Region and BR Sulzer Type 4 (Class 45) for the LMR. On a visit to the Works in August D1036-D1051 and D54-D57 were seen under construction. Rubbing shoulders with these new machines were two Victorian L&YR locos, 0-6-0 saddle tank No. 51412 and 0-6-0 No. 52312, used as Works shunters.

159

ON SHED

B.R. 14300/99

District Manager
C. R. STUART
Telephone
STOKE-ON-TRENT 44121
Ext.
Telex No. 3629
(A.B. RAIL STOKE)
Telegraphic Address
TRAFFIC RAIL STOKE

BRITISH TRANSPORT COMMISSION

District Manager
London Midland Region
British Railways
Stoke-on-Trent

Our Reference PX3/MPD
Your Reference

21st May 1962.

Mr. J. A. Holland,
xxxxxxxxxxxxxxxx,
xxxxxxxxxxx
xxxxxxxxxxxx

Dear Sir,

Thank you for your letter of 19th May.

I regret that as Crewe Motive Power Depots are closed to the public on Saturdays and Mondays I am unable to arrange for your visit on this day.

If you will please state the name of your school party I shall be pleased to make the arrangements for Sunday 29th July.

Yours truly,

for C. R. Stuart.

Well it was worth a try! Apparently Crewe North shed was closed to the public on Saturdays and Mondays. Sunday was always the best day to visit any shed as nearly all of its locos would be present but the only downside to this was that Sunday train services were extremely restricted. The Sabbath was still treated fairly seriously even in the early 1960s.

Crewe North  5A

Up until 1965 Crewe had two very large loco sheds – Crewe North (5A) supplied locos primarily for main line passenger duties and Crewe South (5B) supplied locos mainly for freight and shunting duties. Crewe North, reached by a footbridge from the north of Platform 1 of Crewe station, was located to the west of the main line to the north of the station. An alternative route was a five-minute walk from the station via an alleyway and Station Street.

The shed was fairly modern having been built as a half roundhouse as recently as 1950 and its allocation during the '50s included many top link locos for service on the West Coast Main Line, including Stanier 'Princess' and 'Coronation' Pacifics – all of them built in the 1930s at the nearby Crewe Works.

Despite creeping electrification and the diesel interregnum, the shed's allocation in November 1961 was still fairly impressive with a total of 96 steam locos and 30 diesels. Apart from a few Ivatt Class 2-6-2 and Stanier Class 4 2-6-4 tanks, all of the steam locos were definitely for main line duties and included 45 Stanier 'Black Five', 22 'Jubilee' and nine 'Royal Scot' 4-6-0s, one 'Princess Royal' and seven 'Coronation' Pacifics and the unique No. 71000 'Duke of Gloucester' Pacific. The entire diesel allocation was made up of three of the original named 'Peaks' (Class 44) and 27 English Electric Type 4 (Class 40).

Crewe North was closed in May 1965 but Crewe South lingered on until November 1967.

Crewe North in the 1950s, and amongst the miscellany of motive power gathered beneath the coaling towers is 'Jubilee' Class 4-6-0 No. 45586 'Mysore' (built by NBL in 1934, withdrawn from Crewe South (5B) in January 1965), Fairburn 2-6-4 tank No. 42121 (built at Derby in 1949 and withdrawn from Birkenhead (8H) in July 1966) and Stanier 'Black Five' No. 45300 (built by Armstrong Whitworth in 1937 and withdrawn from Holyhead (6J) at the end of 1965).

In April 1960 Crewe North only possessed one 'Britannia' but by April 1965 there were no less than 28 that had returned back to their birthplace. Many of these had found their way from Norwich via March after dieselisation in East Anglia. However, No. 70018 'Flying Dutchman', seen here at Crewe North, was one of several that had originally been allocated to Cardiff Canton (86C) for working expresses to Paddington. After a move to Carlisle Canal (12C) the 'Brit' ended up at 5A where it was seen on March 24, 1963. It was withdrawn from its final shed, Carlisle Kingmoor (12A), at the end of 1966.

A view from inside Crewe North's semi-roundhouse in the early 1960s. In the foreground is 'Coronation' class 4-6-2 No 46256 'Sir William A. Stanier F.R.S.' and an unidentified 'Black Five'. On the 70ft turntable is 'Coronation' Class 4-6-2 No. 46232 'Duchess of Montrose'. The latter was withdrawn from Polmadie shed (66A) at the end of 1962 but 'Sir William' lasted nearly two more years until withdrawn from Crewe North in October 1964.

161

Often working in multiple with a combined power output of 3,200bhp the ex-LMS Ivatt-designed prototype diesels were a common sight on the WCML in the 1950s and early 60s. Here, the 13-coach down 'Royal Scot' breasts Summit Cutting at Shap on August 1, 1958 headed by Nos 10000 (carrying 'Royal Scot' headboard) and 10001. Built at Derby in 1947 and 1948 respectively, Nos 10000 and 10001 were withdrawn in 1962 and 1966.

DASTARDLY DIESELS AND ELECTRICS!

Pioneers of main line diesels in Britain, the LMS Ivatt-designed Co-Co locos No. 10000 and 10001 were built at Derby Works in 1947 and 1948. With a power output of 1,600hp No. 10000 was introduced in November 1947 and entered revenue earning service under BR on the Midland route early in 1948. The two locos were transferred to the Southern Region in 1953 to run trials with that region's home-grown diesel locos Nos. 10201-10203. The locos then returned to work, often coupled together, on the LMR in 1955. Both 10000 and 10001 were finally allocated to Willesden (1A) with the former being withdrawn in 1962 and the latter in 1966. Another prototype produced at Derby in 1950 was the unusual 2Bo-Bo2 2,000hp Fell diesel loco No. 10100 which entered service on the Midland line between Manchester and St Pancras. It was withdrawn in 1958. The final LMS prototype was No. 10800, which was built by the North British Locomotive Company in 1950 for use on secondary routes. With a power output of only 827hp it remained in BR service until 1959, when it became a research loco for Brush Traction. It was not scrapped until 1976. The prototype English Electric Co-Co 'Deltic' DP1 also saw service on the LMR until it was withdrawn in 1961.

Following the publication of the 1955 Modernisation Plan, the LMR ordered several successful classes of diesel-electric locos. Some of these were home-grown and included the Derby-built 2,300hp Class 44 'Peak' Class 1Co-Co1 locos (D1-D10) introduced between 1959 and 1960 which saw sterling service, firstly on the West Coast Main Line and then the former Midland route from St Pancras before migrating to Toton (18A) where they were employed hauling heavy freight trains. These were soon followed by the more powerful Class 45 'Peaks' (D11-D137) which were built in two batches at Derby

A notebook from a visit to Derby Works in June 1962. It was busy on the last batch of BR Sulzer Type 4 (Class 46) main line diesels.

Seen here at Basford Hall Junction on July 7, 1958, the forerunner of the Class 55 diesels, the 'Deltic' prototype, was a familiar sight on the WCML. Also known as DP1, it was built by English Electric at their Vulcan Foundry in 1955 and was finished in a striking powder-blue livery with cream side stripes and speed whiskers. The twin-Deltic marine engines had a combined power output of 3,300hp. It was withdrawn in 1961 and has since been preserved as part of the National Collection.

Forerunner of the Class 50 diesels, English Electric prototype DP2, built at Vulcan Foundry in 1962, is seen here heading a test train on the WCML near Warrington in March 1963. The loco was withdrawn following a serious accident at Thirsk on the ECML in July 1967.

Gone are the Stanier Pacifics and double-headed Class 50 diesels - Class 86 electric loco 86232 takes the climb to Shap Summit with ease as it heads the 16.45 Euston to Glasgow express on May 11, 1974.

Built by English Electric the Type 1 (Class 20) diesels were introduced in 1957 and were often to be seen working in multiple. Here Nos. D8000 and D8006 head an up goods at South Kenton in June 1960. D8000 has since been preserved as part of the National Collection.

Between 1962 and early 1964, Crewe Works built 44 'Western' Class diesel hydraulic locos (D1030-D1073) for the Western Region. On a visit to the works in August 1962, D1037-D1051 were seen in various stages of construction, while D1036 was receiving last minute attention before delivery. The first of these handsome locos be built at Crewe was D1035, which had rolled out the month previously. The building of D1030-D1034 was switched from Swindon to Crewe, and consequently these five locos were the last to be built.

A total of 327 BR Sulzer Type 2 (Class 25) main line diesels were built between 1961 and 1967. Although all had been withdrawn by 1987, 20 have since been preserved. Two members of this class, Nos. 7601 and 7600, are seen climbing to Peak Forest Summit with a lime train on August 31, 1972.

and Crewe between 1960 and 1962 and the Derby-built Class 46 'Peaks' (D138-D193) between 1961 and 1963. Along with a large batch of the less powerful Class 40 English Electric Type 4 1Co-Co1 diesels these locos had soon usurped steam power on many main line routes on the LMR by the early 1960s. Both designs were successful with the 'Peaks' remaining in service until 1984 and the Class 40s until 1985. Other successful first-generation diesels included the Class 24 Bo-Bo BR Sulzer Type 2 (D5000-D5150) and Class 25 Bo-Bo BR Sulzer Type 2 (D5151-D5299 and D7500-D7677) most of which were built at Derby or Crewe and many of which went on to see service on the LMR between 1958 and 1987.

Other later successful and long-lived main line types employed by the LMR were Class 20 English Electric Type 1 Bo-Bo (D8000 onwards) introduced in 1957, Class 47 Brush Type 4 Co-Co (D1500 onwards) introduced in 1963 and the ever-popular Class 50 English Electric Type 4 (D400-D449) introduced in 1967. The latter were initially employed, often double-headed, on West Coast Main line services between Crewe and Glasgow until electrification of the route in 1974. They were then transferred to the Western Region where they remained in service until 1994.

The only real duffer among the LMR main line diesels was the unreliable Class 28 'Metrovick' Co-Bo (D5700-D5719) which had been introduced in 1958. They were originally used on the 'Condor' express freight service between London (Hendon) and Glasgow but their unreliability led to this service being taken over by Class 24 locos in 1961. The entire class was reallocated to Barrow-in-Furness and was withdrawn by 1969.

With the new M6 motorway in the background, English Electric Type 4 (Class 50) D435 heads an up express near Tebay on February 1, 1970. Developed from prototype DP2, a total of 50 of these locos were introduced between 1967 and 1968. They initially worked on the WCML north of Crewe but upon electrification of that route were transferred to the Western Region. D435 was later named 'Ark Royal' and has since been preserved.

On completion of the WCML electrification in 1974, the entire fleet of Class 50 locos were transferred to the Western Region. Here 50018 (formerly 'Resolution') takes the empty stock of the 13.50 from Paddington out of Birmingham New Street on June 8, 1977. Sister engine 50013 (formerly 'Agincourt') waits in the centre road. Both locos were withdrawn less than a year later.

Shap

ALTHOUGH NOT A FAMOUS JUNCTION OR MAJOR STATION, THE NAME SHAP CONJURES UP EVOCATIVE MEMORIES FOR THOSE OF US LUCKY TO REMEMBER STEAM ON BRITISH RAILWAYS.

By the early 1960s, this windswept hillside on the Westmorland Fells had become a Mecca for railway photographers keen to capture the raw beauty of steam locomotives powering up the gruelling 1 in 75 gradient from Tebay to Shap Summit – 914 ft above sea level.

Shap is located on the West Coast Main Line between Carnforth and Penrith and the first railway to be built along this route was opened by the Lancaster & Carlisle Railway in 1846. Engineered by Joseph Locke and built by Thomas Brassey, the heavily engineered line between Lancaster and Carlisle took 10,000 navvies only 2½ years to complete.

The hardest approach to Shap Summit is from the south, with the final five miles from Tebay having a gradient of 1 in 75. Here, at Scout Green signal box, just north of Tebay, many famous railway photographers took their finest pictures of Stanier's 'Coronation' Pacifics powering their 12-coach expresses northwards. Although these trains, such as the 'Royal Scot' and the 'Caledonian', normally climbed Shap unassisted, others, such as heavy freights, received help in the rear from banking engines stationed at Tebay. From the north the final approach to Shap Summit was a ten-mile gruelling climb on a gradient of 1 in 125.

With the end of steam on BR less than a year away, the summer and autumn of 1967 saw many railway enthusiasts make their final pilgrimage to witness the spectacle of scheduled steam over Shap.

With its 12-coach train of, all but one, 'blood and custard' coaches BR Standard 'Clan' Class 4-6-2 No 72001 'Clan Cameron' struggles up Shap, banked in the rear by Fowler 2-6-4 tank No. 42424 (built Derby 1934, withdrawn from Stockport Edgeley shed (9B) September 1964), with a Blackpool to Glasgow express in June 1957. Introduced in 1951, the 'Clans' were never a complete success and the ten members of the class were split equally between Carlisle Kingmoor (12A) and Polmadie (66A). 'Clan Cameron' was built at Crewe in 1951 and withdrawn from Polmadie shed at the end of 1962. The last surviving member of the class, No. 72008 'Clan MacLeod' was withdrawn in April 1966. None has been preserved.

By 1967 the Tebay 2-6-4 tanks had been replaced by BR Standard Class 4 4-6-0 locos as bankers up Shap. Seen from the cab of banking engine No. 75026 (built at Swindon 1954, withdrawn from Tebay (12E) end 1967), a train of tankers is hauled up Shap Bank by Stanier '8F' 2-8-0 No. 48074 of Heaton Mersey shed (9F) on October 19, 1967.

Raw Stanier power up Shap – then allocated to Carlisle Upperby (12B), ex-LMS 'Coronation' Class 4-6-2 No. 46225 'Duchess of Gloucester' makes a fine sight as she powers up Shap in the early 1960s. The 'Duchess' was built at Crewe with a streamlined casing in 1938, de-streamlined in 1947 and withdrawn from Upperby in October 1964.

Carlisle Kingmoor 'Black Five' 4-6-0 No. 44727 makes a fine sight as it waits for rear end assistance at Tebay before tackling the climb to Shap Summit in October 1967. Built at Crewe in 1949 No. 44727 was withdrawn from 12A at the end of the month.

Assisted in the rear by Tebay banker Fairburn 2-6-4 tank No. 42110, 'Black Five' 4-6-0 No. 44677 heads a down freight near Scout Green early on June 1, 1966. A 20mph speed restriction was in place here due to buckling of the track in recent hot weather. The Fairburn tank was built at Derby in 1949 and withdrawn from Tebay shed (12E) only ten days after this photo was taken. The 'Black Five' was built at Horwich in 1950 and withdrawn from Carlisle Kingmoor (12A) in October 1967.

167

Carlisle

TOGETHER WITH CREWE, CARLISLE WAS, AND STILL IS, ONE OF THE MOST IMPORTANT RAILWAY JUNCTIONS IN BRITAIN. BOTH ARE LOCATED ON THE IMPORTANT WEST COAST MAIN LINE BETWEEN LONDON EUSTON AND GLASGOW.

In comes the new, out goes the old – with only six months to go before the end of steam in the Carlisle area this contrasting line-up at Citadel in July 1967 consists of, from left to right, Brush Type 4 (Class 47) D1874 on a Glasgow to Liverpool train, a sleeping car, English Electric Type 3 (Class 37) D6737 light engine and BR 'Britannia' class 4-6-2 No. 70051 (minus 'Firth of Forth' nameplate and smokebox door numberplate) heading a Glasgow to Morecambe train. The Class 47 was built at Falcon Works in 1965 and withdrawn as No. 47224 in 2007. Built at Vulcan Foundry in 1962, D6737 spent 1999-2000 working in France before being purchased for preservation in 2003. Finally, No. 70051 was built at Crewe in 1954 and withdrawn from Kingmoor shed (12A) in December 1967.

Carlisle's railway history is incredibly complex with a total of seven different routes and companies reaching the city by 1876. In their order of opening to Carlisle they were: Newcastle & Carlisle Railway (1838); Maryport & Carlisle Railway (1845); Lancaster & Carlisle Railway (1846); Caledonian Railway (Glasgow to Carlisle 1848); North British Railway (Edinburgh to Carlisle 1849); Glasgow, Dumfries & Carlisle Railway (1850 via Gretna Junction on CR); Midland Railway (Settle to Carlisle 1876).

It is amazing that only one of the above routes was closed under the Beeching cuts – the former North British Railway route to Edinburgh via Hawick, known as the Waverley Route, closed in 1969 although that company's branch line to Silloth had already been shut in 1964.

The present imposing façade of Carlisle Citadel was designed by Sir William Tite in 1847 but the station was considerably extended by the Midland Railway on the opening of the Settle & Carlisle route in 1876. By BR days the number of engine sheds had gone from nine to three: Kingmoor (12A), Upperby (12B) and Canal (12C).

Naturally, Carlisle was a paradise for trainspotters especially during the summer months when extra trains were run for the annual Glasgow Fair Holiday and by CTAC (Creative Tourist Agents Conference). With a multitude of routes converging on Carlisle it was possible at least until the mid-1960s to spend a rewarding day at the station – although diesels in the shape of 'Peaks' (Classes 44-46) and English Electric Type 4s (Class 40) had arrived on the scene by 1960 – and spotting a vast range of steam loco classes ranging from the Stanier Pacifics, 'Britannias', 'Clans' and 'Royal Scots' on WCML duties, 'Jubilees' and 'Black Fives' on trains from Leeds over the Settle & Carlisle to Glasgow St Enoch and ex-LNER 'A3' Pacifics and 'V2' 2-6-2s on trains to Edinburgh via the Waverley Route. Even at night Carlisle was busy with the comings and goings of Travelling Post Office and Anglo-Scottish sleeper trains.

Built in 1912, ex-NBR Class 'C-15' 4-4-2 tank No. 67458 was seen on station pilot duties at Carlisle in May 1950. The loco's home shed was Carlisle Canal (12C) from where it was withdrawn in 1956.

Carlisle Kingmoor locos with two evening departures from Carlisle in 1964 – on the left Ivatt Class 4 2-6-0 No. 43121 waits to depart for the Langholm branch with the last train of the day while, on the right, BR 'Britannia' Class 4-6-2 No. 70005 (minus 'John Milton' nameplate) heads an express for Glasgow. No. 43121 was built at Horwich Works in 1951 and withdrawn from Kingmoor shed in November 1967. Built at Crewe in 1951, No. 70005 initially worked expresses on the GER main line out of Liverpool Street and was withdrawn from Kingmoor in July 1967.

Another Kingmoor loco, this time 'Royal Scot' class 4-6-0 No. 46140 (minus 'The King's Royal Rifle Corps' nameplate), heads the 9am Perth to Euston train at Carlisle on Easter Monday 19 April 1965. Originally built with a parallel Fowler boiler in 1927, this loco was rebuilt in 1952 and withdrawn from Kingmoor in October 1965.

ON SHED

A busy scene at Kingmoor shed on July 1, 1962 – in view are a vast array of locomotive types including BR Standard Class 5 4-6-0, 'Jinty' '3F' 0-6-0 tank, Fowler '4F' 0-6-0, 'Crab' 2-6-0, 'Black Five' 4-6-0, 'Coronation' 4-6-2 and 'Britannia' 4-6-2. On the right is 'Jubilee' Class 4-6-0 No. 45691 'Orion' which was withdrawn from Blackpool shed (24E) at the end of 1962.

Carlisle Kingmoor 12A

Originally opened by the Caledonian Railway in 1876, Kingmoor went through various rebuilds and improvements under the former owners and, later, by the LMS. Its large allocation of steam locos provided motive power for both freight and passenger services on the WCML and former GSWR/MR routes north and south of Carlisle. Not a difficult shed to visit, Kingmoor was located on the east side of the main line about a 45-minute walk north of Carlisle station.

The shed's large allocation reflected its importance for mixed-traffic locos and included half of the entire class of BR 'Clan' Pacifics and an enormous quantity of 'Black Five' 4-6-0s. Even with the onset of the dieselisation of main line passenger services, by November 1961 Kingmoor's allocation of 127 fairly 'modern' steam locos (made up of 13 different classes) was still at full strength and included in the mixed traffic category were 22 'Crab' 2-6-0s, 48 'Black Five' and nine 'Jubilee' 4-6-0s and five BR 'Clan' Pacifics. By this date Kingmoor was also home to some fairly impressive top link locos, relegated here after being ousted by dieselisation elsewhere, and included a solitary 'Princess', eight 'Coronation' and four 'Britannia' Pacifics. One oddity was a sole member of the ex-WD 2-10-0 Class of heavy freight locos.

The shed managed to stay open nearly to the end of steam on BR, finally closing at the end of 1967.

80071	44677ᴮ	44672
80073	D6789	46257
D3528	45055ᴮ	D3087
70003	70013	46244
48765	46132	45118
45245ᴮ	70030	44669
D293 Carstairs Carlisle	12A.	92130
44887ᴮ	D5310	44792ᴮ
45028ᴮ	D5225	92021
45195	45527	92233
45629	70037	45588
42125	70035	45742
44128	70038	46255
42214	76094	45013
45176	45521	92009
45120ᴮ	45163ᴮ	44702ᴮ
44795ᴮ	46162	45096ᴮ
64404	47515	47471
12084	42353	45254ᴮ
12083	46132	45336ᴮ
1E 18M	5ST 4D	

By 1964 Kingmoor shed had a number of displaced 'Britannia' locos. Six were seen during a visit on July 29, along with three 'Coronation' Pacifics, three 'Royal Scots' and three 'Jubilees'. Three other 'Britannias' had also been spotted between Carstairs and Carlisle earlier in the day.

Then allocated to Kingmoor, 'Princess Royal' Class 4-6-2 No. 46201 'Princess Elizabeth' was seen on shed on April 25, 1962 – only six months before withdrawal. Designed by William Stanier this powerful express passenger loco was built at Crewe in 1933. The 'Lizzie' was bought for preservation and initially kept at the Dowty Railway Preservation Society's base at Ashchurch, north of Cheltenham in Gloucestershire. She was subsequently moved to the Bulmer's Railway Centre in Hereford before moving to her final home at the Midland Railway Centre at Butterley in Derbyshire.

Carlisle Upperby

During the latter years of steam on the LMR locos were banned from operating under the electrification wires south of Crewe. This restriction was denoted by a yellow diagonal stripe painted on the cabside. Here, complete with stripe and only one month before withdrawal, green-liveried 'Coronation' Class 4-6-2 No. 46237 'City of Bristol' was seen at Upperby shed on August 30, 1964. Behind is '4F' 0-6-0 No. 44009, withdrawn 'Princess Royal' Class 4-6-2 No. 46200 'The Princess Royal', 'Royal Scot' 4-6-0 No. 46110 'Grenadier Guardsman' and rebuilt 'Patriot' 4-6-0 No. 45545 'Planet'.

Located south of Citadel station, there had been a loco shed at Upperby since 1846 when the Lancaster & Carlisle Railway opened for business. Following various enlargements and rebuildings by the L&NWR the depot was completely rebuilt as a large roundhouse and adjacent straight shed by British Railways in 1948 - in fact it was probably the most modern steam shed on BR. With its allocation of mixed-traffic and top link steam locos, Upperby - a 20-minute walk from Citadel station – was a popular shed with trainspotters in the 1950s and early '60s.

Unlike Kingmoor shed, Upperby also became home to a few of the first generation main line diesels which, by November 1961, had reached a total of one named 'Peak' (Class 44) and six English Electric Type 4s (Class 40). By this date Upperby's importance had already started to decline and its steam allocation had dropped to a total of 77, including 23 'Black Five', two 'Royal Scot', three unrebuilt 'Patriot', three rebuilt 'Patriot' and 16 'Jubilee' 4-6-0s and six 'Coronation' Pacifics. The shed closed to steam at the end of 1966.

'Coronation' Class 4-6-2 No. 46241 'City of Edinburgh' was seen visiting Upperby at the end of July 1964. Built at Crewe with streamlined casing in 1940 and de-streamlined in 1947, No. 46241 was withdrawn from Edge Hill shed (8A) in September 1964.

Surrounded by vegetation but, strangely, with its nameplate still intact, recently withdrawn 'Royal Scot' Class 4-6-0 No. 46118 'Royal Welch Fusilier' waits in the condemned line at Upperby on July 29, 1964. This loco was built with a Fowler parallel boiler by the North British Locomotive Co. in 1927 and rebuilt with a taper boiler in 1946.

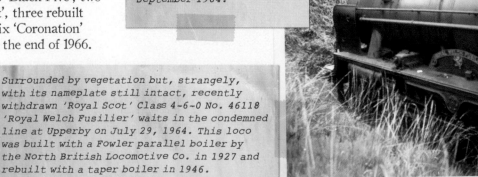

Part of the line-up of ex-LMS preserved locos that were gathered behind a security fence at Bold Colliery near St Helens Junction on May 23, 1980. They were being prepared as part of a cavalcade the next day to commemorate the 150th anniversary of the opening of the Liverpool & Manchester Railway. From left to right: Fowler '4F' 0-6-0 No. 4027 (built at Derby in 1924 and withdrawn as No. 44027 from Workington (12D) in November 1964); ex-S&DJR '7F' 2-8-0 No. 13809 (built at Derby in 1914 and withdrawn from Bath Green Park (82F) in June 1964); Johnson Midland Railway 'Spinner' 4-2-2 No. 673 (built at Derby in 1897 and withdrawn in 1928).

The Great Escape

A total of 103 steam locos from the LMS and its constituent companies have been preserved, including an ex-Mersey Railway 0-6-4 tank that has become a museum exhibit in Australia.

However, a number of the older examples, such as the Liverpool & Manchester Railway's 'Rocket', 'Sans Pareil' and 'Lion' and examples from Scottish pre-Grouping companies are currently static museum exhibits in the UK. Included in the total figure are 33 ex-LMS locos rescued from Dai Woodham's Barry scrapyard. These include examples of Class 2MT 2-6-2 tank, Class 5MT 'Crab', Class 4F 0-6-0, Class 5MT 'Black Five' 4-6-0, Class 2MT 2-6-0, Class 3F 'Jinty', Class 8F and ex-S&DJR 2-8-0.

Noteworthy examples of ex-LMS main line express passenger locos preserved include four 'Jubilee' and two 'Royal Scot' 4-6-0s, and two 'Princess Royal' and three 'Coronation' Pacifics together with 18 examples of mixed-traffic 'Black Five' 4-6-0s. One example of a Stanier 8F 2-8-0 has also been saved from a scrapyard in Turkey.

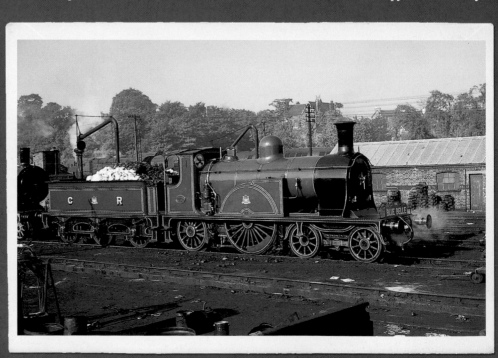

Seen here at Norwood Junction on September 15, 1963, Caledonian Railway 4-2-2 No. 123 was built by Neilson in 1886 as an exhibition locomotive and was withdrawn as LMS No. 14010 in 1935. This unique loco is currently on static display at Glasgow Museum of Transport.

Gathered around the Barrow Hill turntable, from right to left: Midland Railway half-cab '1F' No. 41708 which was shedded at Barrow Hill for some 18 years up to 1965 as part of the Midland Railway's agreement with nearby Staveley Iron and Steel Works to supply motive power for 100 years; LMS Midland 0-6-0 '4F' No. 44482 which was also a local engine during those years. Making up this entirely credible tableau is LMS Midland 0-6-0T '3F' No. 47630 and L&YR 'Pug' 0-4-0 tank No. 51218, making a guest appearance.

(below) The one that didn't escape! Allocated to Wick in 1962, Highland Railway 'Small Ben' Class 4-4-0 No. 14398 'Ben Alder' became the last survivor of its class and, as BR No. 54398, was justly set aside for preservation. It was stored at both Loch Gorm Works, Inverness and Boat of Garten before moving to Grangemouth. Preservation was ultimately rejected on the grounds that it did not carry its original Highland Railway boiler and in the 1960s - that rampant decade of mass destruction - it was broken up for scrap in 1966, an action that has been widely regretted ever since. Complete with snow plough the 'Ben' is seen here, still with its old LMS number, at Aviemore on March 27, 1948.

Saved from closure in the 1980s by public outrage the scenic 72-mile Settle to Carlisle route is now the premier route for steam-hauled enthusiasts' specials.

One of four Stanier 'Jubilee' Class 4-6-0s preserved, No. 5690 'Leander' was built at Crewe in 1936 and withdrawn from Bristol Barrow Road (82E) in March 1964. Since preservation the loco has travelled widely on main line tours and is currently based on the East Lancashire Railway.

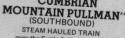

THE CUMBRIAN MOUNTAIN PULLMAN
STEAM HAULED TRAIN

Souvenir Ticket

CARLISLE to PRESTON, HELLIFIELD and Back
Also available for one journey (2118)
from and to...... EUSTON

by connecting services as shown in organisers itinerary

Issued subject to the Regulations and Conditions in the Publications and Notices of the British Railways Board. Not Transferable (M)

Organised by SLOA Marketing in association with British Rail and including Steam Haulage.

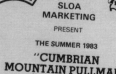

SLOA MARKETING PRESENT

THE SUMMER 1983

"CUMBRIAN MOUNTAIN PULLMAN"
(SOUTHBOUND)
STEAM HAULED TRAIN
over the Settle & Carlisle route
on
Wednesdays
June 29th, July 27th, August 24th and September 14th

34092 'City of Wells' on the Cumbrian Mountain Pullman 1982.

Railway Miscellany

Watching the trains go by – a lone trainspotter watches as ex-works unrebuilt 'Patriot' Class No. 45503 'The Royal Leicestershire Regiment' restarts a mixed goods train near Hartford station, south of Weaver Junction, on February 17, 1952. Built at Crewe in 1932, the 'Pat' was withdrawn from Carlisle Upperby in August 1961.

Sunday diversion – 'Deltic' (Class 55) D9017 'The Durham Light Infantry' enters Carlisle on July 16, 1967 with the 10am Edinburgh to King's Cross diverted via Hawick, Hexham and North Wylam because of a blockage on the ECML near Acklington.

The last full summer of steam to Windermere – watched and recorded by a handful of enthusiasts, 'Black Five' 4-6-0 No. 45295 leaves Oxenholme with the Windermere portion of the summer Saturday 11.55am train from Euston on August 12, 1967. Built by Armstrong Whitworth in 1937, the 'Black Five' was withdrawn from Carlisle Kingmoor at the end of 1967.

(right) Class 50 No. 410 leaves Carlisle on October 6, 1973 with the 10.30 Glasgow to Birmingham train. On the left is preserved 'A4' Class 4-6-2 No. 4498 'Sir Nigel Gresley' after working the A4 Locomotive Society's 'The Hadrian' special from Newcastle.

(below) One of the stars in steam at the Tyseley Open Day on September 29, 1968 was preserved Stanier 'Jubilee' Class 4-6-0 No. 5593 (BR No. 45593) 'Kolhapur'. Built by the North British Locomotive Co. in 1934, 'Kolhapur' had been withdrawn from Leeds Holbeck shed (55A) in October 1967. Fortunately the loco was purchased for preservation early in 1968 and is currently based at Barrow Hill Roundhouse.

BR Standard Class '4' 4-6-0 No. 75024 from Tebay shed (12E) banks a down freight hauled by 'Britannia' Class 4-6-2 No. 70021 ('Morning Star') at Shap Wells on October 17, 1967. Transferred from Croes Newydd shed (6C) in May, No 75024 was withdrawn only six weeks after being photographed here – only 14 years after emerging new from Swindon Works.

NORTH EASTERN REGION

Leeds

WITH TWO MAJOR STATIONS AND FIVE ENGINE SHEDS, LEEDS WAS AN IMPORTANT CENTRE FOR TRAINSPOTTERS UP UNTIL THE MID-1960S.

Ex-LNER 'D49' Class 4-4-0 No. 62773 'The South Durham' stands at Platform 10 at Leeds City with a stopping train to Harrogate on June 26, 1950. Note the ancient clerestory roof coach immediately behind the engine. Built in 1935, No. 62773 was allocated to 50D (Starbeck) at the time of this photo and was withdrawn in August 1958.

At that time Leeds boasted two stations, Central and City. Leeds Central opened in 1854 and was operated jointly by the Lancashire & Yorkshire, Great Northern and North Eastern Railways. Until the arrival of the English Electric Type 4s (Class 40), 'Peaks' (Class 45/46) and 'Deltics' (Class 55), trains north to York and Newcastle and south to Doncaster and King's Cross were often in the hands of Copley Hill (56C) shed's allocation of Peppercorn 'A1' Pacifics. Named trains on these routes included 'The Queen of Scots Pullman', 'The Yorkshire Pullman', 'The Harrogate Sunday Pullman', 'The West Riding' and 'The White Rose'. Copley Hill shed closed in 1964 and Central station closed in 1967, with its services diverted to the modernised Leeds City station.

Leeds City station was born out of the combining of New station (a through station opened jointly by the L&NWR and NER in 1869) and the adjacent Wellington station (a terminus opened by the Midland Railway in 1846) by the LMS in 1938. Although City station was modernised in 1967 it was deemed necessary to expand it

Whitehall Junction, Leeds in the 1950s - 'Royal Scot' Class 4-6-0 No. 46109 'Royal Engineer' heads out of Leeds with the northbound 'Thames-Clyde' express while ex-LNER 'D49' 4-4-0 No. 62764 'The Garth' heads in with a local passenger train from Harrogate. The latter locomotive, also known as a member of the 'Hunt' or 'Shire Class', was built in 1934 and withdrawn in October 1958. 'Royal Engineer' was originally built in 1927, rebuilt with a taper boiler in 1943 and withdrawn in December 1962.

(opposite) Magnificently turned-out by King's Cross shed, 'A4' Pacific No. 60003 'Andrew K. McCosh' departs from Leeds Central at 3.32pm with the up 'White Rose' to King's Cross in November 1961. Built in 1937 and originally named 'Osprey' the 'A4' was withdrawn just over a year later at the end of December 1962. 'The Queen of Scots' Pullman train can be seen on the left.

further to its current 17 platforms when it was rebuilt in 2002. As a branch of the East Coast Main Line, electrification of the route to King's Cross via Doncaster was completed in 1988.

In the late 1950s and early '60s ex-LMS locos such as 'Jubilees', 'Royal Scots' and 'Black Fives' plus a handful of 'Britannias' from Holbeck shed (55A) were a common sight on trains from Leeds City north to Carlisle via the Settle & Carlisle line and south to Sheffield and St Pancras via Chesterfield and to Manchester and beyond. Despite the early introduction of 'Peak' diesels on named trains such as 'The Thames-Clyde Express' and 'The Waverley', steam haulage continued to be seen on trains north from Leeds until the autumn of 1967 when Holbeck shed closed.

Steam remained active around Leeds up until late 1967 when Holbeck Shed (55A) closed in October. Here, on February 12, 1964, ex-LMS 'Jubilee' Class 4-6-0 No. 45597 'Barbados' marshals parcels vans under the new overall roof at Leeds City station. 'Barbados' had been a Holbeck engine for years and was finally withdrawn in January 1965.

ON SHED

Leeds Holbeck 55A

Opened by the Midland Railway in 1868, Holbeck consisted of two roundhouses and was located on the west side of the Woodlesford line about ½ mile south of Leeds City station.

With a shed code of 20A until 1957, Holbeck was the principal LMR shed in Leeds and provided motive power for trains on the former Midland route north to Carlisle and Glasgow St Enoch via the Settle & Carlisle route and south to Sheffield, St Pancras, Birmingham and even to Bristol.

Although absorbed into the North Eastern Region, Holbeck retained its allocation of ex-LMS locos until the very end when, in October 1967, it became the last shed in Leeds to close to steam.

By November 1961 the shed had lost its 'Royal Scots' but still had an allocation of 59 locos, including only four diesel shunters. Of note were the 15 'Jubilee' 4-6-0s and three 'Britannia' Pacifics.

Holbeck shed on August 23, 1966 - left to right 8F 2-8-0 No. 48283, 'Jubilee' 4-6-0 No. 45697 'Achilles' and 8F 2-8-0 No. 48158. The 'Jubilee', a Holbeck engine by that date, was built at Crewe in 1936 and withdrawn in September 1967.

Under new management - ex-LMS 'Black Five' 4-6-0 No. 44849 stands under Holbeck's coaling plant on October 3, 1948. 'Jubilee' 4-6-0 No. 45561 'Saskatchewan' gets ready to move under on the adjoining track. The pre-Nationalisation 'serif' numberplates on the smokebox doors soon gave way to the more modern 'sans serif' style known to most spotters.

A beautifully clean 'Jubilee' No. 45593 'Kolhapur' is ready for its next turn of duty in 1967. This loco, complete with diagonal yellow stripe on its cab, was withdrawn from Holbeck in October 1967 before being saved for preservation.

Leeds Neville Hill

Opened by the North Eastern Railway in 1894, Neville Hill shed originally had a code of 50B until 1960 when it changed its code to 55H.

Located on the north side of the Cross Gates line about two miles east of Leeds City station, the shed consisted of a four-road roundhouse shed until 1960 when half of it was rebuilt as a diesel depot. Consequently by 1961 it had a strange mix of ex-LNER steam locos and a large allocation of brand new main line diesels.

Neville Hill's mid-November 1961 allocation totalled 55 locos of which nearly half were diesels - of these 18 were 'Peaks' (Class 45/46). Despite only 29 steam locos being still on the books, eight different classes were represented, notably the four Gresley 'A3' Pacifics.

With its cabside number barely distinguishable and a grimy nameplate, 'B1' Class 4-6-0 No. 61031 'Reedbuck' was seen at Neville Hill in the summer of 1962. The 'B1' Class had a very short working life - No. 61031 was built in 1947 and withdrawn in November 1964.

Allocated to York shed (50A) Peppercorn 'A1' Class Pacific No. 60154 'Bon Accord' stands over Neville Hill's ash pit in June 1962. Another class with a ridiculously short life - No. 60154 was built in 1949 and withdrawn in October 1965. Although none of this class were preserved we are now fortunate to witness brand new 'A1' Class No. 60163 'Tornado' operating on the main line.

With a sack tied over its chimney, Gresley 'A3' Pacific No. 60081 'Shotover' awaits its fate in Neville Hill shed in November, 1963. Built at Doncaster in 1924 this loco had been withdrawn from service in October 1962. On the right 'J39' Class 0-6-0 No. 64857 also waits for the summons to the cutter's yard.

181

ON SHED

56 A

Wakefield

Located on the east side of the Pontefract line about a 20-minute walk south of Wakefield Kirkgate station, Wakefield shed was a large 10-road dead-end building opened by the Lancashire & Yorkshire Railway in 1893. Formerly coded 25A under the LMR, it was transferred to the North Eastern Region in 1956 when it was rebuilt and became 56A.

Serving a heavily industrialised area of West Yorkshire, the shed provided motive power for heavy freight including the output from many local coal mines. Wakefield's allocation of 64 freight locos in November 1961 reflects its importance in the region. There were eleven different classes represented, among them diesel shunters and two ancient ex-L&YR 3F 0-6-0s dating from 1889. The most numerous classes were the 44 ex-WD 2-8-0s, followed by eight ex-LNER B1 4-6-0s. The shed closed to steam in June 1967.

A development of the LNWR 'G2' heavy freight loco, 75 of the Fowler 7F 0-8-0 engines were built at Crewe between 1929 and 1932. Here, No. 49610 awaits its next turn of duty at Wakefield on April 30, 1949. The last of this class was withdrawn in 1962.

Seen here on September 9, 1967, the silent coaling plant, turntable and long lines of withdrawn engines tell the sad story of both steam's and Wakefield's demise. The shed had closed to steam three months earlier and all of these once-fine machines were destined for the scrapyard.

With fireman and driver posing proudly for John Goss's photo, Peppercorn 'A1' Pacific No. 60120 'Kittiwake' looks every bit a powerful machine at Wakefield in June 1962. Then allocated to Copley Hill (56C), this loco was one of the first batch of this class built by BR at Doncaster in 1948. 'Kittiwake' was withdrawn in January 1964 after only 15½ years' service.

Built in 1947 'B1' class 4-6-0 No. 61022 'Sassaby' (minus nameplate) is seen here looking rather the worse for wear in its last few months of life at Wakefield on August 23, 1966. This loco was withdrawn in November of that year.

York

ASTRIDE THE EAST COAST MAIN LINE, YORK HAS ALWAYS BEEN AN IMPORTANT RAIL CENTRE WITH SERVICES SOUTH TO DONCASTER AND LONDON KING'S CROSS, NORTH TO NEWCASTLE AND EDINBURGH, WEST TO LEEDS AND MANCHESTER AND LEEDS VIA HARROGATE AS WELL AS EAST TO SCARBOROUGH AND TO HULL VIA MARKET WEIGHTON.

Apart from the last-named route all of the others are still open to traffic. The fiercely independent and ramshackle Derwent Valley Light Railway, with its headquarters at York Layerthorpe, has also long closed apart from a short section at Murton Lane which is now preserved.

The current York station with its curving platforms and overall arched roof was opened by the North Eastern Railway in 1877 and, at that time, was the largest station in the world. The station was enlarged in 1909 and suffered considerable bomb damage during World War II. With its two loco sheds (North and South) and a considerable amount of through traffic, York was a magnet for trainspotters in the late 1950s and early '60s.

Showing off its graceful lines a Gresley 'V2' 2-6-2' accelerates a northbound parcels train away from York c.1960. In the foreground, Class '04/8' 2-8-0 No. 63612 trundles along with a coal train from South Yorkshire. The Class '04/8' were a 1944-rebuild (including a 'B1' boiler and new cab) of the Robinson-designed 'O1' locos built for the Great Central Railway in 1911. The last members of this class were withdrawn in April 1966.

Peppercorn 'A1' Pacific No. 60143 'Sir Walter Scott' leaves York with an up evening express made up of mainly 'blood and custard' stock in March 1957. Built at Darlington in 1949 and fitted with a Kylchap exhaust, this loco had a very short life and was withdrawn in May 1964.

Below: Class 40 No. 40172 leaves York with a Scarborough to Edinburgh train on August 2, 1975. Between 1958 and 1962 180 of these locos were built by English Electric at Vulcan Foundry and 20 by Robert Stephenson & Hawthorns of Darlington. No. 40172 was built by English Electric in 1962 and started life painted in BR green and numbered D372. Withdrawal took place in 1983.

Until the arrival of the English Electric Type 4s (Class 40), 'Peaks' (Class 45/46) and 'Deltics' (Class 55), ECML expresses were totally in the hands of ex-LNER Gresley 'A3' and 'A4', Thompson 'A2' and Peppercorn 'A1' Pacifics. Other ex-LNER types that were common at York were the 'B17' (Sandringham Class) and 'B1' 4-6-0s, 'V2' 2-6-2s and, until the late 1950s, the graceful 'D49' (Hunt/Shire Class) 4-4-0s. Trains from the northeast to the Midlands and southwest often changed engines at York with ex-LNER locos giving way to ex-LMS types such as 'Jubilee' or 'Royal Scot' 4-6-0s for their onward journey via Leeds. By the summer of 1963 nearly all ECML passenger services were diesel-hauled, although steam continued in use on freight and local services for a few more years.

Steam was finally ousted in June 1967 when York North shed closed and ECML services remained diesel-hauled, firstly by 'Deltics' and secondly by HSTs, until electrification of the entire route in 1990. Despite this, some services are still operated by old HST sets.

ON SHED

50 A York

York once boasted two large steam engine sheds: York South, which housed LMS locos and York North, which housed LNER locos. Consisting of two roundhouses, York South was located in the triangle of lines on the west side of the ECML south of York Station. Access was via a boarded crossing from Platform 16.

Due to rationalisation, the shed was closed to steam in 1961 and its allocation moved to North shed. York North consisted of four adjacent sheds – two roundhouses, one dead end shed and one through shed. It was located on the west side of the ECML, a 10-minute walk north of York station.

Gathered around the turntable in York shed one day in May 1964 are (left to right) 'V2' Class 2-6-2 No. 60886; an un-identified WD Austerity; 'B1' Class 4-6-0 No. 61031 'Reedbuck' and Peppercorn 'A1' Class 4-6-2 No. 60146 'Peregrine'. The 'A1', a York loco, was withdrawn in October 1965.

Ex-LMS Stanier 2-cylinder 2-6-4 tank No. 42548, built by the North British Locomotive Company in 1936, poses on the turntable inside York roundhouse on August 25, 1964. On the right, with its smokebox door open for cleaning, is BR Standard 9F 2-10-0 No. 92211 – although designed for hauling freight trains, members of the 9F Class were also known for their smooth running at high speed while hauling passenger trains on the East Coast Main Line.

A wintry scene, c.1960 as ex-LNER 'K3' Class 2-6-0 No. 61981 reverses under York's coaling plant. Designed for the Great Northern Railway by Nigel Gresley a total of 193 of these locos were built between 1920 and 1937. Withdrawals took place between 1959 and 1962.

A handsome lineup at York on an undisclosed date in the 1960s. On the left is Peppercorn 'A1' Pacific No. 60121 'Silurian' while in the foreground 'V2' Class 2-6-2 No. 60876 obscures the identity of the 9F 2-10-0 behind it. Both Nos 60121 and 60876 were allocated to York and both withdrawn in October 1965. Note the visiting SR 'Merchant Navy' on the right!

Following the closure of South shed in 1961, North shed's allocation totalled 185 locos including 21 English Electric Type 4 (Class 40) diesels and 36 diesel shunters. The steam roll call included nine ex-LMS locos, two BR Standard 2-6-0s, 11 ex-WD 2-8-0s and 106 ex-LNER locos. Among the latter were nine 'A1' and seven 'A2' Pacifics, 33 'V2' 2-6-2s, 23 'B1' (of which seven were named) and 19 'B16' (nearly all of the remaining members of this class) 4-6-0s and ten 'K1' 2-6-0s.

North Shed closed to steam in the summer of 1967 but operated as a diesel depot until 1984. The buildings and site have now been incorporated as part of the National Railway Museum.

No doubt the subject of a deep discussion, Doncaster-allocated 'B1' Class 4-6-0 No. 61042 waits to move on to the turntable inside York roundhouse on March 31, 1966. Its shed mates include BR Standard 9F 2-10-0 No. 92231 and fellow 'B1' No. 61019 'Nilghai'. The latter was built in 1947 and withdrawn in March 1967.

Darlington Works

OPENED IN 1863
BY THE STOCKTON &
DARLINGTON RAILWAY,
THE RAILWAY WORKS AT
NORTH ROAD WENT ON
TO BUILD LOCOMOTIVES
FOR THE NORTH EASTERN
RAILWAY, THE LNER
AND BRITISH RAILWAYS.

Located near North Road station on the Darlington to Bishop Auckland branch, the Works was about a 30-minute walk from Bank Top station on the ECML.

As well as building many mixed-traffic, freight and shunting locos for the NER, Darlington was also responsible for building the five 'A2' Pacifics designed by Vincent Raven. The first two of these were built by the NER in 1922 with the other three being built after the Big Four Grouping by the LNER in 1924.

With Nigel Gresley as CME, Darlington went on to build a batch of K3 2-6-0s, 52 B17s ('Sandringhams'), D49 4-4-0s ('Hunt/Shire'), 261 'J39' 0-6-0s, six 'K4' 2-6-0s for the West Highland Line, batches of 'V2' 2-6-2s and the 'Hush-Hush' 'W1' 4-6-4 in 1929. Under Edward Thompson the Works built his 'A2/1' Pacifics, a batch of 'B1' 4-6-0s and 30 'L1' 2-6-4 tanks, before continuing with a batch of 22 Peppercorn 'A1' Pacifics, all of which were built under BR management between 1948 and 1949.

By the mid-60s the last few ex-LNER Pacifics to receive works attention were handled at Darlington instead of Doncaster. Here Class 'A2/3' Pacific No. 60522 'Straight Deal' and Class 'A2' Pacific No. 60530 'Sayajirao' are seen inside Darlington North Road Works. No. 60522 was built in 1947 and withdrawn in June 1965. No. 60530 was built at Doncaster in 1948 and spent its short working life allocated to Scottish sheds before being withdrawn from Dundee Tay Bridge (62B) in November 1966.

Darlington North Road Works in the 1950s with a motley collection of boilers, ex-NER and ex-LNER locos. Ex-NER J27 0-6-0 No. 65874 is in the left foreground. Introduced in 1906, 36 of the 'J27' Class lasted until the very end of steam on the North Eastern Region operating coal trains. The last 'J27' in service, No. 65894, was withdrawn from Sunderland shed in 1967 and has since been preserved.

In ex-works condition ex-NER 'Q7' 0-8-0 No. 63460 trundles past Darlington Works 1930s-style office on September 20, 1963 having been saved from the scrapyard the year before and preserved as part of the National Collection. Introduced in 1919 only 15 of these heavy freight locos were built and ended their lives allocated to Tyne Dock (52H) for hauling heavy iron-ore trains to Consett. They were all withdrawn in 1962 and replaced by BR Standard 9F 2-10-0s.

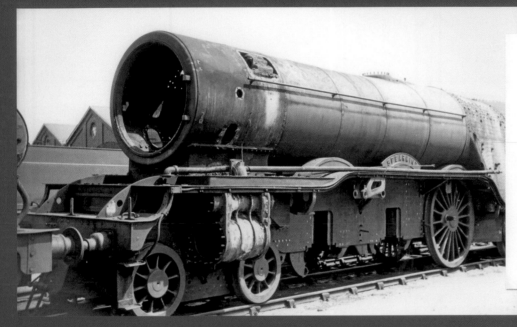

'Flying Scotsman' was the most famous Gresley 'A3' Pacific, but a contender for second place was No. 60100 'Spearmint'. For years she was the pride of Edinburgh Haymarket (64B) and features prominently in railway folklore. Dieselisation of the East Coast Main Line caused 'Spearmint' to be transferred to Edinburgh St Margaret's (64A) in 1962 where she remained until withdrawn in June 1965. She was despatched promptly to Darlington and breaking up proceeded in July. This sad picture shows the thoroughbred partly dismantled but with nameplates still in position.

After Nationalisation, work continued on building the entire class of 65 BR Standard Class 2 2-6-0s and ten of the BR Standard Class 2 2-6-2 tanks along with a batch of what became known later as the Class 11 diesel shunter. Construction of steam locos at Darlington then ceased but, from 1953, the Works continued to build diesels with batches of the Class 08, Class 09 and Class 10 diesel shunters. Main line diesel loco production at Darlington consisted of a batch of BR Sulzer Type 2 (Class 24/25). The three unusual pairs of Class 13 'cow and calf' shunters were also built at Darlington in 1965 for use at the Tinsley Marshalling Yard in Sheffield.

Darlington Works closed in 1966 – however, that is not the final story as the brand new 'A1' Pacific No. 60163 'Tornado' was out-shopped from the new locomotive works in Hopetown Lane. Costing £3 million, paid for by donations and sponsors, 'Tornado' made its first moves under steam in July 2008.

Introduced in 1949, a total of 70 Peppercorn 'K1' Class 2-6-0s were built for the Eastern and North Eastern regions of BR by the North British Locomotive Company. Here, No. 62041 in gleaming lined BR black poses for our photographer outside Darlington Works after a major overhaul in 1964. Withdrawn in 1967, the last engine in this class was No. 62005 which has since been preserved.

Darlington

IN ADDITION TO THE EX-NORTH EASTERN RAILWAY WORKS AND LOCOMOTIVE SHED, DARLINGTON POSSESSED (AND STILL DOES) TWO RAILWAY STATIONS.

When the grey accountants declared steam-hauled trains uneconomic, no consideration was given to the fact that they were a source of healthy occupation for millions of youngsters, a fact confirmed by this picture of Darlington Bank Top station looking north from the south end of the Up main platform on October 10, 1953. Gresley 'A4' Pacific No. 60006, 'Sir Ralph Wedgwood' heads 'The Northumbrian' alongside one of the lovely Class 'A8' 4-6-2 tanks which were Gresley re-builds of Raven 'D' Class 4-4-4 tanks.

North Road, on the line to Wearhead via Bishop Auckland and to Penrith via Barnard Castle, is the more historic of the two stations as it is the site of the terminus of the world's first public railway - the Stockton & Darlington Railway that opened in 1825. It is also located close to the site of the former North Eastern Railway Works. However, the only trains that stop here now are those on the Bishop Auckland branch.

Bank Top station, however, is located on the East Coast Main Line, and the present building dates from 1887, when it replaced a much smaller station. Still busy with services on the electrified ECML and to Middlesbrough, Redcar and Bishop Auckland, Bank Top was once a great place to spot not only the Gresley Pacifics on main line expresses such as 'The Talisman', 'The Northumbrian', 'The Heart of Midlothian' and 'The Aberdonian' and L1 2-6-2 tanks on stopping trains to Richmond, but also BR Standard Class 4 and Ivatt Class 2 2-6-0s on the trans-Pennine route to Penrith. Freight traffic from industrial Teeside and the Durham coalfields was particularly heavy and brought many different types of ex-NER and LNER freight locos to the Darlington area. The end of steam came in Spring 1966 when the nearby Darlington shed (51A) closed.

By 1964 the East Coast Main Line expresses had been totally dieselised. On February 12 English Electric Type 5 'Deltic' (Class 55) D9013 'The Black Watch' pauses at Bank Top station with the southbound 'Tees-Tyne Pullman'. One of a class of 22 locos built by English Electric between 1961 and 1962, D9013 was finally withdrawn from service in December 1981.

Far from home. Ex-SR 'Schools' Class 4-4-0 No. 30925 'Cheltenham' and ex-LMS '2P' 4-4-0 No. 40646 pause at Bank Top station on May 13, 1962 at the head of an RCTS special train, 'The East Midlander', before returning to Nottingham. 'Cheltenham' has since been preserved and is part of the National Collection at the NRM, York.

191

ON SHED

Looking in almost immaculate condition Darlington-allocated 'V2' 2-6-2 No. 60885 simmers outside the shed on September 20, 1963. This loco was still on the shed's books in April 1965 and was one of the last batch to be withdrawn. To the left is ex-works ex-NER 'Q7' 0-8-0 No. 63460 which had been saved from the scrapyard the year before and preserved as part of the National Collection.

Darlington

With its important railway works, large engine shed and Bank Top station sitting astride the East Coast Main Line, Darlington was a favourite destination for trainspotters. There had been an engine shed in Darlington since 1825 when the world's first public railway, the Stockton & Darlington, was opened. This shed was located at North Road close to where the North Eastern Railway later built its Works.

The main shed at Darlington, consisting of a roundhouse opened in 1866 by the NER and a nine-road through shed opened in 1940 by the LNER, was located on the east side of the main line only a five minute walk north from Bank Top station. Its allocation of mainly mixed-traffic and freight locos reflected the importance of freight traffic, particularly from Teeside, in this industrialised region of northeast England. In addition the shed also supplied locos for secondary route passenger services to Penrith via Barnard Castle and Stainmore Summit, the Richmond branch and to Teeside via Stockton.

Fitted with German-style smoke deflectors and a double Kylchap exhaust, Gresley 'A3' Class 4-6-2 No. 60045 'Lemberg' reverses up to the turntable on August 11, 1964. This handsome loco was originally built by the LNER as an 'A1' Pacific in 1924 and rebuilt as an 'A3' in 1927. Withdrawal took place in November 1964.

Allocated to Leeds Neville Hill (55H), 'K1' Class 2-6-0 No. 62007 was seen in ex-works condition at Darlington in April 1965. Built by the North British Locomotive Co. a total of 70 engines of this class entered service between May 1949 and March 1950. They had all been withdrawn by 1967 but one, No. 62005, was saved for preservation.

In the Autumn of 1961, prior to the closure of the trans-Pennine route, Darlington's allocation totalled 68 steam locos plus 27 diesel shunters. Twelve different classes of steam locos were represented of which the two 'A3' Pacifics – 60053 'Sansovino' and 60075 'St Frusquin' – were the stars of the shed. There were also nine 'B1' 4-6-0s (including two named – 61032 'Marmion' and 61037 'Redgauntlet'), a solitary named 'V2' 2-6-2 (60809 'The Snapper, The East Yorkshire Regiment, The Duke of York's Own'), 11 'K1' 2-6-0s, 15 J94 saddle tanks and 12 ex-WD 2-8-0s. Darlington shed finally closed its doors to steam in Spring 1966.

A fine panoramic photo of Darlington shed viewed from the turntable in the 1950s. From left to right are 'B1' Class 4-6-0 No. 61299, 'A5' Class 4-6-2 tank No. 69838, a 'B16' 4-6-0 and an ex-works 'V2' 2-6-2.

Newcastle

DESIGNED BY JOHN DOBSON WITH THREE CURVED AND ARCHED TRAIN SHED ROOFS, NEWCASTLE CENTRAL WAS OPENED IN 1850 AS A JOINT STATION FOR THE YORK, NEWCASTLE & BERWICK RAILWAY AND THE NEWCASTLE & CARLISLE RAILWAY.

Along with other constituent companies, these soon merged to become the North Eastern Railway. The station was approached over the High Level Bridge which was designed by Robert Stephenson to carry both road and railway over the River Tyne. However, until the King Edward VII Bridge was built in 1906, through trains on the East Coast Main Line had to reverse at Central Station. The station also underwent an extension in the 1890s and a suburban third-rail electric train service to Tynemouth started operating from the east side in 1904. The NER claimed that the complex rail junction with its multitude of diamond crossings on the approach to the station was the largest in the world.

Despite the introduction of diesels on ECML trains, Central station was still popular with trainspotters in the late 1950s and early '60s. For a few years the new English Electric Type 4 (Class 40), 'Peak' (Class 45/46) and 'Deltic' (Class 55) diesels could be seen rubbing shoulders with Gresley's magnificent 'A3' and 'A4' Pacifics, along with Thompson 'A2' and Peppercorn 'A1' Pacifics. Named trains were a'plenty and included 'The Flying Scotsman', which made its one scheduled intermediate stop at Central, the morning and afternoon 'Talisman', 'The Northumbrian', 'The Heart of Midlothian', 'The Queen of Scots Pullman' and 'The Tees-Tyne Pullman'.

It wasn't just a continual stream of ex-LNER Pacifics to be spotted at Newcastle Central. Here a 'Q6' 0-8-0 struggles with a long string of coal empties at the western approach to the station. Introduced by the NER in 1913 the 'Q6' Class remained more-or-less intact until the 1960s with the last members being withdrawn as late as 1967.

Still carrying its old 50A shed plate ex-NER Class 'J72' 0-6-0 tank No. 68736 performs station pilot duties at Newcastle Central on September 29, 1963. The longevity of this class was astonishing with a total of 113 locos being built in nine batches between 1898 and 1951. The last 'J72' was withdrawn in 1964.

Alongside these stars of the show were the mixed traffic 'B1' 4-6-0s, 'V2' 2-6-2s and more humble locos including 'V1' and 'V3' 2-6-2 tanks on local and empty coaching stock duties, and for some years Gateshead's diminutive 'J72' 0-6-0 tanks (vintage 1898), some repainted in LNER green, could be seen pottering around Central station on pilot duties. Now all this is gone – the 'Deltics' were replaced by HSTs in the late 1970s and they, in turn, were replaced by Intercity 225 trains on completion of ECML electrification in 1991.

The suburban electric trains to Tynemouth were withdrawn in 1967 and replaced by diesel multiple units but these were also withdrawn in 1980 when the Tyne & Wear Metro commenced service. Consequently the east side of the station has now become a car park.

Young spotters watch the arrival of 'The Queen of Scots Pullman' in Newcastle headed by ex-LNER 'A2/1' Class Pacific No. 60510 'Robert the Bruce'. One of four locos built at Darlington in January 1945 as a Pacific version of Gresley's 'V2' 2-6-2 this loco spent much of its life at Haymarket shed (64B) and was withdrawn in November 1960.

Peppercorn 'A1' Pacific No. 60155 'Borderer' waits to depart from Newcastle on August 8, 1964. One of five 'A1s' fitted with Timken roller bearings this loco was built at Doncaster in 1949 and withdrawn in October 1965. Needing a works overhaul on average every 120,000 miles these five locos were probably amongst the most reliable steam engines ever built in Britain.

Gresley 'A3' Class Pacific No. 60051 'Blink Bonny' restarts vigorously from Newcastle on August 8, 1964. Allocated to Heaton shed (52B), this loco was built in 1924 and withdrawn only three months after this photo was taken, in November 1964.

Ex-LNER 'A3' Class Pacific No. 60099 'Call Boy' enters Newcastle Central with an up Car-Carrier train in September 1961. An English Electric Type 4 (Class 40) waits to take over the train to London (Holloway). The cost of conveying a car and its driver (2nd Class) from Newcastle to London was then £9 10s (single). A Haymarket (64B) loco at this time, 'Call Boy' was built in 1930 and withdrawn in October 1963.

ON SHED

Gateshead

Ex-LNER Class 'J39' 0-6-0 No. 64701 takes a drink of water at Gateshead on June 5, 1950. Built in 1926 this standard LNER goods loco was allocated to 52A at that time and was withdrawn from Sunderland South Dock (52G) in October 1962.

The principal depot for East Coast Main Line motive power in the Newcastle area, there had been an engine shed at Gateshead since 1839. Located on the north side of the line west of Gateshead West station, the depot finally ended up with four square adjoining roundhouses and a straight three-road shed for the larger North Eastern Railway Pacifics. By the late 1950s and early '60s Gateshead, with its impressive allocation of Gresley Pacifics, held a magnetic attraction for trainspotters. However, by late 1961 the writing was on the wall for these magnificent locos as increasing numbers of main line diesels arrived at the shed. By this time there were 78 diesels allocated including four 'Peaks' (Class 45), 26 English Electric Type 4 (Class 40) and six of the mighty 'Deltic' (Class 55).

This invasion had seriously reduced the steam allocation which, by now, was down to a shadow of its former self with only 42 locos. Despite this, there

Seen here in Gateshead shed in June 1950, ex-LNER Class 'Y1' 0-4-0 geared steam loco No. 68141 was built by the Sentinel wagon works in 1929. Despite withdrawals in the 1950s several survived as departmental locos until the 1960s. One member of this class, No. 68153 has been preserved.

Designed by W Worsdell for the North Eastern Railway Class 'G5' 0-4-4 tank No. 67260 was a visitor to 52A when pictured here in June 1950. Built in 1896 this loco spent its last years operating out of Sunderland South Dock shed and was withdrawn from there in 1952.

were still some beauties, including eight 'A4' and 11 'A3' Gresley Pacifics and some old-timers in the shape of six of Worsdell's NER J72 0-6-0 tanks of 1898 vintage, some of which had been repainted in their old NER livery for their duties as station pilot at Newcastle Central station. Three of Worsdell's 1902 NER 'N10' 0-6-2 tanks were still on the books, but they faced imminent withdrawal.

Part of the depot was converted to a diesel maintenance depot in 1964 and the shed finally closed to steam in the Autumn of 1965. The diesel depot was subsequently closed in 1991 following electrification of the ECML to Edinburgh.

Originally introduced by the NER as far back as 1898 a final batch of 'J72' 0-6-0 tanks were built at Darlington between 1949 and 1951. Here No. 69028, the last member of this class to be built and painted in NER green for its station pilot duties at Newcastle Central, was photographed at Gateshead on July 24, 1964 shortly before withdrawal.

With its smokebox door hinges picked out in silver, ex-LNER 'Class 'V3' 2-6-2 tank No. 67628, previously allocated to Helensburgh shed (65H), was photographed at Gateshead on November 24, 1962. The last surviving 'V3s' were withdrawn in 1964.

Final Days

The dawn of 1967 still saw 16 steam sheds operating in the North Eastern Region. Covering a large industrial area ranging from Bradford Manningham and Huddersfield in the southwest to North and South Blyth in the northeast, steam would not live to see 1968.

On occasions when ECML trains were diverted from Ferryhill to Northallerton via Stockton on Tees (thus avoiding Darlington) it was usual for the Darlington (51A) standby Pacific to be kept at Eaglescliffe or Bowesfield. Here, Peppercorn Class 'A1' No. 60124, formerly 'Kenilworth' and here minus nameplates, leaves Eaglescliffe on its return to Darlington on September 26, 1965. This loco was built at Doncaster in 1949 and withdrawn from Darlington shed in March 1966.

By June steam had ceased to operate from York (50A), Hull Dairycoates (50B), Goole (50D), South Blyth (52F), Stourton (55B), Huddersfield (55G), Wakefield (56A), Mirfield (56D) and Bradford Manningham (55F). Next to follow, in September, were the remaining ex-LNER steam sheds in the Newcastle area (51C West Hartlepool, 52F North Blyth, 52G Sunderland and 52H Tyne Dock) with their ex-WD 2-8-0s, 'K1' 2-6-0s, 'J27' 0-6-0s and 'Q6' 0-8-0s,

The last four NER steam sheds to close were the former Midland Railway roundhouse at Leeds Holbeck (55A) and the former L&YR shed at Low Moor (56F) in October, the former LMS shed at Royston (55D) in November and the former L&YR shed at Normanton at the end of December. By January 1, 1968, all steam had disappeared from the region.

Looking very shabby and hauling a solitary brake van Ivatt Class 4 2-6-0 No. 43137 trundles through the closed Redmarshall station near Stockton-on-Tees on September 28, 1966. Never likely to win a locomotive beauty contest, a total of 162 of these locos were built between 1947 and 1952 with nearly the entire class remaining in service until the last few years of steam. One example, No. 43106, has since been preserved.

The last four remaining steam sheds in the Newcastle area all closed on September 9, 1967. Here, Class 'Q6' 0-8-0 No. 63395 of Sunderland shed (52G) makes a dramatic approach to Seaton with a coal train on August 31. Obviously designed for longevity, a total of 120 of these powerful heavy freight locos were built for the NER between 1913 and 1921. Fortunately No. 63395 was saved for preservation and can be seen on the North Yorkshire Moors Railway.

With barely a week to go before the end of steam in the Newcastle area, Class 'J27' 0-6-0 No. 65882 from North Blyth shed (52F) looks a pretty sight as it heads a train of empties for Silksworth Colliery on August 31, 1967. One Class 'J27', No. 65894, has since been preserved.

Ex-WD 2-8-0 No. 90459 takes on water at West Hartlepool shed (51C) in 1965. A total of 935 of these 'Austerity' heavy freight locos were built by the North British Locomotive Company and Vulcan Foundry during World War II. Originally designed for use in Europe after D-Day, a total of 733 ended up on British Railways' books. No class in Britain's railway history was more neglected - they were always filthy and could be heard approaching from long distances by the 'plonk' of banging bushes. For trainspotters, they were the hardest of all British classes to 'clear', as 733 of them roamed Britain from dozens of different sheds and often on work which involved complex inter-colliery transfers.

DASTARDLY DIESELS!

Despite the northeast of England remaining as one of the last outposts of steam on BR – West Hartlepool (51C), North Blyth (52F), Sunderland (52G) and Tyne Dock (52H) sheds not closing to steam until September 1967 – the East Coast Main Line had virtually become dieselised by 1963.

By the early '60s the sleek Gresley Pacifics had been replaced by Class 40 English Electric Type 4 1Co-Co1, Class 46 'Peak' 1Co-Co1 and Class 55 English Electric Type 5 'Co-Co 'Deltic' main line diesels. With the introduction of the more powerful Class 47 Brush Type 4 Co-Co in 1963, the Class 40 and Class 46 locos were gradually diverted to more mundane duties. The 'Deltics' finally disappeared in 1981 when they went on to be replaced by HST sets.

The inaugural molten metal train from Cargo Fleet to Consett approaches South Pelaw on August 4, 1969. Headed by English Electric Type 3 (Class 37) diesels D6832 and D6712 the train is formed of a dynamometer car, three 'torpedoes' and barrier wagons. Introduced between 1960 and 1965 the Class 37 has been so successful that some are still on active duty today.

Prototype Co-Co diesel HS4000 'Kestrel' gets ready to depart from Heaton carriage shed with the empty stock of the 16.45 Newcastle to King's Cross on October 28, 1969. Built by Brush Traction in 1968 'Kestrel' was powered by a 4000hp Sulzer engine and finished in a yellow ochre and dark brown livery. Following trials, the loco was refitted with lighter bogies and went into service on the ECML. The loco was withdrawn in 1971 and sent to Russia as a research vehicle and has not been seen since!

Deltic' (Class 55) D9012 'Crepello' stands at the head of a King's Cross to Newcastle train at Platform 9, York station on June 27, 1964. Built by English Electric at their Vulcan Foundry and named after a famous racehorse, 'Crepello' came into service in September 1961. Allocated for most of its life to Finsbury Park (34G), it was finally withdrawn in May 1981.

From 1961 the Class 24 Sulzer Type 2 Bo-Bo also became a common sight on passenger and freight workings in the northeast. A batch of these (D5096-D5113) was fitted with air pumps and allocated to Gateshead (52A) in 1965 to take over the Tyne Dock to Consett iron-ore trains from BR Standard 9F 2-10-0s. Working in multiple, the '24s' continued to operate this service until March 1974 when it was rerouted. From that date Class 37 English Electric Type 3 Co-Co locos took over iron-ore trains on a new route from Redcar to Consett until the steel works closed in 1983.

English Electric Type 4 (Class 40) No. 272 rumbles through the sun-streaked columns of Newcastle Central with a stopping train from Edinburgh in the early 1970s. Later numbered 40072, this loco was introduced in 1960 and withdrawn from service in 1977.

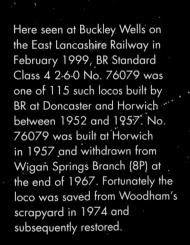

Here seen at Buckley Wells on the East Lancashire Railway in February 1999, BR Standard Class 4 2-6-0 No. 76079 was one of 115 such locos built by BR at Doncaster and Horwich between 1952 and 1957. No. 76079 was built at Horwich in 1957 and withdrawn from Wigan Springs Branch (8P) at the end of 1967. Fortunately the loco was saved from Woodham's scrapyard in 1974 and subsequently restored.

The Great Escape
BR Standard Locos

IT IS NOT SURPRISING THAT 46 BR STANDARD CLASS LOCOS HAVE BEEN PRESERVED AS MOST OF THEM WERE AMONG THE NEWEST AND THE FINAL STEAM LOCOS TO BE WITHDRAWN.

Built at Crewe, Standard Class 7 4-6-2 No. 70000 'Britannia' was the first of 55 such locos delivered to BR between 1951 and 1954. After spending many years allocated to Norwich Thorpe (32A), No. 70000 ended her days at Carlisle Kingmoor (12A) where she was withdrawn in June 1966. Failing to be included as part of the National Collection due to her poor mechanical condition, this loco was preserved privately and returned to the main line in 1991.

Developed from the Standard 'Britannia' Class Pacifics and built at Crewe in 1954, the unique Class 8 Pacific No. 71000 'Duke of Gloucester' was never a great success on BR due to its poor steaming and heavy coal consumption. It was withdrawn in 1962 after only eight years' service and sent, via Cashmore's of Newport, to Dai Woodham's scrapyard at Barry. Here it languished, with many of its parts already removed, until it was saved for preservation in 1974. Following 13 years of rebuilding and major modifications, the 'Duke' returned to main line steam operations in the early 1990s. Complete with its 'Phoenix' plaque, the loco is seen here heading north from Hereford on the third leg (Bristol to Preston) of a UK tour on April 8, 2007.

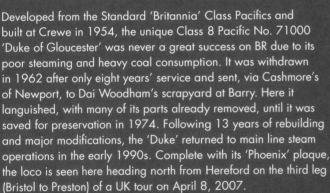

What is amazing is the shortness of life of what were highly successful designs – in some cases only a matter of five years between being built and being withdrawn with many being replaced by untested and unreliable diesel locos. Once again we have Dai Woodham to thank as 38 of these locos were saved from Barry, including the unique BR Standard Class 8P No. 71000 'Duke of Gloucester'. Other stars of preservation include No. 70000 'Britannia', one of the last active steam locos in BR days No. 70013 'Oliver Cromwell', and the last steam loco to be built at Swindon No. 92220 'Evening Star' (which was also the last steam engine built for BR).

Despite the success of most of the BR Standard Class locos there are four classes that have not been preserved. These are the Class 6P5F 'Clan' Pacific, the Class 3 2-6-0, the Class 3 2-6-2 tank and the Class 2 2-6-2 tank (although a replica has been built using parts from a Class 2MT 2-6-0). There are currently plans to build a new 'Clan' Pacific, No. 72010 'Hengist'.

BR Standard Class 5 4-6-0 No. 73096 was built at Derby in 1955 and withdrawn in November 1967. After languishing at Woodham's scrapyard in Barry, the loco (without its tender) was saved for preservation in 1985. A new tender was built and the restored loco was outshopped in BR lined black. It is seen here in mint condition at Ropley on the Mid-Hants Railway on October 30, 1993.

Railway Miscellany

The first railway station to be built inside York's city walls opened in 1841 and remained in use until the present York station was opened in 1877. However, it became a carriage store, as seen here in this 1950s photo, until 1965 when it was largely demolished.

A suburban third-rail electric train service came into service between Newcastle Central and Tynemouth in 1904. Electric parcels car No. E9439E is seen here leaving Newcastle Central on September 14, 1955. The electric trains were withdrawn in 1967 and replaced by diesel multiple units. On the right of the photo is ex-NER 'D20' Class 4-4-0 No. 62383, a member of a long-lived class that was introduced in 1899 with the last withdrawal in 1957.

Class 'A4' Pacific No. 60009 'Union of South Africa' crosses King Edward Bridge in Newcastle with the up 'Jubilee Requiem' on 24 October 1964. Already transferred to Aberdeen Ferryhil (61B) and the last steam loco to be overhauled at Doncaster No. 60009 continued in useful service in Scotland until mid-1966 hauling the 3-hour Glasgow to Aberdeen expresses. This locomotive was built in 1937, withdrawn in June 1966 and subsequently preserved.

With 47 members of this class allocated to York (50A) in 1960, the ex-LNER 'B16' Class 4-6-0s locomotives were a very familiar sight on the route between York and Scarborough. Here, one of the Gresley rebuilds, 'B16/2' No. 61455, hustles a Scarborough to Manchester express through the countryside near Malton in Yorkshire in 1961.

For 77 years the former Stockton & Darlington Railway 0-6-0 'Derwent' was on static display at Darlington Bank Top station. The loco was built in 1845 by William and Alfred Kitching at their Hopetown Works in Darlington and can now be seen at the Darlington Railway Centre and Museum at the historic North Road station.

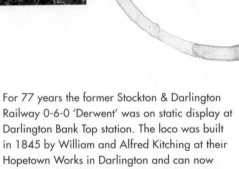

An English Electric Type 5 'Deltic' diesel passes through Manors on the north eastern approaches to Newcastle on August 22, 1961. On the right is green-liveried Bo-Bo electric loco No. 26500 on its way from Trafalgar Yard to Heaton shed (52B). No. 26500 was one of two such locos fitted with both pantograph and third-rail pickup which were built by BT-H and Brush for the North Eastern Railway in 1903-1904 and remained in operation until 1964. No. 26500 is now part of the National Collection and on display at Shildon.

R 29
(1 2) 60532 (2)   30/7/64
(3) 60825   (Tay Bridge)
(4) 70038   com[ ] out of Perth West shed)
(5) 46128 at Perth shed

628
80090	61292	D5308
D2746	60919	Dundee-
64576	60822	Perth.
60532	61403	0359
60528	60818	80123
60973	64558	D5122
64597	65319	70038 P
60979	73145	73148
61278	WEST SHED	D5333
61180	60825	63A
64541	60834	46128 P
64602	D5122	D8033
80124	D2745	D6123
61340	D2709	D2444
61262	D2713	D2412
	D2711	

BRITISH RAILWAYS

SCALE OF MILES

SCOTTISH REGION

First introduced in 1862 the 'Royal Scot' was once the premier express train between Glasgow and London Euston. From the late 1930s the mainstay of motive power for this famous train was provided by LMS Stanier 'Coronation' and 'Princess Royal' Pacifics. Here, watched by a crowd of admirers, 'Coronation' Class 4-6-2 No. 46240 'City of Coventry', resplendent with tartan headboard and allocated to Camden (1B), waits to depart from Central station with the up 'Royal Scot' c.1956. 'City of Coventry' was built at Crewe in 1940 and withdrawn in October 1964.

Glasgow Central

Opened by the Caledonian Railway in August 1879, Glasgow Central became the major city terminus for local trains to Clydeside and the company's southerly route to Edinburgh as well as the important Anglo-Scottish expresses via Carlisle.

Although not as architecturally appealing as the nearby Glasgow & South Western Railway's St Enoch station, Central station during the 1950s and early '60s daily witnessed the humble comings-and-goings of the ex-LMS Fairburn and BR Standard tanks on intensive local services. Central had a much more glitzy side to it than just this in the form of the Anglo-Scottish expresses such as the 'Royal Scot', 'Mid-Day Scot' and 'The Caledonian' as well as overnight sleeper and TPO trains to the south. Stars of this show were primarily the Stanier 'Coronation' Class Pacifics which were ousted in the early '60s by English Electric Type 4 diesels (BR Class 40) and later by the English Electric Type 4 'Hoovers' or what later became BR Class 50. Needless to say these, in turn, were all swept away on electrification of the West Coast Main Line in 1974. Tilting electric multiple units are now the order of the day!

By 1966 the Clydeside suburban electrification wires had reached Glasgow Central and all main line passenger trains from here were now officially diesel-hauled. However, watched by a lone spotter, steam was still in evidence on local Clydeside services and empty coaching stock movements. Here, BR Standard Class 4 2-6-4T No. 80045 is seen waiting to depart on a local Clydeside service in April.

The 17.50 train to Motherwell and Hamilton pulls away from Central station behind Fairburn 2-6-4 tank No. 42126 on July 5, 1961. Allocated to Motherwell (66B) this loco was built at Derby in 1949 and withdrawn in October 1964.

ON SHED

66A Glasgow Polmadie

Allocated to 66A, ex-LMS 'Coronation' 4-6-2 No. 46224 'Princess Alexandra' is seen at rest at its home shed in April 1962. Built at Crewe with a streamlined casing in 1937, this loco was de-streamlined and fitted with smoke deflectors in 1946. After 26 years service hauling heavy expresses on the West Coast Main Line it was withdrawn from Polmadie in October 1963.

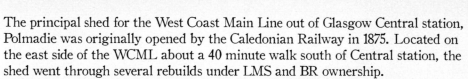

The principal shed for the West Coast Main Line out of Glasgow Central station, Polmadie was originally opened by the Caledonian Railway in 1875. Located on the east side of the WCML about a 40 minute walk south of Central station, the shed went through several rebuilds under LMS and BR ownership.

During the 1950s the shed's allocation of top link locos such as ex-LMS 'Princess' and 'Coronation' Class Pacifics provided motive power for some famous Anglo-Scottish expresses such as 'The Royal Scot', 'The Mid-day Scot' and 'The Caledonian'. Despite the onslaught of dieselisation in other parts of Scotland by the early 1960s, even as late as October 1961 Polmadie had no allocation of the new main line diesels.

Despite the influx of large numbers of the short-lived Clayton Type 1 diesels, Polmadie shed could still muster a good display of steam in 1964. Of interest on a visit to the shed on August 2 were the three Class 'A2' Pacifics (Nos 60524, 60530 and 60535) reallocated there following dieselisation of the ECML, visiting 'A1' Pacific No. 60118 'Archibold Sturrock' and solitary 'Coronation' Class Pacific No. 46255 'City of Hereford'.

With its regimental crest clearly visible, ex-LMS 'Royal Scot' No. 46107 'Argyll & Sutherland Highlander' poses at Polmadie in April 1962. This loco was built in 1927, rebuilt in 1950 and withdrawn at the end of 1962. The name was later carried by 'Deltic' (Class 55) D9021 which was withdrawn in 1981.

Apart from 22 diesel shunters, it was still an all-steam shed with a total allocation of 136 locos representing 18 different classes. Of note were representatives of no less than five former Caledonian Railway classes, five 'Royal Scot' 4-6-0s, nine 'Coronation', three 'Britannia' and five 'Clan' Pacifics. A visit to the shed at the end of March 1964 revealed a large allocation of the extremely short-lived Clayton Type 1 (Class 17) diesels alongside 41 steam locos – stars of the show then were the three ex-LNER 'A2' Pacifics – 60522, 60530 and 60535 – reallocated to Polmadie following dieselisation of the East Coast Main Line. Sadly, by this date there was just one solitary 'Coronation' Pacific (46257 'City of Salford') and one 'Royal Scot' (46155 'The Lancer') on shed.

Polmadie finally closed to steam in May 1967 and a part of it went on to be utilised as a diesel depot.

Another 66A 'Coronation', No. 46230 'Duchess of Buccleuch' was photographed at Polmadie in September 1962. This time looking rather uncared for, this 'Duchess' was built at Crewe without a streamlined casing in 1938 and withdrawn in November 1963. The loco was involved in a nasty derailment at Douglas Park just south of Glasgow on May 26, 1949 hauling the 10.10pm heavily-loaded sleeping car train from Glasgow Central to Euston. The driver overran a home signal set at danger and the loco was derailed on a refuge loop facing point.

The end is nigh – 'A4' Pacific No. 60024 'Kingfisher' reverses slowly out of Buchanan Street after hauling a three-hour express from Aberdeen on August 23, 1966. Allocated to Ferryhill (61B) the 'A4' was one of the last two members of this class (the other being No. 60019 'Bittern') to remain in service until withdrawal two weeks later.

Glasgow Buchanan Street

ONE OF FOUR RAILWAY TERMINI IN GLASGOW, BUCHANAN STREET STATION WAS OPENED IN 1849 AS THE TERMINUS OF THE CALEDONIAN RAILWAY.

Seen here at Buchanan Street on July 26, Peppercorn Class 'A2' Pacific No. 60532 'Blue Peter' was also a regular on the three-hour expresses from Aberdeen in 1966. Allocated to Dundee Tay Bridge shed (62B) until withdrawal at the end of that year, 'Blue Peter' was saved from the cutter's torch by an appeal launched in conjunction with the BBC TV children's programme of the same name.

Prior to closure the station provided services to Edinburgh, Aberdeen via Perth and Forfar, Inverness via Perth, Oban via Stirling and Callander and Dundee via Perth. Although diesels in the shape of Birmingham R. C. & W. Type 2 (Class 26/27) and the unlamented North British Type 2 (Class 21) had started appearing on some services in the early 1960s, Buchanan Street still drew trainspotters from far and wide up to the mid-'60s. The reason for this was the transfer of a number of Gresley 'A4' Pacifics to Aberdeen Ferryhill shed (61B) in 1962 following their displacement by diesels – notably 'Deltics' – on the ECML. Performing their swan song, these magnificent beasts were soon hauling the Buchanan Street to Aberdeen (via Forfar) three-hour expresses, a job they continued to perform very well, along with the occasional 'A2' Pacific, until the Autumn of 1966.

The Scottish Region timetable for Summer 1964 lists four named trains on this 153-mile route: 'The Grampian', 'The Bon Accord', 'The Granite City' and 'The St Mungo'. Until 1963 the Oban via Callander trains were usually hauled by 'Black Five' 4-6-0s but these were replaced by double-headed North British Type 2s until a landslip brought about the early closure of the Dunblane to Crianlarich section on September 27, 1965. After this date Oban trains were diverted to run from Queen Street over the West Highland Line via Crianlarich. However, 'Black Fives' and BR Standard Class 5 4-6-0s could still be seen at work on trains from Buchanan Street to Perth, Stirling and Dundee up until the end. The station closed on November 7, 1966 and has since been demolished.

Ex-LMS Stanier Class 5 4-6-0 No. 44973 waits to depart from Queen Street with a train for Fort William in April 1957. This photo clearly shows the operational problems caused by long trains waiting in the station's short platforms. Built at Crewe in 1946, the 'Black Five' spent some time allocated to Fort William shed (63B), but after dieselisation of the West Highland line ended up at Carstairs (66E), from where it was withdrawn in September 1965.

Glasgow Queen Street

OPENED IN 1842 BY THE EDINBURGH & GLASGOW RAILWAY, QUEEN STREET HIGH LEVEL STATION BECAME THE GLASGOW TERMINUS OF THE NORTH BRITISH RAILWAY (LATER THE LNER).

Glasgow Queen Street provided services to Edinburgh Waverley, Fife and, from August 1894, on the newly-opened West Highland line to Fort William and Mallaig. Suburban services to the east and west called at Queen Street Low Level station. With its rather cramped layout and overall glazed arched roof, High Level station was approached through a tunnel down a 1 in 42 incline. Until 1909 departing trains were hauled by a powerful winch up the incline as far as Cowlairs. After this date trains were banked in the rear by tank locos until the end of steam in 1963 when modern diesels were able to haul their trains up the incline unassisted.

Along with Peppercorn Class A1 Pacifics at the head of two named trains - 'The North Briton' to Leeds City and 'The Queen of Scots Pullman' to King's Cross (both via Edinburgh Waverley), the West Highland Line departures were the highlight of a day's trainspotting at Queen Street. Motive power (often double-headed), supplied by Eastfield depot (65A) for these trains ranged from the ex-NBR 'D34' 4-4-0s (known as 'Glens') and ex-Great Northern Railway 'K2' 2-6-0s (known as 'Lochs') to the ex-LNER 'K4' 2-6-0s and the more modern 'K1' 2-6-0s, ex-LMS 'Black Fives' and BR Standard Class 5 4-6-0s. However, by 1960, with the introduction of the Birmingham R. C. & W. Type 2 (Class 27) and North British Type 2 (Class 21) diesels already underway, the writing was on the wall for steam services out of Queen Street. It became the first terminus in Glasgow to see the end of steam workings and, in November 1966, also took over the services that formerly terminated at the neighbouring Buchanan Street station.

Fitted with small snow ploughs for working on the West Highland line, Birmingham Railway Carriage & Wagon Co. diesel No. 26026 stands in Queen Street station on March 6, 1982. A total of 47 of these locos were built at the company's works at Smethwick between 1958 and 1959. The last members of this class were withdrawn in 1993 and 13 have since been preserved.

ON SHED

Glasgow Eastfield

65 A

Minus its shed code plate, Thompson Class 'A2/3' 4-6-2 No. 60512 'Steady Aim' languishes inside Eastfield shed on March 29, 1964. Built at Doncaster in 1946 this loco was withdrawn from Polmadie (66A) in June 1965.

The principal engine shed for the North British Railway in Glasgow, Eastfield was a large 14-road through shed which opened in 1904 and was located on the east side of the line about a 20-minute walk north of Cowlairs station.

With dieselisation of the West Highland Line already well underway, by October 1961 Eastfield had already lost many of its steam star performers for that scenic route such as the 'D34' 4-4-0s ('Glens'), 'K2' 2-6-0s ('Lochs') and 'K4' 2-6-0s. By that date they had been replaced by 11 Birmingham R. C. & W. Type 2s (Class 27) and 38 of the unsuccessful and short-lived North British Type 2s (Class 21) in addition to 25 English Electric Type 1 (Class 20) and 25 diesel shunters.

The shed's steam allocation then totalled 58, made up of nine different classes including examples of five ex-NBR types – 'D94' 4-4-0 (the last remaining 'Glen'), 'J37' 0-6-0, 'J36' 0-6-0 (1888 vintage), 'J83' 0-6-0 and 'N15' 0-6-2 tanks (used as Cowlairs bankers out of Queen Street station). Other classes included ten 'Black Five', seven 'B1' 4-6-0s and four BR Standard Class 5 4-6-0s. A visit to the shed in March 1964 revealed a total of 111 locomotives of which only 40 were steam.

Eastfield shed finally closed to steam in November 1966 and was replaced by a diesel depot which itself was closed in 1992. The only sub-shed was at Arrochar on the West Highland Line. It closed in October 1959.

An interesting line-up at Eastfield on May 19, 1964. From left to right: 'A4' Class 4-6-2 No. 60010 'Dominion of Canada' (built in 1937, withdrawn from Ferryhill (61B) in May 1965 and since preserved as a static exhibit in Canada); ex-LMS Hughes 'Crab' 2-6-0 No. 42803 visiting from Ayr (67C) (built at Crewe in 1928 and withdrawn in December 1966); ex-LMS rebuilt 'Patriot' Class 4-6-0 No. 45512 'Bunsen' minus centre driving wheel and linkages (built at Crewe in 1932, rebuilt in 1948 and withdrawn in March 1965).

By 1964 Eastfield shed was being swamped by diesels. In among the numerous diesel shunters and English Electric Type 1 diesels were six BR Standard Class 5 4-6-0s of which four can be seen listed here.

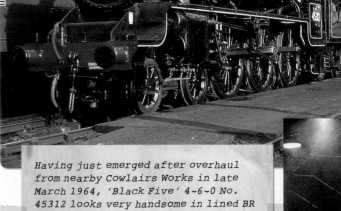

Having just emerged after overhaul from nearby Cowlairs Works in late March 1964, 'Black Five' 4-6-0 No. 45312 looks very handsome in lined BR black livery. One of a batch built by Armstrong Whitworth in 1937 this loco survived until the very last months of steam on BR being withdrawn from Bolton shed (26C) in June 1968. Eighteen members of this class have since been preserved.

Although Eastfield closed to steam in 1966, it continued as a diesel depot until 1992. Here one of the named Scottish Class '37's No. 37043 'Loch Lomond' stands inside the depot on March 6, 1982.

Glasgow St Enoch

**WITH ITS ARCHED WROUGHT IRON AND GLAZED ROOF,
GLASGOW ST ENOCH WAS BY FAR THE MOST IMPRESSIVE
TERMINUS STATION IN THE CITY.**

Opened in May 1876, it later became the headquarters of the Glasgow & South Western Railway and the starting point for services to Renfrewshire, Ayrshire and Dumfriesshire and Stranraer (for Northern Ireland), as well as Anglo-Scottish services via Dumfries, Carlisle and the Midland Railway route to Leeds and London St Pancras via the Settle & Carlisle route.

The principal named train was the 'Thames-Clyde Express' which, in the summer of 1964, took 8 hours 50 minutes on its journey from St Pancras. Haulage of this train was normally undertaken by one of Stanier's ex-LMS 'Jubilee' Class 4-6-0s until the early '60s when 'Peak' (Class 45/45) diesels took over. Sadly, St Enoch was closed on June 27, 1966 and has since been demolished – what a waste! Surviving services were transferred to Central station.

(opposite) Although closed a month before to passenger services, St Enoch continued to be used for a while by mail and parcels trains. Here, BR Standard Class 4 2-6-0 No. 76093, allocated to Corkerhill (67A), carries out station pilot duties at Platform 10 of St Enoch on July 27, 1966.

A busy scene at St Enoch in the mid-1950s with 'Black Five' 4-6-0 No. 44856 waiting to depart with its train of 'blood and custard' coaches for Dumfries and Carlisle. Built at Crewe in 1944 this loco was withdrawn in February 1967.

St Enoch's fabulous arched glass roof can be seen in its full glory here in this photo taken just prior to closure in 1966. A couple of DMUs wait in the central platforms with services to Ayrshire while a BR Sulzer Type 4 (later Class 45) waits at the head of an express for the south via Dumfries and Carlisle. This scene has now completely disappeared.

ON SHED

A grandstand view of Corkerhill taken on September 1, 1954. Ex-LMS locos predominate, notably the three 4P Compound 4-4-0s in the front row. Of these two, Nos 41133 and 41142, are identifiable with an ex-Caledonian Railway Class '29' 0-6-0 tank sandwiched between them. No. 41133 was built at Horwich Works in 1926 and was withdrawn from Corkerhill at the end of September 1954. No 41142 was built by the North British Locomotive Company in 1925 and withdrawn from Corkerhill in July 1956.

Glasgow Corkerhill • 67 • A

Built in what was then a rural location by the Glasgow & South Western Railway, Corkerhill shed opened in 1896. It was located on the south side of the line between St Enoch and Paisley Canal and was only a five-minute walk east from Corkerhill station. At the same time the G&SWR also built an adjacent village to house the 112 employees of the shed and their families.

Rebuilt by BR in 1954, the six-road through shed provided motive power for main line services on former G&SWR routes from Glasgow St Enoch. These included services to Renfrewshire, Ayrshire and Dumfriesshire and Stranraer (for Northern Ireland) as well as Anglo-Scottish expresses (such as 'The Thames-Clyde Express') via Dumfries, Carlisle and the Midland Railway route to Leeds and London St Pancras via the Settle & Carlisle route. Corkerhill's October 1961 allocation totalled 81 locos of which 71 were steam and contained a large percentage of BR Standard types. Of note was a solitary ex-LMS 2P 4-4-0, 14 'Black Five', ten 'Jubilee' and ten BR Standard Class 5 4-6-0s, eight BR Standard Class 4 2-6-0s and 19 BR Standard Class 4 2-6-4 tanks.

A visit to Corkerhill was made on August 5, 1964. The visit recorded 23 locos, of which only one was a diesel. Class 'A2' No. 60535 'Hornets Beauty' seems to have strayed over from its home shed of Polmadie.

On its way back home to Bolton after overhaul at Cowlairs Works 'Black Five' 4-6-0 No. 45312 was spotted at Corkerhill on March 29, 1964. One of a batch built by Armstrong Whitworth in 1937 this loco survived until the very last months of steam on BR, being withdrawn from Bolton shed (26C) in June 1968.

Several 'Royal Scot' 4-6-0s, minus name and numberplates, were spotted stored out of use at Corkerhill during a visit on March 29, 1964. Here, No. 46104 'Scottish Borderer', built in 1927 and rebuilt in 1946, looks decidedly the worse for wear 15 months after withdrawal.

Keeping No. 46104 company on 'death row' at Corkerhill was fellow class member No. 46102 'Black Watch', which had also been withdrawn 15 months earlier. The name (with the prefix 'The') was later given to 'Deltic' (Class 55) D9013 in January 1963.

A visit to the shed in late March 1964 revealed 44 steam locomotives plus six diesel shunters and (a sign of the times!) two 'Peak' diesels (Class 45) – D14 and D18. Included in the steam tally were three 'Royal Scots' and a 'Jubilee'. Later that year, in early August 1964, another visit revealed a total of only 23 locomotives - all steam except for one diesel shunter – which included visiting 'A2' Pacific No. 60535 'Hornets Beauty'.

St Enoch closed in June 1966 and all former G&SWR services were transferred to Central station. Corkerhill closed to steam in May 1967 but continued in use as a diesel depot.

Fitted with small snowplough and single-line token exchanger, 'Black Five' 4-6-0 No. 45366 was also seen at the shed on March 29, 1964. Allocated to 67A, this loco was built by Armstrong Whitworth in 1937 and withdrawn one month after this photo was taken.

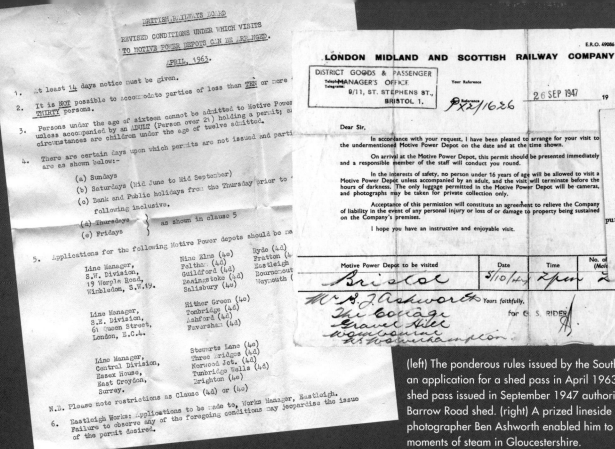

(left) The ponderous rules issued by the Southern Region following an application for a shed pass in April 1963. (above) An LMS shed pass issued in September 1947 authorising a visit to Bristol Barrow Road shed. (right) A prized lineside pass issued to railway photographer Ben Ashworth enabled him to record the final moments of steam in Gloucestershire.

Shed & Works Passes

DURING THE 1950s AND EARLY '60s IT WAS CONSIDERED RATHER A 'CISSY' THING TO APPLY FOR A PERMIT TO VISIT AN ENGINE SHED!

Ex-North British Railway Class 'J37' 0-6-0 No. 64632 was spotted at the coaling plant during a Glasgow 'shed bash' on March 29, 1964. Built in 1921, No. 64632 was an Eastfield loco for many years but finally ended its days at Thornton Junction in 1965.

'Shed bashing', as it was known, was a term used by trainspotters to describe their frenetic trips to as many engine sheds (usually without permits) as was possible in one day.

Without an official permit, some sheds were easier to visit than others, depending on the friendliness of the shed foreman or the deviousness of the trainspotter. All manner of tricks were employed to gain access to the hallowed ground and once inside it was often a game of cat and mouse before we were eventually thrown out. However, many visits were official and highly organised by the myriad railway societies up and down the country, whose members were whisked from shed to shed by the coach load. It was a sad fact that many of these trips had to be made by road but (a) the trips were usually held on Sundays when the work force was at home digging the garden or out ferreting. The sheds were full and, because it was the Sabbath, there was only a limited or non-existent train service to the nearest station, and (b) there was no other practical way to visit such a large number of sheds as unfortunately many of them were located on out-of-the-way goods-only lines.

Naturally, the proper paperwork had been done by the Society and the necessary permits obtained. Annual open days at Crewe, Derby and Swindon for instance also drew large crowds of spotters. To accommodate the young spotter, Swindon Works also allowed visits without a permit on a Wednesday afternoon during the school holidays.

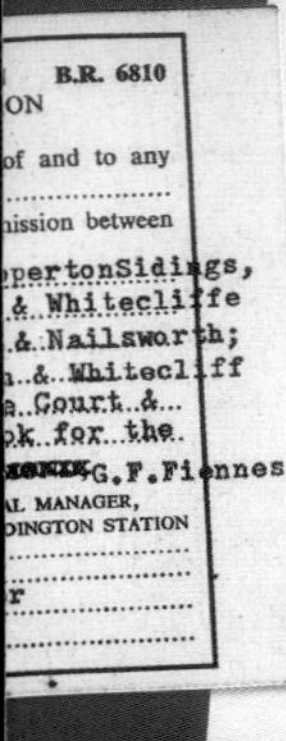

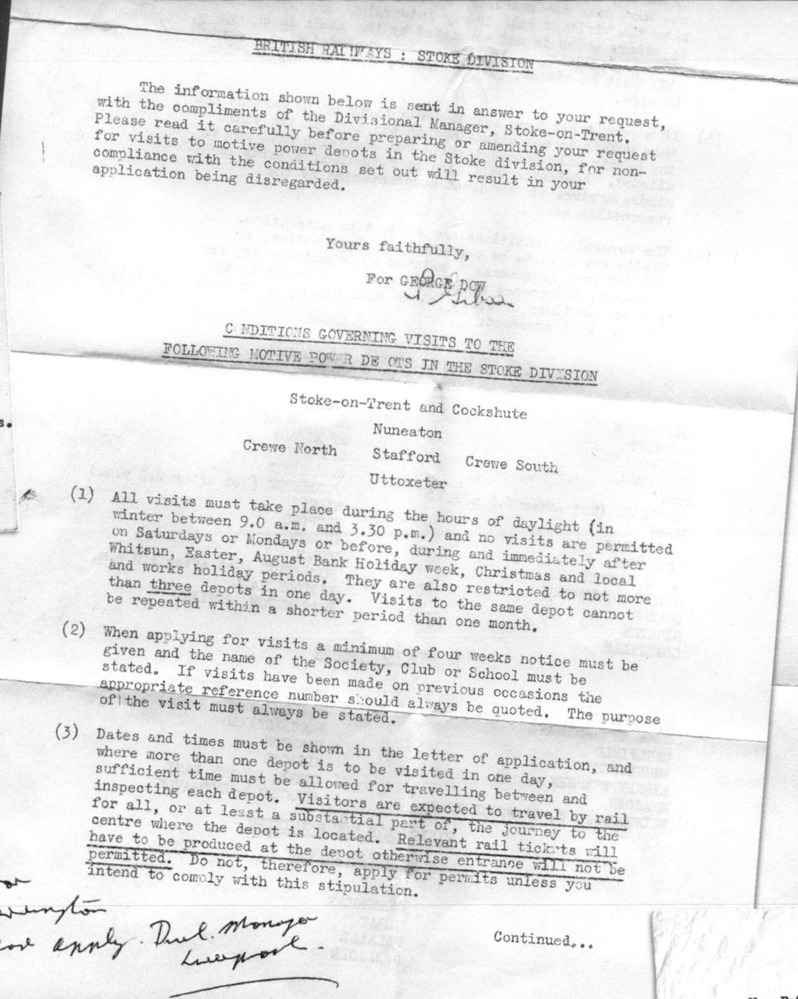

BRITISH RAILWAYS : STOKE DIVISION

The information shown below is sent in answer to your request, with the compliments of the Divisional Manager, Stoke-on-Trent. Please read it carefully before preparing or amending your request for visits to motive power depots in the Stoke division, for non-compliance with the conditions set out will result in your application being disregarded.

Yours faithfully,

For GEORGE DOW

CONDITIONS GOVERNING VISITS TO THE
FOLLOWING MOTIVE POWER DEPOTS IN THE STOKE DIVISION

Stoke-on-Trent and Cockshute

Nuneaton

Crewe North   Stafford   Crewe South

Uttoxeter

(1) All visits must take place during the hours of daylight (in winter between 9.0 a.m. and 3.30 p.m.) and no visits are permitted on Saturdays or Mondays or before, during and immediately after Whitsun, Easter, August Bank Holiday week, Christmas and local and works holiday periods. They are also restricted to not more than three depots in one day. Visits to the same depot cannot be repeated within a shorter period than one month.

(2) When applying for visits a minimum of four weeks notice must be given and the name of the Society, Club or School must be stated. If visits have been made on previous occasions the appropriate reference number should always be quoted. The purpose of the visit must always be stated.

(3) Dates and times must be shown in the letter of application, and where more than one depot is to be visited in one day, sufficient time must be allowed for travelling between and inspecting each depot. Visitors are expected to travel by rail for all, or at least a substantial part of, the journey to the centre where the depot is located. Relevant rail tickets will have to be produced at the depot otherwise entrance will not be permitted. Do not, therefore, apply for permits unless you intend to comply with this stipulation.

For Warrington
Please apply. Dist. Manager
Liverpool.

Continued...

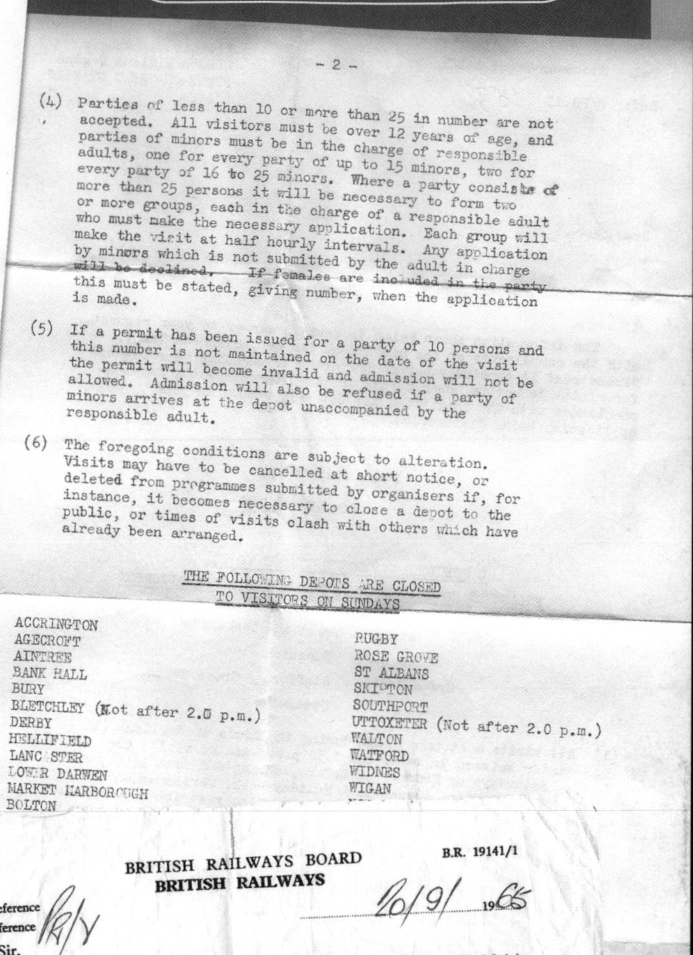

- 2 -

(4) Parties of less than 10 or more than 25 in number are not accepted. All visitors must be over 12 years of age, and parties of minors must be in the charge of responsible adults, one for every party of up to 15 minors, two for every party of 16 to 25 minors. Where a party consists of more than 25 persons it will be necessary to form two or more groups, each in the charge of a responsible adult who must make the necessary application. Each group will make the visit at half hourly intervals. Any application by minors which is not submitted by the adult in charge will be declined. If females are included in the party this must be stated, giving number, when the application is made.

(5) If a permit has been issued for a party of 10 persons and this number is not maintained on the date of the visit the permit will become invalid and admission will not be allowed. Admission will also be refused if a party of minors arrives at the depot unaccompanied by the responsible adult.

(6) The foregoing conditions are subject to alteration. Visits may have to be cancelled at short notice, or deleted from programmes submitted by organisers if, for instance, it becomes necessary to close a depot to the public, or times of visits clash with others which have already been arranged.

THE FOLLOWING DEPOTS ARE CLOSED
TO VISITORS ON SUNDAYS

ACCRINGTON	RUGBY
AGECROFT	ROSE GROVE
AINTREE	ST ALBANS
BANK HALL	SKIPTON
BURY	SOUTHPORT
BLETCHLEY (Not after 2.0 p.m.)	UTTOXETER (Not after 2.0 p.m.)
DERBY	WALTON
HELLIFIELD	WATFORD
LANCASTER	WIDNES
LOWER DARWEN	WIGAN
MARKET HARBOROUGH	
BOLTON	

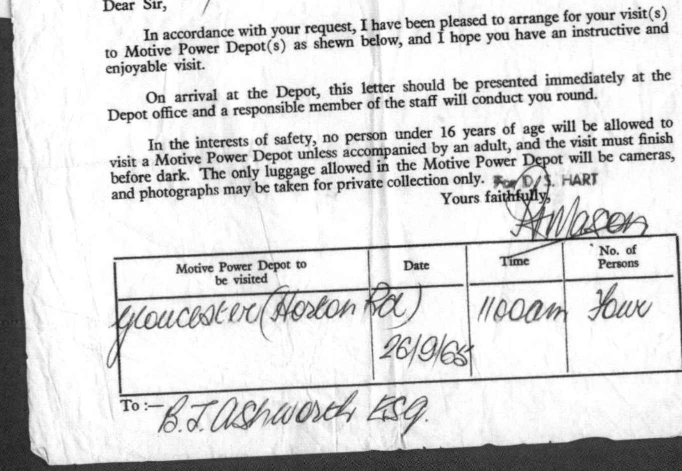

B.R. 6810

...of and to any
...mission between
...perton Sidings,
... & Whitecliffe
...& Nailsworth;
...Court &
...ck for the
...G.F.Fiennes.
AL MANAGER,
...DINGTON STATION

BRITISH RAILWAYS BOARD
BRITISH RAILWAYS

B.R. 19141/1

Your Reference R/Y
Our Reference R/Y
26/9/ 1965

Dear Sir,

In accordance with your request, I have been pleased to arrange for your visit(s) to Motive Power Depot(s) as shewn below, and I hope you have an instructive and enjoyable visit.

On arrival at the Depot, this letter should be presented immediately at the Depot office and a responsible member of the staff will conduct you round.

In the interests of safety, no person under 16 years of age will be allowed to visit a Motive Power Depot unless accompanied by an adult, and the visit must finish before dark. The only luggage allowed in the Motive Power Depot will be cameras, and photographs may be taken for private collection only. For D.S. HART

Yours faithfully,

Motive Power Depot to be visited	Date	Time	No. of Persons
Gloucester (Horton Rd)	26/9/65	11.00am	Four

To:- B.J. Ashworth, ESG.

One memorable 'shed bash' that comes to mind was organised like a military campaign. On April 7, 1963 (a Sunday), the Warwickshire Railway Society took a coachload of members to nearly every shed in South Wales. Joining the coach on its way south in Gloucester at around 5.30am, we were soon traipsing round Lydney (85B sub-shed) before arriving at our next destination, Severn Tunnel Junction (86E) at 7am. During that long day we visited a total of 21 sheds and sub-sheds plus the Barry dump – Cardiff Cathays (88M) was also described in my notebook as a dump! In all we spotted 618 steam locos and only 43 diesels (mainly shunters). Despite the fact that we inexplicably didn't visit Abercynon (88E), it was an exhilarating and very profitable day. Just in time as well, as all of the steam sheds in South Wales had closed by 1965.

A very different 'shed bash' occurred a year later over the weekend of March 28/29, 1964. It may well have also been organised by the Warwickshire Railway Society, when a whole trainload of spotters departed from Birmingham New Street on the evening of the 28th behind No. 46256 'Sir William A. Stanier F.R.S.' – destination Glasgow! Arriving in Glasgow at the crack of dawn on the 29th, several hundred of us were bundled into a fleet of coaches which trundled from shed to shed until we reached Edinburgh Waverley later in the evening. Departure from Waverley was at 10.35pm with arrival at Birmingham New Street at 6am on the 30th. It was my first trip to Scotland and, by the end of the weekend, my notebook was filled to bursting with hundreds of 'foreign' locos. In all we visited ten sheds in the Glasgow and Edinburgh area and spotted a grand total of 349 steam locos and 312 diesels.

(top left) The Stoke Division of the LMR issued detailed conditions for visits to their engine sheds, including the stipulation that visitors must travel by rail! No wonder so many trainspotters 'bunked' sheds without permission. (top right) Prior notification also had to be given if any females wished to travel with the party. Why? (above) A shed pass for Gloucester Horton road shed for a visit on September 26, 1965. Three months later the shed closed to steam. Of interest is the stipulation that any photographs taken were for private collection only.

Day Tripper

Scotland, summer of '64

By 1964 steam was well on the way out in many regions of British Railways. Fortunately, many parts of Scotland held on for a few more years, so making a trip across the border was very worthwhile. I was based in Gourock during late July and early August and from there my trainspotting friend and I sallied forth armed with our Freedom of Scotland Silver tickets (costing 6 guineas). The aim was to travel on as many lines and visit as many sheds in Scotland as possible – this we achieved with resounding success.

On my return home it took several days to trawl through my notebook and then underline 723 cops in my Ian Allan ABC Combined Volume!

Carstairs shed (66E) was visited on July 29. Stars of the show on that day were 'A2/3' Pacific No. 60512 'Steady Aim', 'Royal Scot' 4-6-0 No. 46140 'The King's Royal Rifle Corps' and ex-Caledonian railway 4-4-0 No. 54463.

Coal trains from the Ayrshire coalfields around Dalmellington were usually headed by ex-LMS Hughes/Fowler '6P5F' 'Crab' 2-6-0 locos. No. 42789 was one of 17 of these powerful locos seen at Ayr shed (67C) on July 28, 1964.

July 27 A great day out to Inverness travelling via Glasgow Buchanan St. and Perth. Highlights included: seeing two 'A4s', Nos 60027 'Merlin' and 60034 'Lord Farringdon', on the 3-hour Glasgow to Aberdeen expresses; doubleheading by D5327 and D5127 on a 14-coach train to Inverness; Inverness shed (60A) which by then was totally dieselised and return to Perth behind D5115 and D5124 on a 16-coach train; last leg back to Gourock behind Fairburn 2-6-4 tank No. 42264.

July 28 Into Glasgow Central behind No. 42266; D163 from St Enoch to Dumfries; Dumfries shed (67E) including 'Clan' No.

72009 'Clan Stewart'; Dumfries to Stranraer behind No. 45463; Stranraer shed (67F); Stranraer to Ayr by dmu; Ayr shed (67C) with loads of 'Crabs'.

July 29 Glasgow Central to Carstairs behind D234; Carstairs shed (66E); Carstairs to Carlisle behind D293; Carlisle Kingmoor shed (12A); Carlisle Upperby shed (12B); Carlisle to Edinburgh via Waverley Route behind D24; St Margarets shed (64A); Haymarket shed (64B); Edinburgh Princes St. to Glasgow by dmu.

July 30 Glasgow Queen St. to Haymarket by dmu; Haymarket to Dunfermline by dmu; Dunfermline

CARSTAIR SHED
CCE

D8124	80116	45492	✗✗
42259	70007	44700 B	✗✓✓
42241	D317	42688	✗✓✗
GOURCK-CARSTAIRS 29/7/64	42245	44454	
8012d	D337	45478	✗✗
42266 Gourock to Glasgow	80002	42058	✗✗
73075	D3906	45090	✗✗
42274	D313	42129	✗✗
D4546	D293	42056	✓✓
73061	D3917	60512 P	✗✗
80115	45012 B	46140 P	✓✗
80127	D229	4495?	✗✗
80108	D815	44956 B	✗✗
42264	42695	45173 B	✗✗
D3907	44973	44793 B	✗✗
42259	D2410	44701 B	✗✗
42143	D3285	45172 B	✗✗
42241 Glasgow to Glasgow	D3384	54463 P	✗✗
D234 Carstairs	44952 B	80074	✓✓

British Railways

HERE THERE EVERYWHERE

by train with a Freedom of Scotland ticket

Issued any day March 1 to October 31·1964

"FREEDOM OF SCOTLAND" TICKETS

"FREEDOM OF SCOTLAND" tickets are now available for Seven or Fourteen consecutive days unlimited travel anywhere in Scotland, (also including Berwick-upon-Tweed and Carlisle) where there is a railway service, and on all steamer services operated by the Caledonian Steam Packet Company on the Firth of Clyde and Loch Lomond (where service in operation)

Issued any day during the period

1st March to 31st October

The "SILVER" ticket is valid for seven consecutive days:

SECOND **£6-6-0** CLASS

(FIRST CLASS £9-9-0)

The "GOLD" ticket is valid for fourteen consecutive days:

£10-10-0 CLASS

(FIRST CLASS £15-15-0)

FOR FAMILIES TRAVELLING TOGETHER travelling together, with the "SILVER" ticket ONLY, the cost is (2nd class) and £7-17-6 (1st class). The minimum reduced charge is ONE adult and ONE child

RS AND UNDER 14 YEARS ARE CHARGED HALF THE

Ask for folder at any British Railways Station, Accredited Agency or by post from the Commercial Services Manager, (Scottish Region), Blythswood House, 200 West Regent Street, Glasgow, C.2

60825

45309	65A	80056
D8512	D8103	80027
70003	D2763	D6135
DAWSHOLM 65D	64592	D6110
42195	80063	D6128
42197	D6131	D8074
42131	60846	D3211
76046	60027	D6126
42201	D8013	D6134
78051	D2770	D2765
76102	D2771	D2760
76100	D8009	D2762
76103	D6132	42269
123	D5349	61245
103	D8111	61140
49	D8082	73078
76074	D361	76045
256	D6109	48292
76101	D5365	43024
54348	42194	73105

Before becoming static museum exhibits the four preserved Scottish steam locos were kept at Dawsholm shed for a while. Ex-Great North of Scotland Railway 4-4-0 No. 49 'Gordon Highlander' looked in fine fettle at the shed on August 5.

Noted on the trip back from Carlisle on August 1, the down 'Royal Scot' was hauled by a filthy Britannia Class 4-6-2 No. 70002 'Geoffrey Chaucer', deputising for a failed English Electric Type 4 at Carlisle, on the final leg of its journey to Glasgow Central. It left Carlisle 26 minutes late and achieved a top speed of 72 mph through Crawford and Abington before arriving at Glasgow an hour late!

The four Scottish preserved steam locos were spotted at Dawsholm shed (65D) on August 5: Caledonian Railway 4-2-2 No. 123; Highland Railway 4-6-0 'Jones Goods' No. 103; Great North of Scotland Railway 4-4-0 No. 49 'Gordon Highlander; North British Railway 4-4-0 No. 256 'Glen Douglas'. The next shed on the list that day, Eastfield (65A) revealed 'A4' Pacific No. 60027 'Merlin' lurking among the shed's many diesels.

shed (62C); Dunfermline to Thornton Junction by dmu; Thornton Junction shed (62A); Thornton Junction to Dundee; Tay Bridge shed (62B) and Dundee West shed; Dundee to Perth behind D5122; Perth shed (63A); Perth to Buchanan St. behind No. 73149.

July 31 Gourock to Glasgow Central behind No. 42216; Buchanan St. to Aberdeen behind D5368; Kittybrewster shed (61A); Ferryhill shed (61B); Aberdeen to Buchanan St. behind No. 60019 'Bittern'; Glasgow Central to Gourock behind No. 80110.

August 1 Gourock to Glasgow behind No. 80120; St Enoch to Carlisle behind D87; Carlisle station, Upperby shed (12B); Carlisle to Glasgow behind No. 70002 'Geoffrey Chaucer'.

Our Freedom of Scotland ticket had now run out so we then concentrated on local visits.

August 2 Polmadie shed (66A); Queen St. to Edinburgh by dmu; Dalry Road shed (64C); Haymarket shed (64B); St Margarets shed (64A).

August 5 Dawsholm shed (65D); Eastfield shed (65A); St Rollox shed (65B); Corkerhill shed (67A); Motherwell shed (66B); Glasgow to Gourock behind No. 73061.

August 6 Ardrossan shed (67D); Hurlford shed (67B).

45055	45286	42703
44944	45256	44730
46499	42791	60931
44901	D5108	46255
45736	48742	42874
43045	92249	12085
47614	46426	70002
43981	D214	45742
D525	D6795	45061
D234	D5281	42125
45584	44669	42214
45588	D374	45478
43139	D375	46128
D5180	45295	45705
D6787	44727	45013
45429	45105	60535
44878	42948	72007
45141	48302	44883
44723	45431	70038
44730	48157	D8513
13M	7D	

(opposite) Two stored 'V2' 2-6-2 locos, Nos. 60825 and 60834 were spotted at Dundee West shed on July 30. The shed had closed to steam in 1958 and by 1964 was in use as a diesel depot.

'Jubilee' Class 4-6-0 No. 45574 'India' was spotted at Hurlford shed (67B) on August 6 with its motion removed. Fellow 'Jubilee' No. 45666 'Cornwallis' was also on shed that day.

225

SCOTTISH REGION

Edinburgh Princes Street

With its two city-centre stations, four engine sheds and two sub-sheds, Edinburgh was well-worth visiting for a trainspotting bash in the early 1960s. The two stations, Waverley and Princes Street, were only a short distance apart along Princes Street, but there the similarity ends.

Originally opened in 1870, Princes Street station was the Edinburgh terminus of the Caledonian Railway. By 1893 it had been rebuilt and enlarged as a grand Victorian station with seven platforms and an adjoining hotel. For years it provided long-distance services to London via Carstairs (also served by local services until 1964) and the West Coast Main Line and local services to the north and west of the city and to Glasgow via Shotts. Sleeper trains also departed from Princes Street every evening – although by Summer 1964 this was down to just one with portions for Birmingham, Liverpool (Lime Street) and Manchester (Exchange) departing at 23.30 on most nights.

Motive power as far as Carstairs was normally provided by ex-LMS locos such as 'Black Five' 4-6-0s from nearby Dalry Road shed (64C). Services from Princes Street were gradually run down during the early 1960s and it was closed in 1965. Sadly this grand Victorian edifice was demolished but travellers can still enjoy the Caledonian Railway's grand hotel now renamed Caledonian Hilton.

In winter 1963 a neglected looking 'Coronation' Class 4-6-2 pulls into Princes Street at the head of a lengthy rugby special from Wales for the February 2 international at Murrayfield stadium. Wales won 6-0, their only victory in that year's Five Nations Championship, in which they collected the 'wooden spoon'.

Princes Street station on October 24, 1964 – in the middle distance two Stanier Black 5s sit at the head of the 10.10 express to Birmingham, while in the foreground a driver walks past the train engine for the 09.30 Edinburgh to Manchester Victoria.

(below) Stanier 'Black Five' 4-6-0 No. 45127 eases empty coaching stock away from Platform 1 at Princes Street station on November 2, 1964. In the foreground Fairburn 2-6-4 tank No. 42058 waits by the water column. Ten months later the former Caledonian Railway terminus was closed completely, with all services diverted to the through (former North British Railway) station at Waverley. The 'Black Five' was withdrawn from Dundee Tay Bridge (62B) in November 1966, while the Fairburn tank was withdrawn from Carstairs shed (64D) in August 1966.

Edinburgh Waverley

JUST A SHORT DISTANCE DOWN PRINCES STREET IS THE SECOND LARGEST STATION IN THE UK - EDINBURGH WAVERLEY. LOCATED IN A VALLEY FORMED BY A DRAINED LOCH, THE STATION WAS BUILT BY THE NORTH BRITISH RAILWAY IN 1866 ON THE SITE OF THREE SMALLER STATIONS. IT WAS ENLARGED AFTER THE OPENING OF THE FORTH BRIDGE AND REBUILT AS A 19-PLATFORM TERMINUS AND THROUGH STATION IN 1902.

Waverley has always been a popular station with railway photographers due to the panoramic view of it afforded from North Bridge. It was also popular with trainspotters because of the wide variety of ex-LNER locos to be seen and the diverse destinations served. These ranged from trains to Glasgow Queen Street including the luxury 'Queen of Scots Pullman' and Gresley 'A4' Pacifics from Haymarket shed on romantically named East Coast Main Line expresses such as 'The Flying Scotsman', 'The Elizabethan' and 'The Talisman', to 'A1' and 'A2' Pacifics on trains to Dundee and Aberdeen and 'A3' Pacifics on Waverley Route trains, such as 'The Waverley' to London St Pancras, via Carlisle.

Allocated to Heaton (52B) 'A3' Class 4-6-2 No. 60083 'Sir Hugo' stands in Waverley at the head of a sleeping car train destined for King's Cross on March 29, 1964. This loco was originally built by the LNER as an 'A1' Pacific in 1924, rebuilt as an 'A3' in 1941 and withdrawn just over a month after photographed here.

(opposite) A panoramic view of Waverley in August 1958 that is certain to please both the train and bus spotter.

In the final year of operation of this famous train, 'A4' Pacific No. 60014 'Silver Link' leaves Waverley with the up 'Elizabethan' non-stop express to King's Cross on August 20, 1961. Built in 1935, this loco was the first of its class and was withdrawn from King's Cross shed (34A) at the end of 1962. Some 'A4s' were fitted with corridor tenders to enable a crew-change on this non-stop service.

However, by 1963 Haymarket shed had become a diesel depot and ECML expresses were headed by English Electric Type 4 (Class 40) or 'Deltic' diesels (Class 55) from the nearby Haymarket shed (64B), Waverley Route trains were headed by 'Peaks' (Class 45/46) and services to the north were often in the hands of Birmingham R. C. & W. Type 2 diesels (Class 27). Steam became rarer and rarer until May 1967 when the remaining steam shed in Edinburgh, St Margarets (64B), was closed. Amidst much public consternation, the Waverley Route closed in 1969.

HST sets replaced the 'Deltics' in the late 1970s and these, in turn, were superseded by InterCity 225 trains when electrification of the ECML to King's Cross was completed in 1990.

During the final months of steam at Waverley, 'Black Five' No. 44954, allocated to Carstairs shed (66E), gets ready to depart with a parcels train on July 29, 1966. This loco was built at Horwich in 1946 and withdrawn at the end of September 1966.

ON SHED

64 A

Edinburgh St Margarets

With Birmingham R. C. & W. Co Type 2 diesel D5304 in the background, local boy ex-LMS 'Black Five' 4-6-0 No. 45162 and visiting ex-LNER Class 'V2' 2-6-2 No. 60836 make a fine sight outside St Margarets on 24 April, 1966. The 'Black Five' was built by Armstrong Whitworth in 1935 and withdrawn from St Margarets in November 1966. The 'V2' was built at Darlington in 1938 and withdrawn from Dundee Tay Bridge (62B) at the end of 1966.

A dangerous shed to visit, as it was located on both sides of the main line about 1½ miles east of Waverley station. The original round house at St Margarets was built on the north side of the line by the North British Railway in 1846. Part of the old building was later used for the stabling of smaller steam locomotives.

Although the shed foreman's office was on the north side, the main shed, opened by the NBR in 1866, was located on the south side of the line and using the boarded crossing over the main line could be a perilous matter. Even in October 1961 the rather antiquated and run down St Margarets had a large allocation of mixed-traffic, freight and shunting steam locos on the south site while there were 44 diesel shunters stabled on the north site. The steam tally totalled 134 locos with representatives from 12 different classes including six classes of vintage North British Railway locos. The oldest of these were the seven 'J36' 0-6-0s dating from 1888 including one named example (65224 'Mons'). Other NBR types were 'J35', 'J37', 'J88', 'J83', and 'N15'. Ex-LNER mixed traffic locos totalled 52

Built by BR at Doncaster in 1948, Peppercorn Class 'A2' Pacific No. 60534 'Irish Elegance' simmers away nicely in the yard at Edinburgh St Margarets in August 1962 just four months before her final withdrawal from service in December of that year.

Gresley's 'A3's were every bit as graceful as the famous racehorses they were named after, and their scintillating performances over the East Coast Main Line truly lived up to the association. In later years, the 'A3's acquired double chimneys and German style smoke deflectors, modifications which - although imposing - greatly marred their original beauty. Here, complete with German style smoke deflectors, is No.60041 'Salmon Trout' at St Margarets shortly before withdrawal in 1965.

of which 28 were 'V2' 2-6-2s and 24 were 'B1' 4-6-0s including five named examples. St Margaret's also housed three 'A3' and four 'A2' Pacifics.

A visit to the shed on a weekday in early August 1964 revealed 50 steam locos, six main line diesels, five diesel shunters and seven Clayton Type 1 (Class 17). After the closure of Haymarket (64B) to steam in 1963, St Margarets received a few 'A4' and more 'A3' Pacifics that had been made redundant from that shed. One of the last steam sheds in Scotland it was finally closed down in May 1967.

A detailed close-up of the motion of a Class 'V2' 2-6-2 at St Margarets in May 1966. In the background is Fairburn 2-6-4 tank No. 42128 which was built at Derby and withdrawn from 64A in November 1966.

A much-photographed celebrity by this time, 'A4' Pacific No. 60024 'Kingfisher' looks a magnificent sight on the turntable at St Margarets in September 1966. Fitted with a corridor tender for working the non-stop 'Elizabethan' express, this beautiful engine was withdrawn within a few days of this photograph and cut-up five months later in a miserable North Blyth scrapyard.

ON SHED

64 B

Photographed on 1 May, 1954, examples of ex-LNER Classes 'A3' 4-6-2, 'B1' 4-6-0 and 'V2' 2-6-2 line up outside Haymarket in the days when steam reigned supreme.

Edinburgh Haymarket

A visitor to Haymarket from Heaton (52B) gets ready for a trip home down the ECML from Edinburgh. Thompson Class A2/3 4-6-2 No. 60511 'Airborne' was built at Doncaster in 1946 and withdrawn from Tweedmouth shed (52D) in October 1962.

Although there had been an engine shed at Haymarket since 1848, the building so loved by trainspotters in the 1950s and early '60s was built by the North British Railway in 1894. The shed came under the control of the newly-formed LNER following the 1923 Grouping and mainly provided top link locos for East Coast Main Line trains out of Edinburgh Waverley station. It was located on the north side of the line about a 10-minute walk west of Haymarket station and with its very large allocation of ex-LNER Pacifics Haymarket was a magnet for trainspotters. However, by the early 1960s, its days as a steam shed were definitely numbered.

With the influx of English Electric Type 4 (Class 40) and 'Deltic' (Class 55) diesels, by October 1961 its steam allocation had been reduced to 41 locos of which seven were 'A4', 11 were 'A3', five were 'A1' and three 'A2' Pacifics. Thrown in for good measure were some old timers whose lives were about to be cut short such as two named 'D11' 4-4-0s (62691 'Laird of Balmawhapple' and 62693 'Roderick Dhu') and two named 1891-vintage NBR 'J36' 0-6-0s (65235 'Gough' and 65243 'Maude'). At the same time its diesel allocation included 14 English Electric Type 4 (Class 40), 19 Birmingham R. C. & W. Type 2 and five of the brand new 'Deltic' diesels (Class 55).

Two unkempt Peppercorn Class 'A1' Pacifics line up for duty at Haymarket on 6 October, 1962. On the left is No. 60155 'Borderer', then allocated to Heaton (52B), built by BR in 1949 at Doncaster and withdrawn from York (50A) in October 1965. Behind it is No. 60161 'North British', then allocated to 64B, built by BR at Doncaster at the end of 1949 and withdrawn from St Margarets (64A) in October 1963 – a short life of less than 14 years for such a fine machine. In contrast the NBL 0-4-0 diesel shunter, D2753, was one of three such machines allocated to Haymarket at that time.

Haymarket closed to steam in September 1963 with many of its Pacifics being transferred to other Scottish locations such as St Margarets, Aberdeen Ferryhill and Dundee Tay Bridge. A visit to Haymarket at the end of July 1964 revealed 30 diesels including three 'Deltic', six English Electric Type 4, six Birmingham R. C. & W. Type 2, one of the first Brush Type 4 D1507 (Class 47) and ten of the later batch of the highly unsuccessful Clayton Type 1 (Class 17) diesels. The shed continues in use as a diesel maintenance depot.

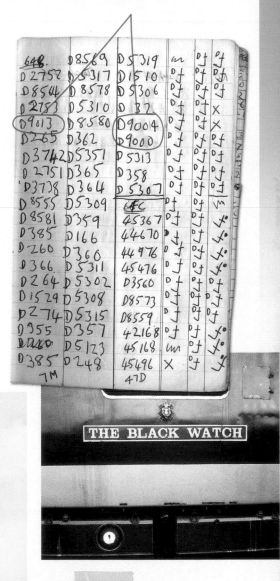

Haymarket shed had closed to steam in September 1963 and its Gresley and Peppercorn Pacifics had been transferred elsewhere and replaced by English Electric Type 4, Birmingham R. C. & W. Co. Type 2 and 'Deltic' Type 5 diesels. Three of the latter class were seen on shed on March 29, 1964 – D9000 'Royal Scots Grey', D9004 and D9013 'The Black Watch'.

Ex-LNER Class 'A3' Pacific No. 60035 'Windsor Lad' looks immaculate in this photo taken at Haymarket in the late 1950s. Built at Doncaster in 1934 and spending much of its life allocated to 64B, No. 60035 was withdrawn in September 1961 and was cut up at its birthplace one month later.

233

Thornton Junction

62 A

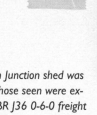

The handwritten shed-spotting list (left):

```
4599                02584   90444
NFERLING A         65922   90117
THORNTO
555                P 61147  64572
Y3338              65287    65925
                   D3340    61118
62A
THORNTON J JUNCTION
61133              61081    61148
D2578              64586    90727
65908              65903    65932
90020              61346    64588
90628              64546    64618
65905              64564    90041
65345              64549    D3337
61132              65410    65916
61330              90319    D264
64591              90705    60034
65904              64595    46463
02583              65907
D2339              65901    64587
61343              65911    61402
02576              90468    61277

ASF  32E  1M  8D
```

Ex-LNER 'B1' Class 4-6-0 No. 61147 was spotted at Thornton shed during a visit on 30 July, 1964. It was built by Vulcan Foundry in 1947 and withdrawn from Dundee Tay Bridge (62B) at the end of 1965. Behind the 'B1' is a Class 'J37' 0-6-0 minus its centre driving wheel and connecting rod.

Apart from seven diesel shunters Thornton Junction shed was 100% steam on July 30, 1964. Amongst those seen were ex-WD 2-8-0 and J37, J38 and ancient ex-NBR J36 0-6-0 freight locos, Nos. 65345 and 65287.

The main engine shed for the former North British Railway and LNER in this coal-mining region of Fife, Thornton Junction's allocation included a large number of heavy-freight and mixed traffic locos. Located on the south side of the Thornton to Dunfermline line, the shed was a good 25-minute walk from the little station at Thornton Junction. The final building on this site was a seven-road through shed opened by the LNER in 1933 and by October 1961 it had an allocation of 52 steam locos and 16 diesel shunters. The mainstay of the motive power was provided by 12 'B1' 4-6-0s, 15 'J38'and eight ex-NBR 'J37' 0-6-0s and 12 ex-WD 2-8-0s. The last surviving 'K4' 2-6-0 No. 61994 'The Great Marquess', built by the LNER for working on the West Highland line, was also allocated to Thornton at this time just prior to withdrawal and preservation.

A visit to the shed at the end of August 1964 revealed 40 steam locos and seven diesel shunters. Even on a visit in late August 1966 our spotter found 14 steam locos and five diesel shunters along with English Electric Type 3 (Class 37) D6859. By then these handsome engines were becoming seen in increasing numbers along with the Brush Type 4 (Class 47) diesels.

Its sub-sheds were at Anstruther (closed 1960), Burntisland (closed 1958), Kirkcaldy (closed 1959), Ladybank (closed 1958) and Methil (closed 1958). Thornton Junction shed closed completely in April 1967.

Allocated to Thornton Junction, ex-NBR Class 'J37' 0-6-0 No. 64570 seems to have received some cosmetic treatment to its front end when photographed at the shed by Colin Garratt in 1965. Introduced in 1914, the final survivors of this class survived until the end of steam in Scotland in 1967.

One of three such locos allocated to Tay Bridge at this time, Peppercorn Class 'A2' Pacific No. 60528 'Tudor Minstrel' looks in fine fettle on 30 September, 1965. Built by BR at Doncaster in 1948 'Tudor Minstrel' was withdrawn from Aberdeen Ferryhill in June 1966. Another ex-62B 'A2', No. 60532 "Blue Peter' was later saved for preservation.

62B Dundee (Tay Bridge)

Up until 1958 there were two steam sheds in Dundee – Dundee West, opened by the Caledonian Railway in 1885, and Dundee Tay Bridge, opened by the North British Railway in 1878. The former was closed in 1958 and used as a diesel depot and for storage of withdrawn steam locos. Tay Bridge, located on the north side of the line a short distance west of Dundee Tay Bridge station, was an eight-road through shed with an allocation of 35 steam locos in October 1961.

A visit to the shed in early August 1964 revealed 28 steam locos including five 'V2' 2-6-2s and ten 'B1' 4-6-0s with two familiar local stars - 'A2' Pacifics No. 60532 'Blue Peter' (since preserved) and No. 60528 'Tudor Minstrel' – and 'A4' Pacific No. 60012 'Commonwealth of Australia'. At the same time West shed had four stored steam locos (two 'B1's and two 'V2's) and 11 diesels (of which nine were shunters). Tay Bridge shed finally closed in May 1967.

Dundee Tay Bridge shed on July 30, 1964. On shed that day were the two local stars, 'A2' Pacifics Nos 60532 'Blue Peter' and 60528 'Tudor Minstrel' and 'A4' Pacific No. 60012 'Commonwealth of Australia'. The latter loco was withdrawn from Ferryhill shed (61B) three weeks later.

Dundee Tay Bridge shed on 1 September, 1954. In the foreground on the turntable is ex-NBR Class 'J35/4' No. 64492, while in the background is an unidentified Class 'V2' 2-6-2. A total of 70 of the Class 'J35' locos were built between 1906 and 1913 by the North British Locomotive Company and at the NBR Cowlairs Works. Used for coal traffic and pick-up goods, the last of the class was withdrawn from service in 1962.

Final Days

DESPITE THE EARLY DIESELISATION OF ALL ROUTES NORTH OF GLASGOW, PERTH AND ABERDEEN BY 1962, STEAM STILL CLUNG ON TO LIFE IN CENTRAL AND SOUTHERN SCOTLAND FOR FIVE MORE YEARS.

By 1965, timetabled passenger services on the Stranraer to Glasgow St Enoch line were operated by diesel multiple units. However, until closure of Stranraer shed (67F) in October 1966, steam continued to be seen on goods trains and the occasional relief passenger train. Here BR Standard Class 4 2-6-0 No. 76001 and BR Standard Class 5 4-6-0 No. 73104 make a fine sight as they cross Kilpatrick Viaduct, near Pinmore, with the 'Empress Voyager' (2.40pm Stranraer to Glasgow relief) on 31 July, 1965. After less than 14 years' service No. 76001 was withdrawn from Ayr shed (67C) in August 1966. No. 73104 was just ten years old when it was withdrawn from Corkerhill (67A) in October 1965.

By the dawn of 1967, the 'A4'-hauled Glasgow to Aberdeen expresses were already becoming a dim memory and the deluge of Type 17 Clayton diesels had already made enormous inroads into previously steam-hauled local freight workings. With the ending of the 'A4' reign on the Glasgow expresses the previous Autumn, it was Carstairs (66D) that became the first steam shed to close in 1967. This was followed the next month by Aberdeen Ferryhill (61B) and then a month later by the Fife freight shed at Thornton Junction (62A) in April.

Despite their age two members of the ex-NBR Class 'J36' (introduced in 1888) survived until the last year of steam in Scotland. Here, No. 65288 was seen in steam during a visit to Dunfermline shed (62C) on 23 August, 1966. Along with its sister engine, No. 65345 (also spotted at Thornton Junction shed on that day), No. 65288 was withdrawn in June 1967.

'A4' swansong - during a shed bash to Thornton Junction, Dunfermline and Alloa on August 23, 1966 the last leg of the journey back to Glasgow from Stirling was behind 'A4' Pacific No. 60024 'Kingfisher' hauling an Aberdeen to Glasgow three-hour express. This fine loco was withdrawn two weeks later.

65903	X	Alloa Shed
90041	X	"
D3345	X	Alloa
D3537	✓	Stirling
D3539	X	"
D5364	X	"
D6126	X	"
D6137	✓	"
D8104	X	"
D1859	✓	"
P76109	X	"	Goods (Nor P
D5333	X	"
D6105	X	"
D8088	X	"
2P (60024)		Stirling - Glasgow
D253	X	Stirling
D6104	✓	
70038	X	St. Rollox
D5360	✓	Buchanan St.
D5364	X	"

Veteran ex-NBR Class 'J36' No. 65267 approaches Lower Bathgate with a train of empties for Westfield Colliery on 10 August, 1965. Introduced in 1888, some members of this class saw active service in France during World War I and were named after famous generals and battles on their return to Scotland. The last members were withdrawn in 1967 but No. 65243 'Maude' has since been preserved.

The final curtain - during the final months of the steam-hauled Aberdeen to Glasgow three hour expresses, Class 'A4' Pacific No. 60034 'Lord Faringdon' enters Stonehaven with the 5.15pm Aberdeen to Glasgow train on 23 August, 1966. Originally named 'Peregrine', No. 60034 was built at Doncaster in 1938 and withdrawn from Ferryhill (61B) the day after this photo was taken. The last regular BR train to be hauled by an 'A4' was also between Aberdeen and Glasgow on 14 September, 1966. One member of this class, No. 4469 'Sir Ralph Wedgwood (originally named 'Gadwall') was seriously damaged during an air raid on York in April 1942 and was subsequently scrapped.

There then followed the closure of all remaining Scottish steam sheds, apart from one, during May. These were Dundee Tay Bridge (62B), Dunfermline (62C), Perth (63A), Edinburgh St Margarets (64A), Glasgow Polmadie (66A), Corkerhill (67A) and Beattock (68D). Motherwell (66B) holds the honour of being the last steam shed to operate in Scotland until its closure on July 1.

Perth

THE GATEWAY TO THE HIGHLANDS, PERTH WAS, AND STILL IS, AN IMPORTANT RAILWAY JUNCTION. IT WAS HERE THAT THE HIGHLAND RAILWAY FROM INVERNESS MET THE CALEDONIAN RAILWAY FROM GLASGOW, ABERDEEN AND DUNDEE AND THE NORTH BRITISH RAILWAY FROM EDINBURGH.

Having deputised for failed 'A4' No. 60034 'Lord Faringdon' at Forfar, 'A4' No. 60009 'Union of South Africa', allocated to Ferryhill (61B) calls at Perth with the 7.10am train from Aberdeen to Glasgow on 29 September, 1965. No. 60009 was built in 1937, withdrawn in June 1966 and has since been preserved. Originally named 'Peregrine', No. 60034 was built in 1938 and withdrawn in August 1966.

Sadly, the former CR lines to Lochearnhead via Crieff (closed 1964) and to Kinnaber Junction via Forfar (closed 1967) have now gone. The Highland line became the first casualty of dieselisation and by 1962 all trains previously hauled by 'Black Five' 4-6-0s to Inverness were in the hands of the Birmingham R. C. & W. Type 2 (Class 27) and BR Sulzer Type 2 (Class 24) diesels.

On a journey from Perth to Inverness in late July 1964 our trainspotter travelled in a 14-coach train double-headed by D5327 and D5127. By then Inverness shed was 100% diesel and the return journey was on a 16-coach train double-headed by D5115 and D5124.

Until the Autumn of 1966 the highlights of a day's trainspotting at Perth were the Glasgow to Aberdeen three-hour expresses which, since 1962, were usually headed by one of Aberdeen Ferryhill's 'A4' Pacifics, reallocated there after the dieselisation of the ECML. Other classes regularly seen at Perth included Polmadie's (66A) BR 'Clan' Pacifics and 'Jubilee' and 'Royal Scot' 4-6-0s often seen at the head of the West Coast Postal or on overnight fish trains, and other local services in the hands of 'Black Five' and BR Standard Class 5 4-6-0s.

(above) Halting under an old Caledonian Railway bracket signal, rather grimy ex-LMS 'Royal Scot' 4-6-0 No. 46166 'London Rifle Brigade' arrives at Perth with a down express in May 1959. Glistening in the low evening sunshine 'Black Five' 4-6-0 No. 44997 waits to take over the train. The 'Royal Scot' was built in 1930, rebuilt with a taper boiler in 1945 and withdrawn in September 1964. The 'Black Five' was built at Horwich in 1947 and withdrawn from Perth shed (63A) in May 1967.

One of the ill-fated diesel designs which helped to bring the once-mighty North British Locomotive Company to its knees. On a summer's day in 1961 Type 2 D6109 and an unidentified sister loco bring the 10.00 Dundee West to Glasgow Buchanan Street to a halt at Platform 1 in Perth station. The NBL Type 2s, built in Glasgow, were prone to go on fire, and were displaced from Aberdeen-Glasgow and Dundee-Glasgow services in a steam 'swansong' between 1962 and 1966. An engine driver from the St Rollox (Glasgow) depot was once asked: "What's the best thing about these NBL Type 2s?". He replied: "The fire extinguisher. I use it more often than the throttle."

Class 'A4' 4-6-2 No. 60019 'Bittern' receives admiring glances at Perth while heading an Aberdeen to Glasgow express on 31 August, 1964. 'Bittern' was built at Doncaster in 1937, withdrawn from Ferryhill shed (61B) in September 1966 and has since been preserved.

Perth

Known as Perth South shed, Perth shed was opened by the Caledonian Railway in the mid-19th century and was replaced by a new eight-road through shed by the LMS in 1938. The shed was located on the west side of the main line about a 15-minute walk south from Perth station. Its allocation in the 1950s included many ageing Caledonian Railway locos and a large number of 'Black Five' 4-6-0s, used in multiple for working heavily-loaded trains on the Highland line to Inverness. The shed also supplied motive power for trains on the former CR routes to Crieff, Dundee and Aberdeen via Forfar.

SCOTTISH REGION

63 A

'Black Five' country – a panoramic view of Perth South shed in September 1954 at a time when it was home to around 70 'Black Fives'. Only a few are visible in this shot with the others hard at work on the Highland line to Inverness or on the main line to Glasgow and Aberdeen. To the left of the picture a member of this class pounds southwards with its train of 'blood and custard' coaches en route to Glasgow.

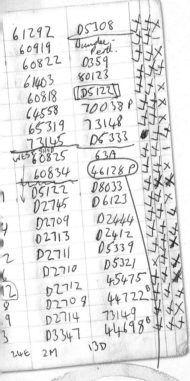

Perth shed was visited on July 30, 1964 and of the 32 locos spotted 24 were steam. Visiting from Carlisle Kingmoor (12A) was 'Royal Scot' Class 4-6-0 No. 46128 'The Lovat Scouts'. This loco was withdrawn in May the following year.

Even the rays of the evening sunshine fail to add any glamour to decrepit 'A4' Pacific No. 60031 'Golden Plover' as it awaits its fate outside Perth shed on 28 August, 1965. Built at Doncaster in 1937 'Golden Plover' was the sole 'A4' allocated to St Rollox shed (65B) in 1965 and was withdrawn in November of that year.

Not far from home, one of Dundee Tay Bridge shed's Peppercorn 'A2' Class Pacifics, No. 60528 'Tudor Minstrel' was spotted visiting Perth shed on 11 January, 1962. Named after the racehorse that won the '2000 Guineas' in 1947 and built by the infant BR at Doncaster early in 1948, this loco was withdrawn from Ferryhill (61B) in June 1966.

By October 1961 its allocation totalled 55 steam locos made up of eight different classes, including a dwindling number of ex-CR types, the oldest of which was a solitary Drummnd 2F 0-6-0 (No. 57345) dating from 1892. By far the largest contingent were the 35 'Black Fives' although, by now, their numbers were dwindling due to dieselisation of the Highland line by a fleet of 27 Birmingham R. C. & W Type 2 diesels (Class 27) based at Inverness. A visit to Perth shed at the end of July 1964 revealed just 24 steam locos (and eight diesels) including 'Royal Scot' No. 46128, 'Jubilee' No. 45629, 'B1' No. 61294 and a solitary CR 2P 0-4-4 tank, No. 55204.

Perth had four sub-sheds – Aberfeldy (closed 1962), Blair Atholl (closed 1962), Forfar (closed 1964) and Crieff (closed 1958). Perth shed closed to steam in May 1967 but continued as a diesel depot until 1969.

In the 1950s Perth was home to around 70 'Stanier 'Black Fives'. Dieselisation of the Highland main line had vastly reduced their numbers but even on July 30, 1964 there were still 16 to be seen on shed. Although withdrawn over 18 months previously ex-Caledonian Railway McIntosh 0-4-4 tank No. 55204 was still languishing there.

A contrasting line-up of steam and diesel power at Perth shed on 20 May, 1964. From left to right: ex-LNER 'V2' Class 2-6-2 No. 60970 was built at Darlington in 1943 and withdrawn from St Margarets (64A) in early 1966; ex-CR '2P' 0-4-4 tank No. 55204 (one of the last members of this class to survive) was built at St Rollox in 1910 and withdrawn from Perth shed at the end of 1962; BR Sulzer Type 2 (Class 24) diesel D5120 and Birmingham R. C. & W. Co Type 2 D5317.

ON SHED

61 A Aberdeen (Kittybrewster)

SCOTTISH REGION

One of only two Class 'Z5' 0-4-2 tanks built for the North British Railway by Manning Wardle in 1915, No. 68192 awaits its fate in the scrap line at Kittybrewster in May 1960. These diminutive locos were built for shunting duties in Aberdeen Docks. To the right veteran ex-NBR Class 'J36' 0-6-0 No. 65247 similarly awaits its fate.

The first shed at Kittybrewster was built by the Great North of Scotland Railway in the mid-19th century. This was replaced at a later date by a half-roundhouse and was modified by BR in 1956. The shed was located two miles northwest of Aberdeen on the west side of the Inverness main line, only about a five-minute walk from Kittybrewster station.

Until closure to steam, the shed, which provided motive power for all of the GNoSR routes north and west of Aberdeen, was famed for its wondrous collection of veteran steam locos from pre-Grouping railway companies including the North Eastern Railway, Great North of Scotland Railway and the Great Eastern Railway plus other ex-LNER and ex-LMS types.

By October 1961 it had lost its steam allocation entirely and had 44 diesels on its books including nine Barclay 0-4-0 shunters for working around Aberdeen Docks, 15 0-6-0 shunters and the final 20 of the luckless North British Type 2 (Class 21). Despite this, on a visit to the shed at the end of July 1964 one lucky spotter found 'A4' Pacific No. 60007 'Sir Nigel Gresley' in store prior to its later preservation.

Sub-sheds were at Ballater (closed 1958), Fraserburgh (closed 1961), Inverurie (closed 1959) and Peterhead (closed 1965). Kittybrewster closed to steam in 1961 but was retained as a diesel depot for a while.

Kittybrewster and Ferryhill sheds were visited on July 31, 1964. The train from Glasgow Buchanan St was headed by D5368 and three 'A4' Pacifics, Nos 60009, 60027, 60034, were spotted en route.

Seen here in 1954, the former GNoSR semi-roundhouse at Kittybrewster was home to an amazing assortment of veteran pre-Grouping steam locos. In the distance an unidentified 0-6-0 tender loco prepares to move down to the turntable.

61B Aberdeen (Ferryhill)

Although famous for its allocation of 'A4' Pacifics in 1964, other, more mundane, steam classes could also be seen in action at Ferryhill. Here, on March 20, are BR Standard Class 4 2-6-4 tank Bo. 80055, ex-works Class 'J37' 0-6-0 No. 64620 and ex-WD 2-8-0 No. 90705. No. 80055 was built at Derby in 1954 and withdrawn from St Margarets (64A) in September 1966. The 'J37', an ex-NBR design introduced in 1914, was one of the final three that were withdrawn from Dundee Tay Bridge (62B) in April 1967. The 'DubDee' was withdrawn from Thornton Junction (62A) only four months after photographed here.

Operated jointly by the North British and Caledonian Railways, the 10-road shed at Ferryhill opened in 1908 and provided motive power for main line services south of Aberdeen to Glasgow via Forfar and Perth and to Edinburgh via Dundee.

The shed was located on the west side of the main line south of the junction with the Dee Valley line to Ballater, and was only a short walk from Aberdeen station. Following the dieselisation of the East Coast Main Line in 1962, the shed was allocated displaced Gresley 'A4' Pacifics to operate the three-hour expresses to Glasgow via Forfar and Perth. During their swan song, these fine locos put up sterling performances until the Autumn of 1966, when all of these trains became diesel-hauled and were diverted via the Dundee route.

A visit to Ferryhill at the end of July 1964 revealed 21 locos of which only three were diesels including English Electric Type 4 (Class 40) D362. On the plus side our trainspotter noted in his excitement that there were seven 'A4' Pacifics (No. 60004 'William Whitelaw', No. 60006 'Sir Ralph Wedgwood', No. 60010 'Dominion of Canada', No. 60012 'Commonwealth of Australia', No. 60016 'Silver King', No. 60023 'Golden Eagle' and No. 60026 'Miles Beevor') on shed. A ride back to Glasgow Buchanan Street behind No. 60019 'Bittern' was a fitting end to this blissful day! No. 60024 'Kingfisher' repeated this treat in late August 1966. Ferryhill shed closed to steam in March 1967.

Ferryhill shed on July 31, 1964 was a wondrous place – on shed that day were no less than seven 'A4' Pacifics, relegated there after the dieselisation of the ECML. The trip back to Buchanan St. was behind No. 60019 making it the twelfth 'A4' seen that day.

One of the seven 'A4' Pacifics seen at Ferryhill on July 31, 1964 was No. 60026 'Miles Beevor'. Employed on the three-hour Aberdeen to Glasgow expresses, the 'Streaks' performed their swansong until September 1966. Built at Doncaster in 1937 and previously allocated to King's Cross (34A) 'Miles Beevor' was finally withdrawn at the end of 1965.

DASTARDLY DIESELS!

North British Locomotive Company Type 2 D6148 arrives at Banchory with a pickup freight for Ballater in 1959. This loco had just been delivered brand new to Kittybrewster shed (61A) and was withdrawn only eight years later at the end of 1967. Along with the Clayton Type 1 the NBL Type 2s were the most unsuccessful of the first generation diesels ordered by BR. They were particularly prone to catching fire!

Although all Highland and Far North lines north of Stanley Junction, the West Highland Line and the Oban line had become dieselised by 1962, steam continued to reign for a few more years in Scotland culminating in the famous Aberdeen to Glasgow 3-hour expresses which remained in the hands of displaced 'A4' Pacifics until the Autumn of 1966. The dieselisation process in Scotland was complete by 1967.

The Class 26 Birmingham Railway Carriage & Wagon Co Type 2 Bo-Bo (D5300-D5346) were one of the first generation main line diesel types to arrive in Scotland. After evaluation on the Eastern Region all members of the class had been allocated to either Haymarket (64B) or Inverness (60A) by 1960 and were often used in multiple for working heavily loaded trains on the Highland Line and the Far North. Some members of this class remained in service until 1993. Introduced in 1961, the Class 27 B. R. C. & W. Type 2 Bo-Bo (D5347-D5415) soon also found their way to Scotland where they were allocated to Eastfield (65A) for working the West Highland Line. Outlived by the older Class 26, the last member of this class was withdrawn in 1987.

The other types of first-generation diesel to arrive in Scotland were the BR Sulzer Type 2 (Class 24) and the Class 21 North British Type 2 Bo-Bo (D6100-D6157). Unfortunately, the latter, unlike the Class 24, 26 and 27 locos, were an unmitigated disaster and a terrible waste of taxpayer's money. After evaluation on the Eastern Region, all members of the class had been allocated either to Eastfield (65A) or Kittybrewster (61A) by 1960 and proved (opposite) English Electric Type 4 (Class 40) D292 leads Stanier 'Black Five' 4-6-0 No. 45161 at the head of a Glasgow to Birmingham express at Wandel Mill in the Clyde Valley in July 1962. The 'Black Five' was built by Armstrong Whitworth in 1935 and withdrawn from Carstairs shed (64D) in November 1966. D292 was built in 1960 and withdrawn in 1982.

(right) Fifty English Electric Type 4 (Class 50) diesels were built at Vulcan Foundry between 1967 and 1968 to haul trains on the non-electrified section of the WCML between Crewe and Glasgow. They normally worked in multiple as seen here with D445 and D412 heading the down 'Midland Scot' express on Beattock Bank on August 1, 1970.

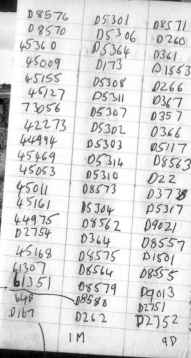

D8576	D5301	D8571
D8570	D5306	D260
45360	D5364	D361
45009	D173	D1553
45155	D5308	D266
45127	D5311	D367
73056	D5307	D357
42273	D5302	D366
44994	D5303	D5117
45469	D5314	D8563
45053	D5310	D22
45011	D8573	D3738
45161	D5304	D5317
44975	D8562	D9021
D2754	D364	D8557
45168	D8575	D1501
61307	D8564	D8555
61351	D8579	D9013
64B	D8580	D2751
D167	D262	D2752
IM		9D

At Haymarket diesel depot (64B) on August 2, 1964, were 12 Clayton Type 1 (Class 17), 11 Type 2 (Class 26/27), eight English Electric Type 4, three 'Deltic' (Class 55) and four 'Peak' (Class 45/46).

English Electric Type 1 (Class 20) No. 8085 draws the empty coaching stock of the 'Thames-Clyde Express' out of Glasgow Central on May 9, 1972. On the left BR Sulzer type 2 (Class 25) No. 7583 waits to draw more ECS out of the station. Delivered between 1957 and 1962, and 1966 and 1968, the Class 20 was a particularly successful class.

to be one of the most unreliable types ordered by BR – sharing this dubious title with their lookalike Class 22 hydraulic cousins on the Western Region and the later Class 17 Clayton Type 1. When operational they were often seen on former Great North of Scotland routes north of Aberdeen or in tandem on the Oban line via Callander. With the bankruptcy of the North British Company in 1962, spares for these locos became difficult to source and many were cannibalised for their parts. Between 1963 and 1965 twenty members of the class were fitted with uprated engines and reclassified as Class 29. By 1968 all Class 21 locos had gone to the scrap heap while the Class 29 only survived until 1971. The final duffer in this Scottish list of failures was the Class 17 Clayton/Beyer, Peacock Type 1 Bo-Bo (D8500-D8616) the majority of which ended up being allocated to Haymarket (64B) and

Polmadie (66A). Introduced between 1962 and 1965, the Class 17 was so unreliable that the last member had been withdrawn by the end of 1971.

The rest of the Scottish diesel scene in the '60s is well known, with the East Coast Main Line being taken over by Class 55 English Electric Type 5 'Deltics' and the West Coast Main Line firstly by underpowered Class 40 EE Type 4 and then by the Class 50 EE Type 4 used in multiple as far south as Crewe. The former Midland/G&SWR route from St Enoch to London via the Settle & Carlisle and, until closure in 1969, the former North British Railway's Waverley route from Edinburgh to Carlisle soon became the stamping grounds for the BR Sulzer Class 45 'Peaks'.

The Great Escape
BR Diesel & Electric Locos

Following the 1955 Modernisation Plan, a myriad of untried and non-standard diesel types were introduced into service on British Railways.

The successful English Electric Type 1 (Class 20) locos were built in two batches: D8000 – D8199 were built at Vulcan Foundry between 1957 and 1962; D8300-D8327 were built by Robert Stephenson & Hawthorns between 1966 and 1968. Some are still in operational condition, and 25 have been preserved including the first member of this class, D8000 (later renumbered 20050), seen here at Crewe Works on May 20, 2000. It is part of the National Collection at the National Railway Museum in York.

Most notable of these were the unreliable diesel-hydraulics built for the Western Region which had a working life that was much less than that of the steam locos they replaced. However, many of those trainspotters who can remember the diesel invasion of the late 1950s and early '60s now have fond memories of these early diesels and it is fortunate that many have since been saved from the breaker's yard. On the other hand it is not surprising that some of the early and unsuccessful examples escaped the preservationists' eye as their lives were so short that they were being withdrawn only a few years after the end of steam.

Classic examples of main line diesels that were never preserved include none of the prototypes apart from 'Deltic' (DP1) or the North British Locomotive Company's five 'Warship' Class diesel-hydraulics (D600-D604). Apart from the English Electric Type 2 'Baby Deltic' (Class 23), all of the other types not preserved were all built by the North British Locomotive Company – Type 1

Built by English Electric at Vulcan Foundry a total of 22 'Deltic' (Class 55) locos were introduced between 1961 and 1962. Designed for high-speed services on the East Coast Main Line, their introduction spelt the end for Gresley's 'A4' Pacifics on this route. They were named after British Army regiments and famous racehorses and, after 20 years of sterling service on the ECML, were withdrawn at the end of 1981 and replaced by HST sets. Six 'Deltics' have been preserved including the first member of this class, D9000 (55022) 'Royal Scots Grey', seen here on a visit to Old Oak Common in August 1991.

(D8400-D8409), retired 1968; Class 21/29 Type 2 (D6100-D6157), retired 1971; Class 22 Type 2 diesel-hydraulic (D6300-D6357), retired 1972; Class 43 Type 4 'Warship' diesel-hydraulic (D833-D865), retired 1971.

From the early 1970s, diesel preservation has gone from strength to strength and currently there are 347 preserved main line diesels in the UK based on the many privately owned railways scattered around the country. In addition to this number, there are more than 200 diesel shunters, numerous diesel multiple units and three ex-GWR railcars.

Some of the main line diesels are also cleared for operating on the main rail system. Apart from the early classes listed above that have not been preserved, examples of every single type of main line diesel are now represented, ranging from the sole surviving members of Class 28 (Metrovick Type 2 Co-Bo D5705), Class 15 (BTH Type 1

Bo-Bo D8233) and Class 17 (Clayton Type 1 Bo-Bo D8568) to 23 of Class 20 (English Electric Type 1 Bo-Bo), 44 of Class 37 (English Electric Type 3 Co-Co) and 37 of Class 47 (Brush Type 4 Co-Co). Other notable classes include representatives of Class 35 'Hymek', Class 42 'Warship' and Class 52 'Western' diesel-hydraulics and Class 50 'Hoovers' and Class 55 'Deltics'. Moves are currently afoot to preserve a Class 58 Co-Co heavy freight diesel.

Not surprisingly there are not too many electric locos preserved, as there are no preserved electric lines on which to run them! Despite this handicap, there are 18 main line electric locos preserved (including a Class 77 in Holland) with representatives of Classes 71, 76, 77, 81-87 and 89.

Non-standard types preserved include no fewer than 18 members of Class 73 Bo-Bo electro-diesels and the Brown, Boveri gas turbine-electric loco No. 18000.

The final main line diesel hydraulic locos delivered to the Western Region were the 74 'Western' Class (Class 52) between 1961 and 1964. Unfortunately, owing to their incompatibility with diesel electric locos, WR's diesel hydraulic 'experiment' ended, and all had been withdrawn by 1977. Luckily, seven have been preserved: D1010 'Western Campaigner', D1013 'Western Champion', D1023 'Western Fusilier', D1041 'Western Prince'. D1048 'Western Lady', D1062 'Western Courier'. The latter locomotive is seen here at Arley on the Severn Valley Railway on May 9, 1987.

Railway Miscellany

51. In the absence of flags

(*a*) Both arms raised above the head denotes Danger or stop :—
   (NOTE.—When riding on or in a vehicle either arm moved up and down denotes stop.)

Rule 51

(*b*) Either arm held in a horizontal position and the hand moved up and down denotes Caution or slow down, thus :—

(*c*) Either arm held above the head denotes All Right, thus :—

49

Instructions for hand signalling of trains as laid out in the British Railways Rule Book for 1950.

The end of the line – far from its home shed of Perth (63A), BR Standard Class 4 2-6-4 tank No. 80093 gets up steam at the tiny Loch Tay shed at the end of the Killin branch on August 4, 1965. The 4¼ mile branch from Killin connected with the Glasgow to Oban line (via Callander) at Killin Junction. Although scheduled for closure in November 1965, the section of line from Dunblane to Crianlarich, including the Killin branch, closed prematurely on September 27, following a landslide in Glen Ogle.

A pair of 'Black Fives' await their next turn of duty at St Rollox shed, Glasgow (65B) on May 19, 1964. St Rollox shed closed in November 1966. No. 45471 was built at Crewe in 1938 and withdrawn from Dumfries shed (68B) in July 1965. No. 45473 was built at Derby in 1943 and withdrawn from Dundee Tay Bridge (62B) in November 1966.

Ex-LNER Gresley 'V2' 2-6-2 No. 60885 passes Monktonhall Junction near Edinburgh with a Saltburn to Glasgow train on July 7, 1962. This loco was built at Darlington in 1939 and withdrawn from Darlington shed (51A) in September 1965. One member of this class, No. 60800 'Green Arrow', has been preserved as part of the National Collection.

Following the end of sweet-rationing decorated toffee tins were very popular in the 1950s. Here, Stanier 'Coronation' Class 4-6-2 No. 46220 'Coronation' heads the 'Royal Scot' through romanticised Highland scenery on a tin of Fillery's Toffees.

Looking a fine sight at the head of three Gresley 'blood and custard' coaches, Class 'K2' 2-6-0 No. 61779 blasts out of Aberdeen with the 8.11am train for Ballater in April 1954. A total of 65 'K2s' were built for the Great Northern Railway between 1914 and 1921 with the last being withdrawn in 1962.

Fitted with a snowplough, 'Black Five' 4-6-0 No. 45117 simmers by the great arch at the entrance to Inverness shed (60A) in May 1961. The shed was closed to steam only a month later when BR Sulzer Type 2 (Class 24) and Birmingham R. C. & W.Co Type 2 (Class 26) took over all of the remaining steam diagrams on the Highland line north of Perth. No. 45117 was built at the Vulcan Foundry in 1935 and withdrawn from Hurlford shed (67B) in October 1965.

ACKNOWLEDGMENTS

Firstly I would like to thank my late mother, Joan, for squirreling away my trainspotting books in her loft for 33 years – without this unique material this book would not have been possible. Thanks are also due to all of the railway photographers out there - in particular Ben Ashworth, John Goss, Tony Harden, Tom Heavyside, Alan Jarvis, and Michael Mensing – and to Ron White of Colour-Rail who have supplied many of the photographs used in this book and to David & Charles for use of their photographic archive.

I am especially grateful to those employees of British Railways who put up with our antics during those 'golden years' – they must have thought the younger generation had gone completely mad! For their companionship I would also like to thank my old trainspotting friends in Gloucester – I am sorry I cannot remember all your names after all this time - and to Robert Meadows with whom I spent many happy weekends and holidays operating his garden railway. Last but not least thanks are also due to Peter Hughes, formerly of Gourock in Scotland, with whom I spent many happy hours 'bunking' engine sheds and travelling around the highways and byways of the Scottish Region in the 1960s.

Finally I would like to thank David & Charles, publishers of this book, who were brave enough to let me off the leash on such a large project - especially to Ali Myer, Neil Baber, Emily Pitcher and to their excellent designer Martin Smith.

ABOUT THE AUTHOR

Author and photographer Julian Holland spent his formative years, notebook and camera in hand, trainspotting on draughty stations and in grimy engine sheds and travelling the highways and byways of the British Railways network in search of that elusive locomotive number or to travel over a soon-to-be-closed line. The repercussions of the 'Beeching Report' and the end of steam on British Railways in 1968 failed to dampen his passion for railways –as benign dictator of the UK he would now renationalise the railway system and reopen many of the long-closed railway lines!

Trained as a graphic designer at the infamous Hornsey College of Art in the late '60s, Julian went on to a successful career creating books for many well-known publishing companies. In more recent years he has contributed to many best-selling books on railways and has also written *Amazing and Extraordinary Railway Facts* (David & Charles 2007), *Discovering Britain's Little Trains* (AA Publishing 2008) and *Great Railways of the World* (AA Publishing 2008).

As a writer and photographer he has also produced *Water Under the Bridge* (Collins & Brown 1998), *Exploring the Islands of England and Wales* (Frances Lincoln 2007) and *Exploring the Islands of Scotland* (Frances Lincoln 2008).

D A Anderson: 167t; 233bl

B J Ashworth: 8/9t; 14t; 15mr; 18b; 25tl; 38t;
39tr; 39bl; 45b; 47t; 52bl; 54bl; 55t; 56t; 57br;
59t; 71br; 74br; 75t; 86b; 89tl; 114/155t; 120br;
121tl; 139t; 139mr; 153m; 172t; 175bl; 179b;
182b; 191t; 205tl; 207br; 222tm; 222tr; 223br

D H Ballantyne: 46t; 73tl; 73b

Peter Bowles: 78t

British Railways: 23tr

Melvyn Bryan: 141bl; 215br; 217br

M Bryce: 211bl

David Bullock: 43ml; 65bl

D E Canning: 91m; 117bl; 165m

I S Carr: 97tl; 153bl; 174bl; 191bl; 200; 202br;
203tr; 206br; 207ml

Jim Carter: 161b

H C Casserley: 178bl; 180bl; 182t; 196t; 198tl;
198mr; 198b

P J Chambers: 163mr

C R L Coles: 63br; 83t; 93ml; 122bl; 155mr

Colour-Rail: 8br; 10br; 11t; 12t; 15bl; 17b; 19r;
20b; 22t; 25b; 41mr; 41bl; 42bl; 43tl; 46bl; 55br;
61tr; 80t; 82t; 82bl; 87b; 92br; 94; 96; 98tl;
102br; 103tl; 106t; 110br; 111t; 112t; 113b;
121mr; 121bl; 122tr; 128t; 129br; 133ml; 140b;
147t; 148t; 166t; 171t; 172b; 185tl; 186b; 189br;
193tr; 197b; 199bl; 199br; 204; 205tr; 205br;
208m; 211tl; 215tl; 217ml; 228t; 230t; 231bl;
233tl; 239t; 240br; 242tl; 244bl; 246; 247tl;
247br; 249ml; 249br

K Connolly: 11br; 23bl; 51b; 139bl; 165bl; 16br;
181br; 185mr

S Creer: 133tl; 155rl

Derek Cross: 40br; 162t; 164t; 168; 244t; 245t;
249tl

C E Dann: 118t

M Dunnett: 97m; 169m; 184/185b; 187tl; 188tr;
194; 203br; 207tl

N F W Dyckhoff: 174t; 177m; 202t

Mike Esau: 12br; 63tl; 89b; 99t; 99b; 141ml;
151m; 151b

J N Faulkner: 157bl

Kenneth Field: 61ml; 88tr; 117t; 143tr; 143ml;
155bl; 157tl; 179tl; 180br; 206tr

J A Fleming: 134m; 134br; 135b; 143bl; 145t;
146b

T G Flinders: 103br

P R Foster: 187b; 231mr

P J Fowler: 27bl; 45mr; 83ml

John Goss: 13tl; 13ml; 15t; 17tl; 21tl; 21tr; 21b;
24b; 29mr; 29bl; 36tl; 38bl; 53tl; 56br; 57bl;
61br; 72bl; 78br; 79bl; 80br; 85tl; 88bl; 93tr;
95m; 110tl; 126; 127tl; 127mr; 131mr; 131bl;
135tl; 170br; 181tr; 181ml; 183t; 189tl; 192t;
192br; 196br; 197tl; 201tr; 201br; 208t; 212t;
213b; 214bl; 217tl; 218; 229b; 232bl; 235tl; 236;
237ml; 237br; 238t; 241t; 248tr

R M Grainger: 85br; 102t; 104t

Tony Harden: 16m; 70t; 105mr; 129ml; 130t;
170t; 188bl; 193b; 216t; 219t; 219b; 220t; 232t;
235bl; 240tr; 242br

Tom Heavyside: 41tr; 48tl; 48br; 50tr; 50bl; 50br;
57t; 58; 60t; 62tr; 62br; 68bl; 69tr; 69b; 70br;
71tr; 72t; 81ml; 84t; 85bl; 89mr; 105tr; 119tl;
125mr; 149bl; 150t; 150br; 152t; 152bl; 153tl;
159ml; 163b; 166br; 167bl; 175mr; 175br; 180tr;
183b; 199t; 241bl; 243tl; 245ml; 248bl

G F Heiron: 10t; 45tl

R W Hinton: 163tl

Julian Holland: 4tl; 4tm; 5; 6bl; 6bm; 16bl; 24tr;
32t; 32br; 33tl; 33tr; 33br; 34bl; 34br; 35mr;
35br; 35bl; 37t; 37bl; 40bl; 41t; 42tr; 42mr; 43tr;
44bl; 52tr; 53ml; 53br; 55bl; 64b; 66t; 67tl; 67bl;
67br; 74t; 75br; 81t; 87t; 100t; 101t; 101m;
101b; 128bl; 137b; 145br; 148br; 149tr; 171mr;
171br; 214t; 216bl; 220bl; 221tl; 221tr; 221b;
222bl; 224tr; 224b; 225tl; 225b; 228bl; 233br;
234tr; 237tl; 239bl; 243br; 249mr; 250ml

Peter Hughes: 137m

Alan Jarvis: 26t; 27tr; 27br; 28br; 30tr; 30br; 30bl;

31tl; 31mr; 31bl; 36br; 38br; 39br; 59m; 65tl; 68t

M C Kemp: 119tr; 123tl; 167mr

R A King: 133br

Michael Mensing: 19tl; 19b; 40tl; 92t; 115bl;
124b; 138t; 138bl; 140tr; 141tl; 159tl; 201tl

Milepost 92½: title page; 7; 22br; 28ml; 28/29t;
54t; 76t; 90; 98b; 105b; 106br; 107t; 107b; 109tl;
109mr; 113tl; 119bl; 124t; 142t; 144t; 144br;
151tl; 154t; 157tr; 159mr; 160b; 173tl; 173br;
176t; 186tl; 189ml; 190; 196ml; 201ml; 209m;
210; 230br; 231tl; 234br

R Montgomery: 97tr

Brian Morrison: 10ml; 123bl; 132

G R Mortimer: 123mr

John K Morton: 79tl; 103bl; 116ml; 127bl; 156;
157mr; 178t; 187mr

Barry J Nicolle: 13br

Ivo Peters Collection: 8bl; 23ml

C. Plant: 164b

R F Roberts: 169tr; 206ml

Gerald T Robinson: 49t; 49br

M L Rogers: 116tl

D Trevor Rowe: 130br; 131tl

W S Sellar: 229tr

John R Smith: 44m

R Smith: 161tl

Frank Spaven: 226b; 226/227t; 227b; 239mr

Mike Turner: 136br

John S Whiteley: 169br

Rev Graham B Wise: 147b; 158t

Dr M H Yardley: 175tl